Coaching Writing in Content Areas

Write-for-Insight Strategies, Grades 6–12

SECOND EDITION

William Strong

Professor Emeritus, Secondary Education

Utah State University

Foreword by Dan Kirby

Boston   Columbus   Indianapolis   New York   San Francisco   Upper Saddle River
Amsterdam   Cape Town   Dubai   London   Madrid   Milan   Munich   Paris   Montreal   Toronto
Delhi   Mexico City   São Paulo   Sydney   Hong Kong   Seoul   Singapore   Taipei   Tokyo

For my National Writing Project colleagues, whose lives
offer insights into quality instruction
and
especially for biology teacher Bob Tierney, who led the writing-to-learn movement

Vice President and Editor-in-Chief : Aurora Martínez Ramos
Editorial Assistant: Michelle Hochberg
Marketing Manager: Krista Clark
Production Editor: Janet Domingo
Editorial Production Service: S4Carlisle Publishing Services
Manufacturing Buyer: Megan Cochran
Electronic Composition: S4Carlisle Publishing Services
Cover Designer: Linda Knowles

Credits and acknowledgments borrowed from other sources and reproduced, with permission, in this textbook appear on the appropriate page within text (or on page ii).

Library of Congress Cataloging-in-Publication Data
Strong, William, 1940-
   Coaching writing in content areas: write-for-insight strategies, grades 6–12/William Strong.—[2nd ed.].
     p. cm.
   Includes bibliographical references and index.
   ISBN-13: 978-0-13-269004-1 (alk. paper)
   ISBN-10: 0-13-269004-7 (alk. paper)
  1. English language—Rhetoric—Study and teaching. 2. Report writing—Study and teaching (Middle school)
3. Report writing—Study and teaching (Secondary) I. Title.
PE1404.S847 2012
808'.0420712—dc22
                      2011001852

Text excerpts: pp. 15–20, 24–25: Reprinted with permission from the National Writing Project. Strong, William. 2003. "Writing Across the Hidden Curriculum." *The Quarterly of the National Writing Project* 25(1):2–7, 38. **pp. 32–34, 37, 39, 42, 57, 121:** Reprinted from Mitchell, Diana. 1996. "Writing to Learn Across the English Curriculum and the English Teacher." *English Journal* 85(5):93–97. Copyright © 1996 by the National Council of Teachers of English. Reprinted with permission. **pp. 41–42, 55–57:** Reprinted from Gere, Ann (ed.). 1985. *Roots in the Sawdust: Writing to Learn Across the Disciplines.* Copyright © 1985 by the National Council of Teachers of English. Reprinted with permission. **pp. 51–53:** Reprinted from Pugh, Sharon, et al. 1992. *Bridging: A Teacher's Guide to Metaphorical Thinking.* Copyright © 1992 by the National Council of Teachers of English. Reprinted with permission. **pp. 65, 104, 107–110, 124:** Reprinted by permission from *Coaching Writing* by William Strong. Copyright © 2001 by William Strong. Published by Heinemann, a division of Reed Elsevier, Inc., Portsmouth, NH. All rights reserved. **pp. 68–70:** Reprinted from Strong, William. 1986. *Creative Approaches to Sentence Combining.* Copyright © 1986 by the National Council of Teachers of English. Reprinted with permission. **pp. 73–74, 101:** Reprinted by permission from *Writer's Toolbox: A Sentence Combining Workshop* by William Strong. Copyright 1996 by McGraw-Hill Inc. etc. **pp. 138–140:** Reprinted from Olson, Carol Booth. 2003. *The Reading/Writing Connection: Strategies for Teaching and Learning in the Secondary Classroom, "Personalized Research Paper."* Reprinted with permission of Pearson Education, Inc. **pp. 167–169:** Reprinted from Graham, Steve et al (ed). 2007. *Best Practices in Writing Instruction.* Reprinted with permission of The Guilford Press.

Printed in the United States of America

10 9 8 7 6 5 4 3 2 1   15 14 13 12 11

www.allynbaconmerrill.com

ISBN-13: 978-0-13-269004-1
ISBN-10: 0-13-269004-7

About the Author

William Strong has coached middle school and high school teachers for over four decades. Besides presenting many conference talks and workshops, he authored *Coaching Writing: The Power of Guided Practice* (Heinemann, 2001) as well as several sentence-combining books for teachers and students. He served on the National Writing Project Advisory Board for a decade and was consulting author in composition for the *Writer's Choice* textbook series (Glencoe/McGraw-Hill, 2001). At Utah State University, he founded and directed the Utah Writing Project for 25 years while teaching content area literacy, English education, and writing. His teaching and research have received college-level awards, and he has often been honored for leadership in teacher education. He enjoys Utah skiing, large motorcycles, and gardening along the river. Readers can contact the author at wcstrong@msn.com.

Contents

About the Author   iii

Preface   vii

Foreword by Dan Kirby   xix

Chapter 1
Writing from the Inside Out   1

Remembered Writing   1

Narration as Knowledge   2

Prompting Narrative   3

Literacy Autobiographies   6

Reflecting on Narrative   9

Content Area Examples   10

Narrative Insights   13

Write-for-Insight Activity   14

Chapter 2
Challenging the Hidden Curriculum   15

Teacher as Writer   15

Resistance to Writing   16

The Hidden Curriculum of Writing   17

Roots of the Hidden Curriculum   18

Writing without Grades   19

Note-Taking and Note-Making   20

Resisting the Hidden Curriculum   22

Making Learning Personal   24

Writing-to-Learn Samples   26

Thinking Outside the Box   28

Write-for-Insight Activity   29

Chapter 3
Exploring Expressive Writing   30

Windows to the Heart   30

Opening Expressive Windows   32

What If . . .?   32

Three Words   33

Take a Stand   34

Letters   34

"You Are There" Scenes   34

Quotation Prompts   34

Guided Imagery   35

Dramatic Scenarios (Cases)   37

Role-Playing   39

Dialogue Writing   41

A Reader/Writer Dialogue   42

Write-for-Insight Activity   44

Chapter 4
Tapping the Power of Metaphor   45

Valentine's Day   45

The Power of Metaphor   46

Exercising Metaphor   48

More about Metaphor   50

Using Semantic Charts   52

Using Pattern Poems   53

Metaphors in Prose   57

Metaphors of Teaching   58
Write-for-Insight Activity   59

Chapter 5
Helping Basic Writers Succeed   61

Basics of Good Teaching   61
Wall Text Basics   63
Back to Human Basics   63
Developing Transcribing Skill   66
Using Content-Based Dictation   67
Summarizing and Paraphrasing   68
Teaching Basics Strategically   71
Sentence-Combining Basics   73
Workshop-Style Teaching   75
A Bridge to Literacy   77
Write-for-Insight Activity   79

Chapter 6
Designing Assignments and Rubrics   80

Darth Vader in Action   80
Assignments by Design   81
Assignments to Motivate   83
Ten Design Principles   85
Context + RAFT = CRAFT   86
Case Study of an Assignment   89
Content Area Writing Tasks   92
Creating Propaganda   92
Ultimate Frisbee   93
"Healthy Choice" Meal Proposal   94
Website Design Proposal   95
Darth Vader Revisited   96
Write-for-Insight Activity   97

Chapter 7
Managing the Writing Process   99

Coaching Writing   99
Visualizing the Writing Process   100
Understanding the Model   102
Guiding Cycle 1 Activities (Prewriting)   104
Guiding Cycle 2 Activities (Revising)   106
Prompting Self-Assessment   109
Strategy 1 (Reading Aloud)   111
Strategy 2 (Reading Imaginatively)   111
Strategy 3 (Rereading with Care)   111
Bumps in Process Teaching   111
Managing Collaborative Writing   113
Write-for-Insight Activity   114

Chapter 8
Coaching and Judging Writing   116

Responding to Writing   116
Thinking About Assessment   118
Coaching versus Judging   118
Getting Ready to Coach   119
Principle 1 (Models)   120
Principle 2 (Rubrics)   120
Principle 3 (Response)   120
Up-Front Coaching   121
Coaching as Response   122
Audiotape Coaching   124
Getting Ready to Judge   125
Judging Portfolios   127
Coaching as a Lifetime Sport   128
Write-for-Insight Activity   129

Chapter 9
Researching Outside the Box   131

A Research Story   131
Personalized Research   133
The Saturation Report   134
A Student Saturation Report   136
The I-Search Paper   137
Multigenre Research Project   140
Challenging Advanced Students   143
Traditional Guided Research   145
The Problem of Fakery   146
Write-for-Insight Activity   147

Chapter 10
Writing in a Digital World   148

Cultural Divide   148
iPod Inspiration   149
WebQuest Nation   150
PowerPoint Pedagogy   152
A Gift of Glogs   154
Guerrilla Journalism   156
Classroom Demonstration   158
Blogging Basics   159
Exploratory First Steps   161
Write-for-Insight Activity   163

Epilogue
Revisiting Insight   164

Listening to Students   164
Coaching with Insight   165
Leveling with Students   166
The "Writing Next" Report   167
Listening to Research   169
Write-for-Insight Activity   170

APPENDIX A   Literacy Autobiography Case Study   171

APPENDIX B   Bob Tierney's Concept-Trigger Words   174

APPENDIX C   Macie Wolfe's Cubing Activity   177

APPENDIX D   Graphic Organizers   179

APPENDIX E   Content Area Writing Assignments   184

References   190

Index   193

Preface

Introducing Insight

> *How can I know what I think until I see what I say?*
> —E. M. Forster

New to This Edition

A new title—*Coaching Writing in Content Areas: Write-for-Insight Strategies, Grades 6–12*—provides focus for the second edition. This book is informed by the "best practice" coaching of expert teachers and updated with important new research. Thanks to workshop feedback and reviewer comments, I've retained the personal voice and practical ideas of the first edition but made changes to improve the book's utility:

- *Electronic Technology.* A new chapter, "Writing in a Digital World," describes how computers and digital media have changed the landscape of content area coaching—through weblogs, podcasting, and interactive composition.

- *Landmark Research.* A new Epilogue, "Revisiting Insight," summarizes findings of a major meta-analysis on effective writing instruction (Graham & Perin, 2007). This "capstone" material confirms key coaching practices in this book.

- *Strategies for Basic Writers.* Classroom-tested ideas—such as Flexible Teaming, Wall Text, and Cubing—are added to help English language learners and special education students find success in using writing as a tool for content learning.

- *Middle School Teacher Profiles.* New profiles of terrific content coaches at the middle school level—Kathy Christiansen (social studies), Laura Miller (English and French), and Macie Wolfe (science)—are now included.

- *High School Teacher Profiles.* New ideas from great high school teachers—Launa Moser (health education and occupations, physical conditioning), Chris Sloan (AP English, journalism, new media), and Jeremy Young (mathematics)—have been added.

- *Student Writing Samples.* New examples of writing-to-learn activities—as well as rubric-assessed public writing—are presented. These writing samples help content area coaches know what to expect from students.

- *Reorganization and Updating.* The Table of Contents has been reorganized, and references have been updated throughout the book. An earlier chapter, "Writing as a Means to Meaning," has been deleted from this edition.

Now a Small Confession

Back in the Dark Ages, when I was a zealous young professor managing a statewide site of the National Writing Project—this with a full teaching load and no released time—a three-word insight dawned on me: *Success is punishment.*

Simply put, the more heroic your effort, the more you get to do. Traveling the wild, windswept outback of Utah, I also learned that the best teachers among us wouldn't have it any other way—though they *do* look for ways to work smarter, not harder.

For me, the second edition revisits the paradox of success—not that I'm complaining. I'm glad the earlier book was useful to content coaches like you. So, my aim remains unchanged: to engage good teachers across great distances of time and space—and perhaps even greater distances of culture and personal experience.

Why? Because I still regard meaningful learning—that is, learning through personal insight—as the core work of any educational relationship, including the one in this book. As used here, *insight* refers to flashes of enlightenment or surprise, a "seeing from within." And to achieve insight, one must be involved, attentive, relaxed.

Like now: Just ☺ if you're with me.

This book explores writing as a tool for learning in *all* content areas. By *writing*, I mean a rich array of activities—note-taking, drawing, journaling, summarizing, charting, brainstorming, metaphor-building, blogging, scripting of podcasts—in addition to traditional school writing assignments like essays, lab reports, and research papers. More specifically, this book focuses on increasing student motivation, enhancing long-term learning, and actually *easing* the workload shouldered by teachers across the middle school and high school grades. As I previously hinted, it's about working smarter, not harder.

I aim to be a friendly, thought-provoking companion to new and veteran teachers in diverse disciplines. I invite attention to strategies that support schooling's most basic goals—emotional and intellectual engagement—and I celebrate the work of those who teach for insight, often against daunting odds.

"Work," as Kahlil Gibran (1923/1975, p. 28) once put it, "is love made visible." To me, this is a perfect description of good coaching in content area classrooms.

Writing and Skiing

I worked hard on the opening sections above, the ones you've read in moments. After all, finished text is seamless, its process of construction invisible. In my opening lines, I hoped to avoid the mind-numbing jargon of education, but I also didn't want to insult your intelligence with the kind of prose that puts its feet on the coffee table.

So the writing was work, but it was also fun. I liked the challenge, just as I enjoy skiing on bright winter afternoons, with my downhill shadow offering instant feedback on how I'm doing. Watching it swoop through Utah turns, there's nowhere else I'd rather be. All that matters is paying attention. For you, the pleasure of paying attention may come from making music, shooting baskets, doing Sudoku and crossword puzzles, or working at a potter's wheel. If you know the feeling of doing something for the challenge and fun of it—what psychologist Mihaly Csikszentmihalyi (1990) calls "flow"—you understand my point about mental and physical focus. Optimal experience, or flow, results from testing our own limits to see what we can do.

Skiing is one such test for me, and writing is another. I try to ski relaxed and alert, free from mental chatter and self-criticism. It's a state of mind in which I give full attention to the moment-to-moment experience—the swells and dips of the terrain, the feel of the snow—instead of worrying about how I look. The same goes for writing. I try to silence self-doubt and inner criticism by first following the thread of unfolding sentences—even though I'm unsure of their direction—and then paying attention to the emerging meaning.

Let me explain. As I whisper what I've written, listening closely and tinkering to get the words right, language itself becomes a kind of "shadow-teacher," showing me the way. Just as I return to the same slopes in different light and snow conditions, I often revisit what I've written, seeing whether I can make the text clearer, tighter, or more vivid. It's interesting to see what I can learn.

To understand this same idea from another angle, consider the words of poet William Stafford (in Murray, 1990, p. 162), one of the great teachers of the twentieth century:

> I'm not alone when I'm writing—the language itself, like a kind of trampoline, is there helping me.

Stafford believed that the act of writing helps us "catch the bounce" of personal insights. In other words, we learn from our own writing to the extent we really pay attention to it.

The point is this: Writing isn't like the multiplication tables, something you learn once and for all. It's something you continually learn how to do, like making love. And for this reason, it's endlessly educational, for both teachers and students.

Learning Together

I share this background because clear, effective writing is among the most demanding tasks most of us will ever do. This book's ideas and activities may challenge you. But as you engage professionally, you'll gain insights from your written reflections. For example, writing a piece of your own literacy story will help you better appreciate the lessons of past experience; but *sharing* that story—and hearing the stories of others—will help you become a reflective practitioner (Schon, 1983) who values student writing and uses this knowledge to excite learning in your field.

Also, this is a book with attitude. At one level, it shares a philosophy of instruction and classroom-tested strategies for all content areas; at another level, it targets fakery as education's Public Enemy Number One. Visit middle school and high school classrooms as I often do, and you'll see students who view learning as boring and pointless. Sure, they go through the motions—handing in reports, taking tests, shuffling from class to class—but the lights have gone out, and nobody's home. Somewhere along the way, busywork and mindless teaching conspired to snuff out insight and the joy of learning. You and I will exacerbate the problem unless we're part of the solution.

Finally, this book asserts the power of collaboration as well as the power of the "I" pronoun. In this edition, several dynamic teachers share great ideas for motivating middle school and high school learners. This book also showcases "public writing" tasks (Daniels, Zemelman, & Steineke, 2007), complete with grading rubrics. While these assignments don't carry double-your-money-back guarantees, they will certainly spark thinking about parallel approaches in your discipline. So, just as my voice will mentor you in this book, the voices of my students and National Writing Project colleagues have helped shape my thoughts about personal insight. I again thank them for their instruction.

And now another small confession: As the first reader of this book, I've reread and rewritten the words many times to get them right. Doing so, I've imagined you as an intelligent and discerning companion, one who often asks, "What next?" and "So what?" Of course, it's my job as a writer to respond.

So, as I read through questioning eyes, I find myself changing words, rearranging paragraphs, adding examples, and tightening language. Yes, the words must make sense to me before they can make sense to you; but it's my *anticipation* of your reading that has somehow enabled me to write as fully and insightfully as I can.

I encourage you to do as I've done—to meet the text halfway, questioning it for answers. In other words, try to be a *responsive* reader, one who is intellectually open and willing to interact. Trust your responses, and write for insight at the end of each chapter. Then share your thinking with others.

Why Writing Matters

Historically, the first national study of secondary school writing linked survey research with 259 in-school observations (Applebee, 1981). The report revealed many eye-opening facts, including these two:

- Only three percent of class time in the observed classes was spent on writing of at least paragraph length.
- Thirty-two percent of the surveyed teachers said they *never* assigned such writing.

(p. 99)

Moreover, homework assignments of paragraph-length writing or more occurred only *3%* of the time (p. 93).

Applebee's snapshot captured school realities decades ago—before *A Nation at Risk* (NCEE, 1983) and other hard-hitting reform documents (Boyer, 1983; Goodlad, 1984; Sizer, 1984) urged an overhaul of American secondary education and increased attention to writing. "Surely things have improved by now," you're thinking.

But in 2006 Applebee and Langer reached a sobering, data-driven conclusion in *The State of Writing Instruction in America's Schools*:

> What is clear is that even with some increases over time, many students are not writing a great deal for any of their academic subjects, including English, and most are not writing at any length. Two-thirds of students in Grade 8, for example, are expected to spend an hour or less on writing for homework each week, and 40% of twelfth graders report never or hardly ever being asked to write a paper of 3 pages or more. (p. 28)

Commenting on national curriculum trends, the researchers lament that "writing seems to be dropping from attention" (p. 29).

A similar tone was adopted by the National Commission on Writing in America's Schools and Colleges. With support of the College Entrance Examination Board (CEEB), the National Commission views writing as "clearly the most neglected" of the traditional three Rs and asserts that it is "increasingly shortchanged throughout the school and college years"—this despite the fact that writing is "how students connect the dots in their knowledge" (CEEB, 2003, p. 3).

Parallel themes are echoed in an ACT report, *Crisis at the Core* (ACT, 2004). For example, of the 1.2 million high school graduates who took the 2004 ACT assessment, only 22% were deemed *ready* for college in the basic academic areas of English, math, and science—and many did not have the skills to succeed in workforce training. In fact, a 2006 survey found that 81% of employers regarded recent high school graduates as "deficient in written communications" (Casner-Lotto & Barrington, 2006; Conference Board, 2006).

The National Commission argues that writing is central to education. "If students are to make knowledge their own," the authors assert, "they must struggle with the details, wrestle with the facts, and rework raw information and dimly understood concepts into language they can communicate to someone else" (CEEB, p. 9). Moreover, writing will assume increasing importance, as our technology-driven, knowledge-based economy makes new demands on workers. To summarize: "Writing today is not a frill for the few, but an essential skill for the many" (p. 11).

Today's college admission tests reflect the new reality. In February and March 2005, writing was added to ACT and SAT assessments. The ACT assessment has objective items related to language skills, plus an optional 30-minute essay prompt. The writing section of the new SAT has multiple-choice items and a required 25-minute essay. Your students will find sample prompts—and test-taking advice—at the ACT and SAT websites.

Good News from NAEP

Periodically, the National Assessment of Educational Progress (NAEP) tests narrative, informative, and persuasive writing. Students are asked to write stories or personal essays, to share knowledge or convey messages clearly, and to take positions that can be supported and developed through logical argument. Most state assessments follow a similar pattern.

Happily, NAEP data from 2007 offers hope for the future. Compared with previous NAEP assessments in 1998 and 2002, average writing scores were higher nationally for students at both eighth and twelfth grades.

At Grade 8 in 2007

- The average writing score was 3 points higher than in 2002 and 6 points higher than in 1998.

- The percentage of students performing at or above the *Basic* level increased from 85% in 2002 to 88% and was also higher than in 1998.

- The percentage of students performing at or above the *Proficient* level was higher than in 1998 but showed no significant change since 2002.

At Grade 12 in 2007

- The average writing score was 5 points higher than in 2002 and 3 points higher than in 1998.

- The percentage of students performing at or above the *Basic* level increased from 74% in 2002 to 82% and was also higher than in 1998.

- The percentage of students performing at or above the *Proficient* level was higher than in 1998 but showed no significant change since 2002.

Source: NCES/NAEP; Salahu-Din, D., Perky, H., & Miller J. (2008).

Additionally, the 2007 NAEP assessment revealed score increases for various minority groups as well as for male students. For example, a 6-point increase in the average writing score for Black students at grade 8 narrowed the White/Black gap in previous assessments.

But let's return to an earlier idea—that writing sometimes gets shortchanged in secondary schools. In its 2002 assessment, NAEP researchers asked eighth-graders how often they wrote in a learning log or journal. The researchers then correlated these self-reports with actual writing performance (scale scores ranged from 0 to 300) and computed averages. Take a moment to compare the average scores of those who "never or hardly ever" wrote in a journal—about 36% of the NAEP sample—versus those who claimed to write "at least once a week," in the following table. Clearly, journal writing pays handsome dividends in terms of increased writing proficiency.

Journal Writing Self-Reports Correlated with Writing Proficiency

Total N = 111,216	Never or Hardly Ever	A Few Times a Year	Once or Twice a Month	At Least Once a Week
Average scale score	143	155	157	158
Percentage	36%	17%	17%	30%

Source: NCES/NAEP, 2002.

The NAEP researchers also wanted to know how often eighth-graders were asked by their teachers to write more than one draft of a paper. They then correlated student self-reports of revision with the average scale scores in writing. Not surprisingly, those students who claimed their teachers "always" asked for revision did significantly better on the NAEP assessment than those who were "never" asked to revise (see the following table). Good teaching helps students achieve.

Revision Self-Reports Correlated with Writing Proficiency

Total $N = 106,722$	Never	Sometimes	Always
Average Scale Score	145	150	159
Percentage	10%	51%	39%

Source: NCES/NAEP, 2002.

As you reflect on the NAEP data for journal writing and revision, maybe you're more inclined to agree with the National Commission on Writing that "writing is every teacher's responsibility" and that "developing critical thinkers and writers should be understood as one of the central works of education" (p. 32).

Writing on the Home Front

To conclude its landmark report, the National Commission on Writing recommended that "the nation's leaders place writing squarely in the center of the school agenda" (CEEB, 2003, p. 26). Three far-reaching recommendations are presented:

- *Time:* The Commission believes that the amount of time most students spend writing should be at least *doubled.* This time can be found through assignments at home and by encouraging more writing during the school day in curriculum areas not traditionally associated with it. . . .

- *Writing across the curriculum:* We strongly endorse writing across the curriculum. The concept of doubling writing time is feasible because of *the near-total neglect of writing* outside English departments. In history, foreign languages, mathematics, home economics, science, physical education, art, and social science, all students can be encouraged to write more—and to write more effectively.

- *Assignments:* We suggest more out-of-school time for writing. . . . *Research is crystal clear: Schools that do well insist that students write every day and that teachers provide regular and timely feedback with the support of parents.*

(p. 28)

It's the "near-total neglect of writing" in content areas outside English that has prompted me to write this book. I take the view—one supported by persuasive research (Langer & Applebee, 1987)—that writing can serve as a powerful tool for content learning, a way of empowering students to construct meaning and develop insights.

What do I mean by this? On a personal level, think about everyday activities when you've set and accomplished written goals—perhaps a shopping list, or a to-do list, or an exercise regimen. Writing gave you power, because it externalized your grocery memory, or created an errand sequence, or set up a record-keeping system for your jogs around the neighborhood. Of course, as a beginning or experienced teacher, you also use writing as a powerful tool to organize instruction.

What works for us works for students as well. Writing helps them collect notes, plan future action, frame questions, monitor their own learning, and engage in an array of tasks, both cognitive and imaginative. For example, as students draw timelines of events, the historical sequence becomes more organized and visual in their minds. As they write imaginatively from a character's viewpoint, they project themselves into stories or problem-solving scenarios. As they organize research notes to develop a media-assisted class report, they rehearse and refine important ideas.

In *Writing to Learn*, William Zinsser sums up the power of writing this way:

> Writing is a tool that enables people in every discipline to wrestle with facts and ideas. It's a physical activity, unlike reading. Writing requires us to operate some kind of mechanism—pencil, pen, typewriter, word processor—for getting thoughts on paper. It compels us by the repeated effort of language to go after those thoughts and to organize them and present them clearly. It forces us to keep asking, "Am I saying what I want to say?" Very often the answer is no. It's a useful piece of information.
>
> *Source:* (Zinsser, 1988, p. 49)

Although writing assists thinking in countless ways, many of us ignore this fact when it comes to schoolwork. Generally speaking, we view student writing as an *assessment tool*—something students do to prove mastery or get a grade—but not as a *tool for learning* (or refining) content knowledge.

Why is this? The answer, I think, goes back to personal experience—and that it's only natural to teach as we've been taught. For many of us, "school writing" conjures up images of book reports, term papers, and essay exams—not to mention grammar worksheets and red pencil comments. Because we often associate school writing with uninspired graded tasks, we tend to discount its potential for helping students learn new ideas. Also, we may be inclined to "assign" writing but not to teach with and through it. That's a huge problem for effective instruction.

Actually, there's a difference between **expressive writing**—brief explorations that assist personal learning—and **public writing** that communicates knowledge to a wider audience. Early chapters discuss how expressive writing can motivate kids to "show what they know." Often ungraded, these exercises help students make personal sense of class lectures, assigned reading, or content discussions. Later chapters build on the expressive writing foundation. Generally, these graded tasks include processes of brainstorming, researching, and organizing, followed by drafting, peer response, self-assessment, revision, and editing. Strategies for coaching quality writing are found in the later chapters.

Of course, process instruction is hardly new. For example, hands-on lab activities, in-class debates, role-playing exercises, and simulations have long been used to invite active learning. Such strategies—as well as time-tested ones like study guides, vocabulary previews, and note-taking worksheets—are often called *instructional scaffolds* (Bruner, 1978) because they help learners construct and internalize knowledge. Thus, the teacher's role shifts from "information dispenser" to "learning facilitator"—and expert teachers are those who orchestrate sequences of increasingly complex activity. They aim not so much to "cover" material as to "uncover" it. They teach for insight.

My framework for linking expressive and academic writing is shown in the following figure. Notice that the three domains of academic writing parallel the categories used by NAEP. Notice too that expressive writing provides "foundation" for the academic domains.

So here's the bottom line: *Writing-to-learn activities help to scaffold the assignments for more formalized—and graded—public writing tasks; the aim of both types of writing is improved content learning.*

Figure I.1

Four Domains of Writing

ACADEMIC ("PUBLIC WRITING") TEXTS		
NARRATIVE & POETIC	**INFORMATIONAL & FUNCTIONAL**	**PERSUASIVE & ARGUMENTATIVE**
These texts give voice to ideas, observations, or experiences.	*These texts convey information or explain facts, ideas, or processes.*	*These texts offer logical or other support for claims or positions.*
Typical school tasks include *stories* (personal, historical, fictional), *poetry* (formula verse, free verse, songs), *scripts* (dialogues, monologues, radio plays, video skits, hypermedia), and *practical texts* (newspaper stories, letters, interviews, obituaries, profiles, parodies, satires, speeches, etc.). To motivate students, many teachers use "real world" genre in this domain—tasks such as the *autobiographical incident, literacy autobiography* (Chapter 1), or *personalized research* (Chapter 9).	Typical school tasks include *test questions, comprehension checks, lab reports, summaries of lecture notes, descriptions, process explanations, biographies of historical figures, and content-centered research papers.* To motivate students, many teachers use "real world" genre in this domain—tasks such as *brochures, business reports, case studies, career plans, directions, guidelines, histories, interviews, how-to manuals, newsletters, pamphlets, posters, resumes, regulations, survey results, web pages*, etc.	Typical school tasks include *letters to the editor, literary or historical analysis, debates, essays focused on policy dilemmas, controversial issues,* and *proposals to solve a problem* (sometimes with research references, surveys, etc.). To motivate students, many teachers use "real world" genre in this domain—tasks such as *awards, advertisements, commercials, tributes, complaints, editorials, eulogies, feature articles, job applications, marketing memos, petitions, requests, reviews, self-assessments, warnings*, etc.
EXPRESSIVE ("WRITING-TO-LEARN") TEXTS		
Expressive writing can take diverse forms, including *lists, sketches, diagrams, maps, and clusters* (both individual and posted as *Wall Text* by teams); *journal or learning log entries* (both traditional and electronic); *freewriting narratives* and *focused freewriting; genre change* and *"text tapping" exercises; responses to reading;* and *letters of advice, affection, apology, complaint, congratulations, invitation, protest, self-direction, sympathy, thanks*, etc.		

Mapping the Chapters

Early chapters in this text show how expressive writing can spark active learning; later chapters emphasize how public writing tasks can develop and extend student knowledge, preparing students for future success in academic and employment arenas.

My first aim is to stimulate your interest, prompt conversation, and motivate writing. As you discuss ideas—and share written notes with colleagues—you'll develop a range of personal and practical insights. My second aim is to engage you in useful activities. For example, I'll invite you to try your hand at creating imaginative writing tasks and rubrics tied to your content area—a welcome diversion from end-of-the-chapter questions.

In Chapter 1, "Writing from the Inside Out," you'll consider the role of narrative knowledge in content learning. In particular, you'll see the usefulness of student-written learning histories in all content areas and how expressive writing can lead naturally to reflective writing. Narrative writing offers great potential to personalize learning.

In Chapter 2, "Challenging the Hidden Curriculum," you'll reflect on teaching practices that often lead to resistance from students. You'll learn how middle school and high school teachers can use learning logs, both traditional and electronic, to motivate expressive writing and in-depth learning—without the workload of correction.

In Chapter 3, "Exploring Expressive Writing," you'll consider quotation prompts, guided imagery, dramatic scenarios (or "cases"), role-playing, and dialogue writing, plus you'll examine brief texts generated by these strategies. These engaging activities, usually ungraded, are ones you can assign "for fun" or as preparation for public writing.

In Chapter 4, "Tapping the Power of Metaphor," you'll examine the soft underbelly of thought—specifically, metaphorical thinking—to consider its potential for forging personal, imaginative links to curriculum content. You'll see how Wall Text can motivate students, spark discussion, and prepare students for academic tasks.

In Chapter 5, "Helping Basic Writers Succeed," you'll consider "flexible teaming"—a useful idea for helping skill-deficient students. You'll also focus on strategic content-based activities that teach basic skills effectively, with a minimum of effort. Here's where you search for ideas to assist kids who may lack academic motivation.

In Chapter 6, "Designing Assignments and Rubrics," you'll see how academic writing tasks can emerge from learning logs and Wall Text. By attending to assignment design and rubrics, you'll learn how to better motivate students, invite collaboration, and help them monitor their own thinking and self-assessment processes.

In Chapter 7, "Managing the Writing Process," you'll revisit the basics of writing process instruction and reflect on the recursiveness principle—how writers "go back" in their writing in order to "move ahead." You'll learn the nuts and bolts of peer response groups and see how such groups can lighten your teaching burden.

In Chapter 8, "Coaching and Judging Writing," you'll explore assessment. This chapter reminds you that feedback matters, and that grading doesn't have to be a black hole that sucks the life out of teaching. You'll find practical, teacher-tested strategies for responding to papers in efficient, helpful ways, plus ideas on portfolio assessment.

In Chapter 9, "Researching Outside the Box," you'll consider alternatives to the traditional research paper, which students pretend to write and teachers pretend to read. You'll see that high-interest formats—Saturation Reports, I-Search papers, and Multigenre Research Projects—provide exciting contexts for inquiry and documentation of findings.

In Chapter 10, "Writing in a Digital World," you'll see what some content teachers are doing to engage students via electronic technology. In fact, you may choose to begin your reading with this important chapter, which is new to the second edition, and use it as a foundation for the other chapters.

Finally, in the "Revisiting Insight" Epilogue, you'll review key points about writing as a tool for learning. In addition, you'll consider a set of research-based techniques for teaching writing to adolescents. This "capstone" material, drawn from an important meta-analysis of many research studies (Graham & Perin, 2007), is also new to this edition.

Five appendixes conclude this book. Appendix A describes a Literacy Autobiography Case Study task for you and your colleagues. Appendix B lists Bob Tierney's "concept-trigger" words, which help students write metaphorically about target concepts in a discipline. Appendix C outlines Macie Wolfe's adaption of a "cubing" prewriting activity, which is useful in all content areas. Appendix D, drawn from development work at the Northwest Central Regional Educational Laboratory (NCREL), offers generic graphic organizers that many content teachers use to support note-taking and writing. Appendix E presents several content area writing assignments (with grading rubrics) to supplement those provided elsewhere in the book.

Acknowledgments

This book is dedicated to my National Writing Project colleagues, for all their insights into quality writing instruction—and especially to biology teacher Bob Tierney, who has shared writing-to-learn workshops since the early 1980s. Bob's great teaching is featured throughout this book, and I thank him for showing us the way.

Let me also acknowledge writing project folks in Utah, with whom I've worked for many years. Colleagues like Chris Crowe, Deborah Dean, Gary Dohrer, Lynda Hamblin, Richard Harmston, Margaret Pettis, Nicole Robinson, Margaret Rostkowski, Jeff Stephens, Denice Turner, and Linda Warren have given to the greater good without hesitation. Utah's literacy instruction would be impoverished without them. For this edition of *Coaching Writing in Content Areas*, I was welcomed into demos and discussions of content area coaching by fine teachers like Randy Christensen, Kathy Christiansen, Curtis Jensen, Laura Miller, Launa Moser, Chris Sloan, DeAnna Stallings, Paul Wagner, Macie Wolfe, and Jeremy Young.

I also need to salute the teachers in my Utah State University classes as well as those in Georgia taught by Professor Dan Kirby. Teachers across the nation love Dan's irreverent sense of humor, classroom wisdom, and inspired teaching. Paralleling his encouragement for this edition were the earlier helpful comments from a convivial response group—namely, Christine, Brock, Keith, Ken, Lynn, Michael, and Sylvia.

As for colleagues farther afield—Ann Bayer, Sheridan Blau, Rebekah Caplan, Sally Hampton, Harry Noden, Tom Newkirk, Carol Booth Olson, Will Pitkin, Tom Romano, Kathy Rowlands, Karen Spear, Nat Teich, Fran Weinberg, Jeff Wilhelm, Denny Wolfe—let me recall a fine sentence of Gabriel Garcia Marquez: "In the end all books are written for your friends."

Several outside reviewers helped improve this book's utility, and I express sincere appreciation to each of them: Margaret Carlock, Lecanto High School; Cathy Fleischer, Eastern Michigan University; Louel Gibbons, The University of Alabama; Madelaine Kingsbury, Overbrook High School; Stephanie Kirby, Maxwell Elementary; Carol Booth Olson, University of California–Irvine; and Mark Reimer, Steinbach Regional Secondary School.

Kudos to my editor, Aurora Martinez, and to editorial assistant Amy Foley for their faith in this project and for shepherding the second edition through production.

Finally, and most importantly, I acknowledge Carol Strong, the woman whose insights about things that matter are both clear and true. In this book I try to honor what this former Professor of the Year has taught me regarding good classroom coaching.

Write-for-Insight Activity

What thoughts did this Preface evoke? That's a question only you can answer. As you jot responses either online or in a traditional learning log and then compare notes with others, you might find your ideas influenced by prior experiences—say, with textbooks (you might dislike them) or with writing (you might secretly write poetry or have a family blog). Also, you might already know something about instructional scaffolds in teaching or have beliefs about the value of writing-to-learn activities. In short, what background do you bring to this reading?

In your learning log, jot down: (1) key ideas of the Preface, (2) your insights about those ideas, and (3) your questions. Reflect on what you bring to the text in terms of experience. In a follow-up workshop, you may be asked to share your log entry with a partner or colleague. Read what this person has to say and talk it over. Afterwards, write briefly about the results of your interchange, explaining how your insights were confirmed, challenged, or extended. As you'll see, this follow-up writing serves to consolidate your learning—helping you "show what you know." Then share a copy of this text (that is, two learning log entries) with your course instructor or workshop leader.

Foreword

What is it about writing that makes people in the secondary schoolhouse nervous and edgy? English teachers know the pressure of being front-line "experts," somehow responsible for improving writing scores on state tests. But teachers of social studies, math, health, science, business, and the arts are feeling the heat as well. Principals and district supervisors, under pressure in the local media, wince at the apparent lack of year-to-year progress. Maybe all of these instructionally intelligent players know that the job of helping young people use written language effectively is everyone's responsibility—and that without a coordinated and collaborative school-wide plan for writing practice, progress will continue to evade us.

Look, I think we're all a little too tense about this writing thing. My local informant, for all things middle and high school, is my daughter Cara, a kid who loves school and loves to write. She writes her own book, has her own blog, and edits classmates' "books" online. This writing craze has taken over a number of her friends as well.

"Well," you say, "with two English teachers for parents, what choice does she have?"

To that I answer, we helped her become a voracious reader—but a chronology of exciting writing experiences in social studies, science, and health classes have helped make her a confident writer. "In sixth grade," Cara reports, "it was the Giant EDLRs (Experimental Design Lab Reports). You know, observations, materials, procedures, and then conclusions on amazing experiments. Also in sixth grade was my epic social studies teacher, Ms. D. One of her favorite things was for us to think outside the box and get the Big Picture. We did this by choosing optional 'Making Connections' assignments, where we'd use a current event or personal experience and link it to what we were currently studying. It would take up a page in our ISN (Interactive Student Notebook), a giant Five-Star spiral that I have to this day and encompassed our entire curriculum for that year."

Clearly, Cara's enthusiasm for writing has been fed by content area teachers who, as Bill Strong suggests, developed inquiry pathways for authentic written products. But let's face it, there are lots of kids in your classes who aren't like Cara—kids who struggle with written language and who don't enjoy those wonderful assignments you've dreamed up. Their writing skills are limited, and they aren't very good readers or thinkers. They turn in bad stuff, and you don't know how to help them fix it. Hey, you know bad stuff when you see it, but you may not know how to help them revise, rethink, or "re-see" their writing.

In this very smart book, Bill Strong has a better idea. He suggests that our task as content area teachers is not so much to *teach* writing (let the English pros do some of the heavy lifting on style, voice, and conventions) as it is to create opportunities for students to *use* writing as a tool for thinking and for content acquisition. Strong affirms throughout that writing promotes deeper and more personal encounters with content. Even more importantly, writing in science, math, and social studies creates opportunities for students to think like professionals in those fields. Such opportunities happen often in the "Reading/Thinking Journal" for Cara's ninth-grade biology class. Her teacher believes that students are more engaged when they record thoughts, questions, and class notes in expressive writing.

I like the way Strong has reworked this second edition to include new ideas, teaching stories, and more emphasis on coaching. The coaching metaphor makes sense for the task of creating authentic writing practice in your classroom.

Shortly after the death of John Wooden, the legendary basketball coach of UCLA, Scott Simon of National Public Radio reprised an interview from several years earlier, in which he'd asked Wooden about his eight national championships and 88-game winning streak. Wooden said that winning games and celebrating championships was nice, but what he enjoyed most was coaching, and what he enjoyed most about coaching was practice. He loved everything about practice time: the routines and rituals of practice, the repetition of practice, the growth and development of players. "It's in practice with insightful and timely coaching," Wooden said, "that great teams are born and learn to win."

Those of us who have spent many years coaching writers say "Amen" to Wooden's observations. Effective coaching happens as we write with students, as well as when we model using writing to learn content. Sometimes it happens at the shoulder level when we kneel beside the desk of a student writer to ask writerly questions. Effective coaching happens up close, often one person at a time—not just to point out or correct weaknesses, but to question and urge further thinking, exploration, and rewriting. Lots of the drudgery of teaching writing comes from the old belief that grading papers is a teacher's most important role. Bill Strong has a different take on that too: "We need to coach more and judge less."

The other important coaching insight I take away from the Wooden interview is his emphasis on the routines, rituals, and repetitions of practice. Writing is complex, high-level human behavior. It can't be learned in one course or one grade level in school. Just throwing out an assignment now and then won't do it. Proficiency requires consistent, repeated opportunities for practice, plus insightful coaching. In the press of teaching our content, however, it's not always easy to come up with the well-designed writing prompt. This book offers plenty of practice activities, assignment ideas, and coaching strategies to engage your students in the content you care about.

One last thought: Successful coaching of writers has as much to do with attitude as it does with technique. The teachers Cara mentioned offered students not only enticing and well-structured writing projects, but also their own personal energy and nurturing spirits as writing coaches. Their love for their content was palpable, their enthusiasm contagious. In working with Bill in summer institutes and in workshops around the country, I've watched him cajole, nudge, and inspire writers toward growth and confidence. As you read this book and listen to Bill Strong's compelling personal voice and warm narrative delivery, you will also come to know exactly who he is as writer, teacher, and coach.

Dan Kirby,
Professor of English Education
Kennesaw State University

Writing from the Inside Out

CHAPTER 1

We write to taste life twice, in the moment, and in retrospection.

—Anaïs Nin

Remembered Writing

"There's a story in your picture," the nun says. Her black sleeves are like bat's wings, a whisper in passing, and her wire-framed glasses catch the light. Outside, a gray Oregon rain makes tiny, trickling rivers on tall schoolroom windows; but inside there is radiator heat, drying wool, and fourth-grade desks in rows, bolted to long wooden runners. The desks are creaky flip-top structures of oak and iron, well-inscribed by other young scholars in parochial school uniforms.

I'm no writer, but I bend to the task, imagining myself astride a pale yellow horse—Palomino, I'll call it—with a dog at my side. The horse is rounded and solid beneath me, and trail-dust covers my boots. It's a rocky landscape shadowed by cottonwoods, a tree I've read about in other stories. The dog moves out ahead, and as he does, I'm recalling a tale told by my father's logging partner about a canyon infested with rattlesnakes. Suddenly the dog freezes, one paw raised. Hidden nearby, just off the trail, a huge rattlesnake lies coiled and hissing, ready to strike. I rein in the horse, quiet him down. Easy, boy, easy. That was a close one.

A few days later, I face more than imagined danger. I'm sent upstairs, past the office of Sister Mother Superior, to the hallowed ground of seventh and eighth graders. I read my paragraphs about how the day was saved by the cowboy's trusty companion. "And this from a fourth grader," the nun says. As the smallest kid in my class but not the dumbest, I catch the drift. She aims to embarrass a sullen audience into better writing. Listening, I nearly wet my pants.

The story appears in the school newspaper, a faded purple-ink publication run off on ditto masters, and there's secret pleasure in seeing my words typed up. I read them over and over. To me, they look "grown up," different from the cursive writing practice that leaves a red welt on my third finger. I take the newspaper home, knowing that being in print confers a new kind of status.

My reading takes place in the kitchen. Home from work in the timber, Dad sits at a chrome kitchen table with laminate top as my mom fixes supper. Reading aloud feels different from reading to the upper grade kids at school. It's less scary in one sense, more scary in another. After all, I *want* them to like it. Dad nods, and I put the story away.

It reappears on a Sunday afternoon at my grandparents' house, a small farm cottage with an oil-burning stove and lace doilies for the horsehair sofa. The after-dinner routine is coffee and homemade cherry pie and adults settling in. My grandfather is lean and white-haired, a Quaker-like man with fourth-grade schooling to match mine; my grandmother is heavy-set, with blunt opinions.

"Billy's story was in the school paper," my mother says, pulling it from her purse.

My grandparents rise on conspiratorial cue. "Oh, let's hear it."

The living room is filled with the steady ticking of an old pendulum clock.

I'm on the spot now, set up by my mother. Yet as I begin to read, I can feel myself again at the center of things, creating and sustaining a world. Dust rises from the trail. Wind moves through the cottonwoods, stirring the leaves. The horse is rounded and solid beneath me, with my family circled around and listening.

"Why, that's very good," they say to me afterwards. And I grin in reply.

Narration as Knowledge

Why do I begin with a small remember story? Because what I know is my experience. And it's this experience plus others—some not so happy—that have shaped my attitudes, beliefs, and skills in the area of writing. Think about it: What each of us truly *knows* about the world—including the world of writing—results from what we've personally experienced, either directly (through life events) or indirectly (through reading, technology, and other vicarious means). Stories show what we know.

Writing "from the inside out"—remembering key experiences and reflecting on their significance—provides our focus for Chapter 1. This simple, basic strategy works in all content area classrooms, as students are invited to recall past events that have influenced their attitudes, beliefs, and skills in an area of study. For example, what are key memories in math and music, science and social studies, or health and humanities? Some experiences will be positive or exciting, others just the opposite. But all of them teach. The point isn't to fixate on the past but to learn from it. And writing is just the tool, regardless of content area, for accomplishing this aim.

Asking secondary students to recall stories of significant learning usually leads to insights. For example, when Michael writes about "being put on the spot and made fun of," you better understand his scowling red face and crossed arms as you try to involve him in a history discussion. When Heather tells of her dad's celebration of her math award, you understand the dynamics of her nose-to-the-grindstone motivation. When Maria praises last year's teacher "who helping to better my English speaking," you're reminded of why you became a teacher in the first place.

Should stories about past learning be graded? For expressive, writing-to-learn work, I recommend simply "checking" the papers and savoring the insights they provide. In reading them quickly, it's helpful to have a packet of sticky notes handy. For each student, jot down a comment or two like the following:

- "Mark, your computer camp story hooked me! Tell me more!"
- "Ali, I hear your concerns. Fresh start in math this year—let's talk!"
- "Emily, how about career goals? I look forward to knowing you better!"

Brief comments like these signal your desire to get students involved in content learning. Later, as they study or work on assignments, you can roam the room, doing on-the-spot mini-conferences—or you can invite students to your desk, with writing in hand. Your comments will set the direction for dialogue, but you can also use general prompts like this one: "Now, Michelle, remind me of your story."

For most students, having a teacher *solicit* and *value* their personal learning story will be a new experience. Expect some students to be a bit wary or tongue-tied, while others may want to share lots of background information. To manage both situations, announce to students your aims for the mini-conference—to know them as individuals, not to evaluate them—and explain that you'll have an egg timer (or some such device) to limit the length of the conferences. Of course, for some students, a quick flip of the egg timer will provide the extra bit of attention they need.

Mini-conferences help students consider the meaning, or personal significance, of their experience. As a responder to writing, or as a mini-conference listener, your key questions or prompts will be ones like these:

- "So, what do you think this experience *taught* you?"
- "Tell me how you could *use* your experience to move forward."
- "Are there *other* stories in your learning history different from this one?"

Inviting students to consider such questions in advance of a mini-conference not only focuses instruction but also encourages in-depth insights, the kind not often seen in some secondary classrooms. Such assessment activities pay long-term dividends in terms of motivation, goal-setting, and willingness to engage in content learning.

Prompting Narrative

Just for a moment, picture yourself at a family celebration—Thanksgiving, say, or maybe a Fourth of July get-together. You're among family and friends, and there's lots of food, while everyone gets reacquainted. Uncle Jake asks, "So how's it going?" And Aunt Marge gives you a big hug and says, "Now tell me everything you've been doing."

Stories frame our lives. Primitive stories like "Milk spill!" are among our earliest utterances, and more complicated summative tales, called obituaries, are our exit stories. Of course, in between our childhood stories and obituaries, we are continually telling stories to Uncle Jake, Aunt Marge, and anyone who feigns the slightest interest. As psychologist Roger Schank puts it, "Communication consists of selecting the stories that we know and telling them to others at the right time" (1990, p. 12).

Telling a story to an interested listener—one who sometimes asks thoughtful questions—encourages the storyteller to revisit and reflect on experience, to see it in larger contexts. An active listener, like any active learner, wants to know more than the bare outline of a story. Interactive talk provides a very powerful rehearsal for narrative writing—including the memories of past content area learning.

Good teachers make processes of active listening explicit through in-class **modeling**. For example, you might share a personal learning story tied to your content area, and let students ask questions to serve as scaffolding for details. Your story might describe the disaster of your middle school science project, or the powerful feelings of your summer visit to Gettysburg, or your current struggles with a graduate statistics course. Such explicit modeling can be followed with a "think-pair-share" activity so that all students can practice storytelling and question-asking about learning, first in pairs and then in small groups. Of course, because students have already practiced their stories—and because they have internalized some of their listeners' questions—they'll write more fluently about past learning events. Remember that a well-developed story provides the basis for reflective *insight*, a form of higher-order thinking.

Another strategy, also based on student-to-student talk, uses **personal artifacts**. As kindergarten teachers discovered long ago, valued objects stimulate storytelling and reflection. What school-related artifacts do students keep in their dresser drawers, closets, or attics? Do they possess achievement ribbons, report cards, photos, old notebooks, yearbooks, trophies, term papers, or other memorabilia? What vivid memories of learning are aroused by artifacts? Again, through teacher modeling, students can be introduced to "time travel" via artifacts; and through think-pair-share activities, they can revisit earlier learning experiences to prepare for writing. Encourage students to reflect on the significance of past learning events—as well as their present-day relevance.

A third kind of prompt to stimulate memory writing involves the brainstorming technique of **clustering** (Rico, 1983, 1997) or free association "mapping." The process begins with a focus word or phrase in the center of a page. Basically, you allow your creative mind to follow random links and associations, however quirky they might seem to your more logical, task-oriented side. You quickly generate words that radiate outward from your central focus and then use these to generate other links or connections. Don't dwell on the associations—just keep them coming as you enjoy the free-wheeling process of memory search. Inevitably, you'll feel or "see" what you want to write about—just as I did for the following cluster. Looking over my cluster in Figure 1.1, you'll recognize some key words for the brief story that opens this chapter.

Figure 1.1

A Writing Memories Cluster

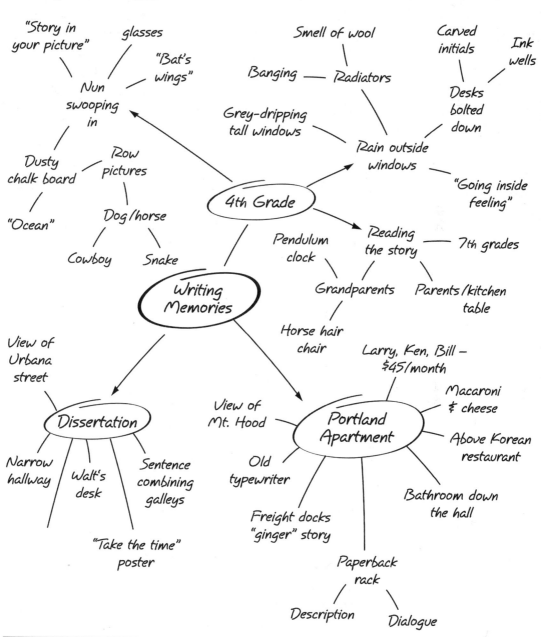

And if you're interested in mind-mapping software for today's tech-savvy students, make sure to check out **Inspiration 9**, the latest iteration of a suite of writing, planning, organizing, and presenting tools designed for students in grades 6 to 12. Like other tools from Inspiration Software, this one is popular with teachers and has won many national awards. A free 30-day trial is available at http://www.inspiration.com/freetrial.

Prompts like these help students create learning histories. It's through such stories that learners begin to understand that they have the means—*because* of self-knowledge—to create positive experiences for themselves. Of course, insights can also be nudged. Suggest to Tony, for example, that when procrastination next rears its head, he can use self-knowledge and self-discipline as twin swords, sending the ugly beast back to his lair.

Literacy Autobiographies

In working with teachers, I've read hundreds of literacy stories, and I always find them fascinating. Each story has its own insights, and each provides a window into a life. Of course, the narratives I value most are those that reflect genuine inquiry into specific personal experiences, not those that lightly skim the surface. It always interests me, too, that as I reread well-told stories years later, I can often picture the individual authors in my mind's eye. Stories have staying power.

Here, for example, is an excerpt from a narrative written by Chris Gooch, a physical science teacher. This paper went through initial drafting, peer response, a reading by me, and final revision. Chris has strong memories of penmanship instruction, which influence his definition of "writing."

> Mr. S. worked hard to help us develop our cursive writing. Over the first few months of fifth grade, I became a student Mr. S. felt comfortable joking around with, even in front of other students. I was turning in an assignment by hand, and I knew full well that I risked the dreaded on-the-spot paper grading. Sure enough, my number was up and he checked my handwriting while I was still standing in front of him. "Chris," he said, "this looks just like chicken scratch."
>
> What he said was true. It did look like a chicken had convulsed on the paper. But that was not why the comment impacted me. The whole class knew that the teacher did not approve of my handwriting. I had always been looked at as an average, or slightly above average, student by my peers in both the academic and athletic spheres. Now, I was being publicly told my handwriting was below average! I handled the situation in a very casual fashion. I did not let on that I had taken a blow.
>
> I turned in countless more assignments on that brown recycled paper. I remember the wide rows divided by dashed lines. I remember using the dashed lines to practice proportion for upper- and lowercase letters. I remember the sound of my pencil on that paper and it still gives me goose bumps, similar to fingernails on a chalkboard. I do not remember, however, getting a positive comment from Mr. S. about my

handwriting, especially not one the whole class heard. While my confidence was partially shaken, my stubbornness was just beginning. I decided I was no longer going to care how my teachers felt about my handwriting as long as they could read my work and the work itself was adequate. If it weren't for the next event I will talk about, I would still have that same attitude.

Do you find yourself drawn into the story that Chris has written—wanting to read more? Of course! You're curious about what happens next, and you're wondering how Chris has used his experience to inform his own work as a teacher. Remember, it is the reporting of experience, plus the reflection about it, that actually creates narrative knowledge. You'll see such reflection in the next sample text.

Music teacher Jennifer Fackrell had a very different sort of literacy narrative, one that centered on being able to cruise through high school with little engagement. As I read and commented on her draft, I tried to be encouraging but also to challenge her exploration of academic fears. The revision process, in Jennifer's words, was "an amazing thing" because "suddenly I was writing to myself." A short excerpt from her courageous final paper—much different from the original—is shown here.

I was able to scrape by with the bare minimum in length and content that was full of "fluff." I knew how to play the system. The teachers were just so grateful to get a readable paper that they didn't really care what was inside. I learned the tricks to a good essay: use five paragraphs, make sure you have an introduction and conclusion, write a good thesis, and support your thesis. This formula did very well for me because it made all of my papers look good. However, I never really learned to write. I remember really struggling with the creative side. I never realized how much this would affect me until I got to college.

My teachers now look for what is inside the paper as well. This has been an eye-opening experience for me. In some ways I feel like I am learning to write all over again. It has been good for me, though. I have been forced to move outside my protective bubble as I share my innermost thoughts with people I barely know. This is something I thought would never be possible, but I think I have finally discovered how to own my own writing and leave my protective bubble behind. It is a great feeling to know that I am capable of writing something with substance. I wish I had discovered this years ago.

I think I have finally discovered the value of writing assignments. If done with proper guidance from a teacher, they can be liberating. As a future teacher, I hope to give all students the opportunity to discover the joys of writing. I think one very important element in all of this is helping them learn to love reading, too. It took me a long time to make the connection between what I read and what I write. I used reading as my protective bubble and feared writing because it forced me to leave that bubble. However, the two are intimately connected. The only way to truly understand what you read is to become connected to it. Writing helps you do that. I don't know why it took me until my last year of college to figure that out, but it will remain with me for the rest of my life. I just hope I can help my students see this while they are still in the public education system.

Finally, consider an excerpt from ESL and language arts teacher Joyce McMullin, a truly compelling memory of middle school fears. Joyce recalled that because she wasn't "talented, smart, funny, popular, or cute," she had to be careful "not to do anything too stupid" that would push her into the "nerd" category. She then painted a scary picture of peer feedback— and illustrated why it's so important for teachers to monitor process writing tasks and provide training on appropriate methods of response. Her piece might well have been titled "When Bad Things Happen to Good Ideas":

Now it was time to share our narrations and get feedback before completing our final draft. I sat across the desk from Heather, a pretty, semi-popular girl who sometimes snickered at the socially backward things I did in school. I stared nervously at the mint-green plaster walls behind her, not wanting to catch her eye. My stomach tied up in knots as her pencil moved across my feeble paper, crossing out, adding on, and filling the paper with corrections. My status as a social outcast grew with every mark of Heather's pencil. I looked down at her paper, which I in turn was supposed to critique. I meekly scratched down a few worthless positive comments: "Good job—I can't see anything wrong." As she handed my paper back, I was completely embarrassed but also terrified, for I now had to conference with Mr. A. himself.

Mr. A. was a perfectly harmless guy. He was funny and friendly to everyone, and most kids liked being in his class. But when you are an insignificant social outcast in the seventh grade, everyone terrifies you, especially teachers. I hoped he wouldn't ream me too hard, since he could see Heather had already set me straight. Sitting across the cluttered piles of paper that camouflaged his desk, I tried to find somewhere to rest my hands, feet, and eyes. He had a sort of confused scowl as his eyes moved back and forth across the scribbled out words. My heart sunk.

Finally he looked at me and I shrank about six sizes into my chair. With the same confused scowl, he asked, "Why did you change this?" I went down another couple of sizes as I blubbered out some answer about how I had written it wrong but Heather had edited it in peer groups. "Change it back," he said.

A few weeks later, after all the papers were written and graded, Mr. A. sat in the center of our semicircle of desks and calmly announced that he was going to read anonymously one example that had scored a perfect five. My stomach dropped and my face went red as I heard the first sentence of my own writing. I put my head down and smiled. No one ever knew it was mine; but I did. For two minutes my writing was in the center spotlight. I had written a paper that my teacher considered a perfect five.

That was probably the most significant writing experience of my life because once I believed I *could* write my desire *to* write was rekindled. I went on to like writing all through high school.

Joyce's story has a happy ending because of her teacher's intervention. Mr. A. respected her writing aims, shielded her from wrong-headed advice, and acknowledged the quality of her work. Given his professionalism, he probably dealt with overzealous peer response before his next assignment, using the training strategies presented in Chapter 7. As always, good teachers make a difference.

Reflecting on Narrative

The landmark book by Judith Langer and Arthur Applebee—*How Writing Shapes Thinking* (1987)—reported on three years of case studies in secondary schools. Langer and Applebee found that although writing took many different forms in content classrooms, it centered on three learning functions:

- Drawing on relevant knowledge and experience in preparation for new activities
- Consolidating and reviewing new information and experiences
- Reformulating and extending knowledge

(p. 41)

Narrative, as considered so far, has the aim of "drawing upon relevant knowledge and experience in preparation for new activities." But can it also "consolidate and review new information" and "reformulate and extend knowledge"?

The answer—if we have students keep ongoing **learning logs**—is yes. As described in Chapters 2 to 5, students construct their own learning about quadratic equations, or photosynthesis, or romantic poetry, or the Great Depression of the 1930s, or some other topic. The ongoing "story line" of a learning log centers on information, but it also reflects doubts, questions, and insights. Because a well-kept learning log offers a first-person account of learning, it makes a great study tool for exams or for the writing of more traditional essays.

Some teachers provide students with weekly single-page sheets, sectioned off by day. Typically, students keep their log sheets in a personal three-ring binder or in a **working portfolio**, which houses the academic work for a term. Other teachers prefer spiral-bound notebooks for learning logs. Writing in the log may occur before a lesson (prediction), during it (questions and response), or afterwards (summarizing). But regardless of format, logs are integrated into the lesson as students share and swap entries or as they volunteer to read aloud. Of course, **weblogs**—or **blogs**—can also be electronically archived on a classroom website as described in Chapter 10.

Regardless of approach, learning logs personalize instruction. So why not have students tell the story of reducing their fast-food intake? Or share their process of researching local history? Or take field notes to document a series of animal behavior observations? Or narrate their personal solution to a math problem? Or do a write-up of make-believe stock market investments over a semester? These aren't school reports in the usual sense—they're imaginative and fun. And they're all story-based.

As students later prepare **learning (or "presentation") portfolios**, they inevitably "reformulate and extend knowledge" because they must showcase selected examples of quality work and include a cover letter to explain the portfolio's artifacts. To construct a learning portfolio, students sequence and evaluate the artifacts, but in their cover letter they must "tell the story" of their learning. As students explain how they came to select certain artifacts—and what each represents—the narrative unfolds "from the inside out." You'll learn more about such portfolios in Chapter 8.

In Mike Rose's *Possible Lives: The Promise of Public Education in America* (1995), math and science teacher Michael Johnson makes a compelling case for using the students' own language, both speech and writing, to teach for insight.

> I have students write narratives in math because it leads to deeper understanding. I'll ask them to explain to me what a decimal is. They'll say, "I'll show you." And I'll say, "No, don't show me. *Explain* to me what a decimal is, what it does. . . ." [Also] each student is linked to a buddy, and those buddies are linked to study groups. We'll take a concept—let's say reproduction in humans—and the students in the study groups cannot move on until everyone understands the concept. The students are teaching other students and are responsible for each other. You'll see a lot of talking going on. (Rose, 1995, p. 219)

Like Johnson, I believe that talk and writing can hook learners into content area instruction. Yes, some students may resort to storytelling as a default strategy on exams and high-stakes assessments because they haven't yet mastered analytic modes of thought. However, with good teaching, narrative provides a foundation for informational forms of writing, just as this chapter builds upon my fourth-grade story.

For balanced learning, students need a rich array of writing activities.

Content Area Examples

"But wait," you may be whispering to yourself. "What would a 'rich array of writing activities' mean in *my* content area?"

Here's a small collection of ideas for expressive writing. Many use narrative, but some draw upon other kinds of thinking skills. Do you see possibilities for your own class here, or assignments you might adapt? Take a moment to browse.

Health and Physical Education

1. Write a biographical sketch of a favorite athlete—or adopt that athlete's voice.

2. Write in letter form, explaining how to play a game or perform a particular feat to someone who doesn't know how.

3. Write to convince a friend or family member to become physically fit.

4. Keep a journal of your calorie intake, exercise regimen, or athletic training.

5. Make up new games, and write descriptions of them, giving strategies and rules.

6. Analyze and critique a gymnastics event, basketball game, or other sporting event.

7. Write self-assessments of your performance from watching video playback.

8. Compare another team's performance, style, or strategy with your own.

9. Write about a sports event on TV as a referee or umpire.

10. Analyze the social class appeals of various games in our culture.

Consumer and Family Studies

1. Create recipes and write them for others after sharing cooked samples.

2. Write paragraphs deciding what should be added or omitted from the recipe.

3. Collect recipes and file them. Write short paragraphs, similar in style to the "Food" section of a newspaper, explaining the appeal of the recipes.

4. Work with others to create handbooks on good grooming, choosing a wardrobe, proper foods for good health, and so on.

5. Make annotated bibliographies for use in specific areas such as child care or preparing foods from other cultures.

6. Evaluate products and publish findings of those that do what they claim to do and those that do not.

7. Write newsletters about ideas for budget management or comparative shopping.

8. Write letters about consumer issues such as pricing, quality, or unfair or unethical business practices.

9. Take notes and write up observations in child care classes; expand these into papers on child behavior or human growth and development.

10. Write and deliver consumer announcements for radio and TV spots.

Fine Arts

1. In music, write lyrics that may be set to music or read with accompaniment.

2. Write assessments of performances or artifacts.

3. Write descriptions of art done by students or established artists.

4. Analyze music with regard to tone, mood, expression, or other elements.

5. Analyze art with regard to color, form, balance, or other elements.

6. Write a letter to a music/art committee describing your preferences for future events.

7. Write a critique of your own artistic performance.

8. Compile a list of music or art for a public showing; then critique the event for different audiences (PTA newsletter, school newspaper, etc.).

9. Explain your motivation for performing or creating a particular work.

10. Write imaginatively from an artist's or composer's point of view.

Mathematics

1. Explain the steps involved in solving a problem to someone else.

2. Write story problems like those in the text or given out as models; swap.

3. Write a description of your own strengths and weaknesses in math and offer suggestions for improvement.

4. Write about how a math skill just studied relates to the one now under study.

5. Create real-life sequences in which math is used to solve a problem.

6. Describe areas of math that you have questions about.

7. Explain math terms in your own words to someone who doesn't understand.

8. Keep a math journal of your insights and frustrations.

9. Study a numerical graph and translate its meaning into sentences.

10. Write weekly letters to parents explaining what you have learned in math.

English and Drama

1. Create character biographies and summaries.

2. Distill and/or analyze the central message in a literary work.

3. Write from the point of view of a literary character.

4. Write up observations of actors or contrasting presentations of a work.

5. Write about sensory experiences that parallel those in literature.

6. Write book reviews that persuade a person to buy a book.

7. Create works in the same form as those under study.

8. Write diaries (from the author's point of view) about intention.

9. Compare a book version with its dramatic rendition on film.

10. Transform fiction or poetry into other literary forms.

Science

1. Keep journals of lab experiments.

2. Write imaginative diaries related to scientific achievements.

3. Write imaginative accounts from inside organisms.

4. Explain a scientific principle to someone who is deaf.

5. Write opinion papers related to pollution, ecology, nuclear energy, or other topics.

6. Describe on paper your process of thinking about an application problem.

7. Write a letter home explaining what you learned this week.

8. Interview a scientist about his/her research and prepare a report.

9. Make predictions about the future based on present trends or data.

10. Compare alternate theoretical explanations for an event.

Social Sciences

1. Write about a single event from different points of view.

2. Explain what two or more events have in common historically.

3. Create a "You Are There" scenario.

4. Conduct field research (interviews and polling) and write up the results.

5. Become a historical figure and create a diary.

6. Explain an event to someone from another planet.

7. Keep a journal recording news references to a particular topic.

8. Extrapolate into the future from present social trends.

9. Create a case study illustrating a psychological principle.

10. Persuade the public through a letter to the editor expressing your views.

Narrative Insights

So let's summarize: Narrative provides the backbone for daily writing in learning logs—the expressive work so fundamental to active learning. The previous array of prompts suggests that logs are limited only by our own imagination. It's through them that students construct ongoing stories of what they understand. Information thus gets transformed into personal knowledge, which can be showcased eventually in exams, traditional essays, or learning portfolios.

To write for insight is to make sense to oneself, first and foremost. At the same time, writing is also a means of communicating with others in a classroom arena. Narrative writing helps students discover meanings in their own experience and connect those meanings to curriculum content through reflection; but shaping one's story for others requires a leap of imagination—keeping readers in mind, asking what they will need from the text, and finding the right words.

Narrative is powerful because it invites students to revisit an experience and learn from it. Moreover, as students share learning stories—and as those stories are validated by others through applause, discussion, and shared laughter—a genuine classroom community is created. Marginalized learners begin to understand, for example, that they're not the only ones who struggle with basic algebra concepts or symbolism in literature. And the well-articulated insights of key students can serve as scaffolding for the entire class, raising the intellectual bar for inquiry.

As you review the Four Writing Domains framework in the Preface, you'll note that learning autobiographies can *either* be an expressive, writing-to-learn activity or a more formalized type of process writing task in the narrative domain. In either case, the writing will help students clarify the meanings of their experience in a particular content area such as history, science, mathematics, or music.

A rationale for narrative knowledge is neatly articulated by Roger Schank (1990), an expert in human memory and artificial intelligence research. Pay close attention to Schank's bottom-line assertion about human learning:

> Our knowledge of the world is more or less equivalent to the set of experiences that we have had, but our communication is limited by the number of stories we know to tell. In other words, all we have are experiences, but all we can effectively tell are stories. . . . *Learning from one's own experiences depends upon being able to communicate our experiences as stories to others.* (italics added)

(Schank, 1990, p. 12)

These ideas link to the head note of this chapter—that "we write to taste life twice, in the moment, and in retrospection." I invite you to *reflect* on these ideas as you brainstorm literacy memories from your past, ones that might become part of your autobiography. True stories lead to personal insights.

Write-for-Insight Activity

Your *beliefs* and *attitudes* toward writing as well as your general approach to writing—your writing *behaviors*—have all been shaped by past experiences. So what memorable experiences made you who you are today? Our aim is to explore this question.

First, make a quick list of school-related writing memories—elementary school, secondary school, and college. Then jot down other memories, such as keeping a diary, writing notes or love letters, and creating imaginative stories or poems for your own pleasure. Look over your lists. Which memories are particularly strong or vivid? Why do you think these memories have stuck with you?

Create a memory snapshot. In your learning log, put yourself in the time and place of your memory and tell the story of what happened. Then comment on what you see as the significance of this particular memory. Your memory of this experience is evidence that it was meaningful to you. So, looking back as an adult, what is the personal learning you now attach to this event?

Share your snapshot with colleagues and hear what they have written. Do any of their stories have relevance to your current teaching? Your course instructor or workshop leader may ask for a copy of your work. Finally, turn to Appendix A for details of the literacy autobiography case study and the assignment's rubric.

Challenging
the Hidden Curriculum

First we shape our institutions, and then they shape us.

—Winston Churchill

Teacher as Writer

Just before class, as young teachers shuffle toward their desks, Kim corners me, asking whether last week's "literacy autobiographies" have been corrected.

"Well, yes and no," I reply. "The essays are coming back today, but no, I don't think I've been correcting them."

"Isn't that your job?" Her voice has a nervous edge.

I shrug. "I try to respond to what you've said and how you've said it because I see honest response as part of good teaching. But merely correcting a paper you won't revise is a little like manicuring a corpse. What's the point?"

Kim looks perplexed. "So what did I get?"

"What do you mean?"

"You know, like grade-wise."

"Well, that depends."

"On what?" Kim asks.

"On whether you work some more on your paper. That's up to you. We're writing to learn, but also writing to communicate. So, decide whether you've written as effectively as you can." I pause to lighten things up. "Of course, there's no extra charge if you'd like to talk it over."

Kim shifts her weight and doesn't smile. "But I thought I was done."

I pull up my Paul Valery quote: "Writing is never finished, only abandoned."

"Hmmm." She knits her brow.

"You know, with luck, some of your students will use revision to explore and develop their ideas. For others, getting by will be the goal."

"Look, all I want is a good grade out of this class."

"I understand that. But you can also learn in the process."

"I don't get it," Kim says.

"Okay, first read my responses, then ask yourself whether you agree with my ideas—and whether my suggestions might help your text. Fair enough?"

"In other words, I have to do more work on it."

"That's really up to you—seriously."

"What's the point?"

"My job is to make sure you assess your own writing and get your money's worth for your hard-earned tuition."

"Uh-huh, sure."

"The idea is to write for insight."

"I really don't get it," she says again.

Resistance to Writing

Kim is an extreme example of the new teacher who doesn't "get it" in lots of ways. But she (or he) does attend preservice and in-service classes, even those that use writing as a tool for making knowledge personal, connected, and accessible to self.

In Chapter 1 you learned that literacy autobiographies prompt reflection. However, Kim didn't like the idea that writing could make her an open book, one that others might read. She resisted writing-to-learn activities and had plenty of questions as we began drafting and sharing: How long does it have to be? Why write about your past experience? Do spelling and punctuation count? Why waste time in response groups?

I read her paper with interest. Aside from its technical flaws, the writing was detached and cool, describing with smugness how she'd eased through secondary schools without writing a single essay. Her strategy was to trade math skills for the writing talents of others. She'd dictate a few key points to friends, who'd do "the dirty work" that she'd recopy or download. When it came to reports and term papers, the issue for Kim was not so much ethics as efficacy—a division of labor.

Through cunning, Kim suggested, it was easy to beat the system. Fakery made sense because it reduced the workload.

"So who wrote *this* paper?" I asked in the margin, forcing a smile.

To veteran teachers, it will come as no surprise that Kim could mouth platitudes to cover up her limited knowledge. On the other hand, she viewed all teachers (me included) as faceless functionaries in a long, weary line of grade dispensers. She saw schooling as a game, the main goal being to outwit those in positions of authority. Left unanswered was the question of why she'd even want to teach, given her cynical beliefs about the fraudulent nature of the enterprise—or how she'd treat learners in her own classroom.

Despite my best efforts, Kim saw personal meaning-making as "bogus." She regarded writing-to-learn activities as ways to keep kids in line, a kind of no-nonsense behavior management tool. She viewed grades as "the whole point of school, the only reason students show up." As she voiced these ideas in our conferences, her ideas about teacher and student roles became clear. The teacher's task was to assign, correct, and grade writing; and the student's job was to "psyche out" the teacher and write to specifications. Kim wanted me to lead in traditional ways, telling her exactly what to do.

Reviewing my suggestions, she was totally amazed and unsettled that a grade might be open-ended, with opportunities for revision extended over time, or that I might raise questions or discuss alternatives but not focus narrowly on correction. Being asked to use the "I" pronoun and think independently prompted anxiety. Her coping strategy was to ask repeatedly, "Is this good enough? So what do you want?"

The Hidden Curriculum of Writing

As I work in schools, I have to conclude that Kim is a product of the hidden curriculum—"school experiences that result in unintended, unplanned, even unsuspected and undesired student learning" (Shaver & Strong, 1982, p. 1). The hidden curriculum of writing certainly isn't found in national standards, in state frameworks, or in colorful scope and sequence charts. Rather, it exists in messages that students read "between the lines," as we use (or abuse) writing in middle schools and high schools. Ask yourself whether any of these statements ring perversely true.

1. Writing in school is something you do to get a grade, and school is something you do to get a diploma or certificate.

2. The main purpose of writing in school is to tell the teacher what the teacher already knows, not to explore a topic or idea.

3. A second main purpose of school writing is to provide diversionary busywork (or "time filler") so that the class is occupied.

4. A third main purpose of school writing is to serve as a management threat to students or as actual punishment for misbehavior.

5. The central intellectual activity in school writing is to guess what the teacher wants, not to figure out what's worth saying or how to say it most effectively.

6. Information about required length is essential in school writing in order for you to pad appropriately or to minimize the possibility of doing extra work.

7. Successful school writing takes no chances with ideas, thereby avoiding the risk of saying something interesting, important, or thought-provoking.

8. Good school writing uses a stilted, objective, and artificial voice—preferably heavy with ponderous words and vague abstractions.

9. The best school writing uses a safe, conventional approach (short sentences, formulaic paragraphs, and mindless banalities) so that errors are minimized.

10. Personal writing (or writing on which one claims to have worked hard) automatically deserves a high grade, regardless of its other features.

11. Features of writing such as intelligence, quality of development, clarity, and logical support are merely the subjective opinions of the teacher.

12. Feedback from the teacher (responses, suggestions, and questions) are really corrections in disguise, and their purpose is to justify the grade.

Of course, our official goals for writing are quite different from those listed. Indeed, we use jargon like "assessing comprehension" and "developing critical thinking" to justify writing instruction. But despite our noble aims, the hidden curriculum of writing often gets taught in subtle, powerful ways—for example, when students are routinely assigned low-level worksheets, when objective exams are the assessments of choice, and when misbehaving students are given written reports as punishment.

Roots of the Hidden Curriculum

Let me be clear that in describing Kim my purpose isn't to blame the victim, as so often happens in discussions of classroom practice. Instead, I use this real case to ask why so many secondary teachers continue to view writing mainly as a tool for assessment and class control rather than as a means of learning.

Consider testing practices. Today, many teachers use tests instrumentally—that is, as tools to motivate reading or to prompt the learning of skills and content. And many of us (though we rarely admit it out loud) continue to use quizzes, tests, and other academic work to control or manage student behavior. For example, when students act out or become unruly, they might get extra homework or busywork (such as preparing a 500-word report). So imagine my reaction when one of my student teachers shared this journal entry involving Scott, her cooperating teacher:

> I did the listening quiz at the very beginning, and I should've waited until later. It didn't calm them down any, though. We didn't get much done. Fortunately, Scott was in the room working on something else, so afterwards he gave me some discipline pointers that he would have done in my place. So, next time I'll have some ideas. Mostly he told me when to throw the book at them. He told me that halfway through the period he'd have given up and given them an essay test due at the end of class. Next time I'll try that.
>
> (Anonymous, personal communication, 2003)

By coupling an aversive aspect of schooling with the threat of a low grade, we force misbehaving kids to "shape up." But after such lessons, should we be surprised that kids develop bad attitudes toward our content area and toward writing? Learners aren't stupid, and our punishing activities are ones they long remember.

The idea that *all* writing gets a grade—and that students write mainly to get a grade—is embedded in the hidden curriculum. Of course, real learning requires risk, and risk leads to mistakes, and mistakes can result in low grades. So students learn, quite naturally, to play it safe. The grades that follow writing bring elation or anguish, relief or resentment, indifference or confusion. But these emotions are incidental to their learning, which occurs—if it occurs at all—during writing.

Stated simply, grades often interfere with our efforts to use writing as a tool for learning. Learners focus on "psyching out the teacher" and "writing to specifications," as Kim put it, and teachers focus on grading stacks of student work instead of merely sampling the texts for evidence of learning—and providing the feedback that might inform tomorrow's instruction.

Thus, traditional ideas about grading deliver a double whammy to write-to-learn activities. If the teacher is the sole audience, and if students view writing only in terms of grades, they usually adopt strategies of pleasing the teacher and playing it safe, rather than strategies of exploring ideas, raising questions, and making personal connections. And if content teachers think they have to grade all the miserable scraps of writing produced by all their classes, they don't assign any writing-to-learn activities. So here is Strong's First Law: *If the amount kids write is limited by what teachers have time to grade, there's no way they'll write enough to learn curriculum content.*

Clearly, the hidden curriculum of writing needs an overhaul. For Kim, it led to a single-minded fixation on grades and an unwillingness (or inability) to think on her own. Because she had never used a learning log to think about subject matter, her reasoning skills were weak; and because she'd never written for purposes other than a grade, her strategies for gaining insight were impoverished. Closed and fearful—and crippled by writing anxiety and a traditional view of teacher and student roles—Kim seemed disadvantaged as both a learner and future teacher.

As my poster child for fakery, Kim personifies the insidious effects of writing's hidden curriculum. At the root of such pathology, I believe, are adversarial roles for teacher and student. School is a game, and the score is kept with grades. Fakery is valued, and personal insight devalued. But it doesn't have to be that way.

Writing without Grades

I'm now certain that Kim had too few teachers like my friend Bob Tierney, a legendary biology teacher and coach from the San Francisco Bay Area who was a front-line fighter in the guerilla war against the hidden curriculum. "When you get a teaching certificate," Bob liked to say, "you get an unlimited supply of [grading] points."

Bob's aim was to make learning a discovery experience. As students made daily discoveries about biology, he made discoveries about how to assist their learning. Often he pulled questions from their spiral-bound **learning logs** to focus his follow-up teaching. This dialogue generated additional writing. Students got points for participation; but Bob wasn't buried under an avalanche of grading work.

Writing-to-learn activities were a regular classroom routine. Kids used drawing and writing to make personal sense of biology concepts, then shared these notes during small-group discussions and labs—in effect, teaching one another through high-engagement activities. And most of them loved such learning.

Bob's basic approach was to outsmart his students. Their overarching goal, he knew, was to get *him* to do all the intellectual work while they daydreamed. Of course, one tried-and-true way to accommodate the student agenda was first to assign biology homework and then, when they didn't do it, tell them what they should have learned. So Bob took a different approach. Dressed as Mr. Wizard in a goofy lab coat, he let the students interrogate him. And just for the fun of it, he sometimes gave wrong answers.

"That isn't right!" his students would say, scrambling for their books.

"What do you know," Bob would have to concede. "I stand corrected again."

Bob used writing-to-learn in all kinds of ways—to open class, to explore concepts during class, to summarize learning at the end of class, and to anticipate reading for the next day's class. Students often swapped learning logs or papers to respond in dialogue fashion to each other's ideas. All of this written work was ungraded, but points did provide an incentive for staying on task. Each check mark in Bob's grade book was worth a set amount, but he would sometimes offer double points for special learning log activities—or even, on rare occasions, triple points.

"No kidding?" Bob's students would ask. "Triple points?"

"This is important material," Bob would reply.

"Wow—triple points!"

As a management strategy, Bob had students keep learning logs in the classroom, using separate color-coded boxes for each class. At the end of a period, kids didn't close their notebooks but instead left them folded open to the current day's work and deposited them in the box. Each log entry had the date and the student's name at the top. Of course, having the logs already open saved Bob time. He could spot-check a stack in minutes. And he could use sticky notes to flag entries of special interest, ones he wanted to use as a bridge to follow-up teaching. Writing opened a window onto each student's learning.

The brighter biology kids soon saw that points mattered little when everybody had amassed roughly the same total number, all earned through active participation. But by then it was too late, because they had been hooked on writing to learn. What they had learned about biology truly felt good—and this was apparent in end-of-semester assessments. Generally speaking, writing-to-learn activities enabled students to better understand concepts, and this understanding made the material more memorable.

In other words, Bob felt that learning, not grades, represented the true mortar of Western civilization, not to mention our best hope for the future.

Note-Taking and Note-Making

One of Bob Tierney's strategies for active learning was a two-column framework called the **double-entry journal**. Students began by making a simple T-chart in their notebooks or by folding worksheets lengthwise ("hotdog-style"). The left column was for taking notes, the right column for making notes. To keep this activity from becoming drudgery, students had opportunities to compare notes with friends, and to use notes on certain assessments.

Note-taking involved pulling key ideas and facts from written text or a lecture, whereas note-making involved thinking about the ideas and facts—for example, making judgments, giving personal examples, or asking questions. The note-taking column recorded information in "nugget" form, with big ideas set to the left and subordinate ideas indented. In contrast, the note-making column gave personal meaning to the information. Thus, the right column might include a drawing, an angry retort, or a memory triggered by information in the left column. Figure 2.1 shows the note-taking and note-making work on "The Cell" done by one of Bob's general science students (personal communication, 2004).

Figure 2.1

Note-Taking/Note-Making

Protozoa

Note-Taking	Note-Making
"Unicellular" supposedly one cell, but there may be a question	How big can they get?
They are divided into classes by how they move. 1. cilia – hair-like structures 2. flagella – whip-like structures 3. pseudopods – means false foot, it just flows 4. flotation – they go with the flow like amoeba or white blood cells	Flagella look the fastest. This is fun.
Protozoa 1. Take in O_2 by diffusion 2. Respiration by Kreb's cycle 3. Aerobic 4. Take in food by oral groove or just engulfing it	We learned that diffusion and respiration stuff in chapter 4. It's starting to make sense.
Reproduction asexual – splitting, mitosis sexual – exchange DNA, more variety	When paramecia just split in half, is that the cloning? Is cloning asexual?

Always interested in innovation, Bob also developed an imaginative and effective variation on two-column notes; he asked his basic, or remedial, students to keep notes in the four-part framework shown here. Bob found that this structure invited an interplay of thinking, with the drawing serving to clarify concepts and the "So What?" paragraph leading to reflection and insight.

Note-Taking	Note-Making
Drawing	"So What?" Paragraph

Still another Tierney innovation was the **Neuron Note** (Tierney, 2002, p. 15). With it, Bob asked general science students to summarize, in homework writing, what they thought they understood, but without the support of their textbooks or notes. He emphasized that it was okay if they didn't understand, but they needed to realize this fact. Students got full credit if they wrote a Neuron Note, but no credit if they didn't. Of course, Bob used insights from Neuron Notes to assess whether students were ready for upcoming tests. Here's a typical Neuron Note written by a basic writer:

> Osmosis is to do with water and cells. Osmosis is the absorbing of water by cells, or pass through. I don't know what it does exactly when it's inside. Osmosis is not the only way, but the one that is used the most is diffusion. I would like to know where they got a name like osmosis for it? Osmosis is different from any other form, but still gets the job done. When it occurs water actually passes through a somewhat membrane so as to equalize the amount on both sides of the cell or whatever kind of membrane it is.

> (Tierney, 2002, pp. 15–16)

Bob wanted proof that such writing activities had positive effects on student learning. Therefore, in an action research study with matched groups, he tested the writing-to-learn method against traditional methods and found that students who wrote regularly learned every bit as much as their control group counterparts—and in addition, *retained* what they had learned in delayed post-tests of biology content (Wotring & Tierney, 1981).

Bob shared the instructional potential of writing in a methods monograph, *How to Write to Learn Science* (Tierney & Dorroh, 2004), reminding us of the root sense of the word *education*—"drawing out" student understanding—in contrast with the hidden curriculum's emphasis on "stuffing in" information.

Resisting the Hidden Curriculum

With the image of Bob Tierney's class in mind, let's now consider some practical writing-to-learn exercises—brief, functional, and usually ungraded. These may occur in students' response journals or learning logs, but they may also occur as stand-alone activities. Many teachers use writing-to-learn to prompt large-group discussion, with students first sharing their writing with a partner or small group, or as a springboard into more formal writing tasks. However, anonymous writing can also work.

One such activity is the **exit slip**. Instead of letting students shut down mentally during the last five minutes of class, challenge them to summarize what they've learned, ask an unresolved question, or think about personal connections to the lesson. Then stand by the door and collect the exit slips. More often than not, these brief writings provide a bridge to the next day's lesson. This is an easy strategy to implement, and one that often yields serendipitous results, a foothold for tomorrow.

Of course, you can also prompt specific responses on exit slips rather than leaving them open-ended. Here are a few leads:

- A friend was absent today. Write him or her a note, telling what happened.

- Pick a favorite quote from today's reading and explain why you like it.

- What questions do you have about next week's exam?

- From the discussion, jot down your three big "take away" ideas.

- How should we approach the problem we had in class today?

I suggest using 3×5 cards (or small handout sheets) for exit slips. These are easier to manage than papers ripped from notebooks. For a cool primer on the exit slip approach, see Corbett Harrison's workshop handout, "Exit Tickets across the Curriculum," available at the popular WritingFix website, sponsored by the Northern Nevada Writing Project (http://www.writingfix.com/WAC.htm). Harrison's full handout is available at his personal website (http://www.corbettharrison.com).

A parallel activity—but slightly more complicated—is the **admit slip**. These are short, anonymous writings, often a half-page or less, that students use to gain admission to class. Typically, writings are collected, and you read a few of them aloud. Thus, admit slips are an alternative to reading quizzes used by many teachers, but with basically the same aim: to force students to prepare for class. And what happens when students show up without admit slips? Some teachers send those students out to the hallway to do the writing; others record a zero for the day's preparation grade.

To work well, admit slips should be sharply focused. But whatever the focus, admit slips can provide openings for discussion or other follow-up activities:

- Ask for a specific response to assigned reading (e.g., summary, question, personal example, evaluation).

- Ask for a real-world example of a discussion topic or a real-world application of a principle or strategy.

- Ask for a solution to a hypothetical problem or issue that draws upon recent in-class or out-of-class work.

As an alternative to teacher reading, shuffle the slips and have students read anonymous slips aloud. Or have students exchange admit slips and write comments. Or have volunteers give voice to their own admit slips.

Finally, there are ubiquitous **Quick-Writes**, which can be used to begin a class or as a change-of-pace activity at some point during the hour. A unique twist on Quick-Writes in mathematics is used by Jeremy Young, a personable and dynamic math teacher at Bear River High School in northern Utah. Young is also a teacher/consultant with the Wasatch Range Writing Project, based at Weber State University.

To open each class, students take a five-question math quiz. The quizzes are immediately corrected and serve as a discussion bridge to the day's lesson. In this discussion, Mr. Young seeks to foster interchange about "specific concepts, processes, and procedures." But then, as follow-up homework—often begun in class—he wants students to respond, in writing, to a set of reflective questions on the *back* of each quiz. The weekly quizzes come back to him every Monday so that he can compile points. "I don't *grade* the written responses," he writes, "but they are required for quiz scores to be *counted.*"

Thus, Jeremy Young aims for a "paradigm shift"—from "assessments *of* learning to assessments *for* learning" (Young, personal communication, 2010). It's a powerful idea. Through daily group discussion and follow-up Quick-Writes, students analyze their math learning, item by item. The goal, as he puts it, is to "drive students toward self-assessment and metacognition." Undaunted by the whine of some students, he focuses instead on kids who clearly benefit from reflective writing. In other words, he teaches for insight.

A large screen interface, called SmartBoard technology, also contributes to Jeremy Young's excellence as a math coach. Using the SmartBoard like a touch-screen laptop, he can project and rotate images, pose thought problems, introduce new topics, download relevant material, archive lessons, and post material to a class webpage. Like Chris Sloan, a SmartBoard guru featured in Chapter 10, Young uses technology with real intelligence—to engage students in discussion, focused note-taking, and reflective writing.

Making Learning Personal

Ungraded writing-to-learn activities help students develop writing fluency. In order to develop fluency, students need to write a lot—far more than they now do in many secondary schools. Of course, learners develop *thinking* skills to the extent they use language functionally and purposefully. So, what mental processes do we hope to stimulate?

The following list shows basic thought processes worth attending to, plus content area examples. Of course, these processes can be adapted to all subject matter areas as students work in real or virtual learning logs.

- *Assessing:* Find out what students already know (or don't know) about a topic, theme, or issue. For example, "Tomorrow we start a new unit called 'The Holocaust.' Write what you already know about this topic."

- *Predicting:* Encourage students to consider what might happen next. For example, "Now that you've seen the lab demonstration of what happens under condition X, write about what you predict will happen under condition Y."

- **Recording:** Ask students to jot down their observations and reactions. For example, "Using notes from the debate, what are your impressions of the styles of the two speakers? Write about each speaker's strengths."

- **Questioning:** Have students take active questioning roles. For example, "Write down three questions you would like to ask the author of this text. What are you unsure about in your reading? What would you like to know more about?"

- **Responding:** Invite students to make journal entries about in-class or out-of-class reading. For example, "What do you imagine the Palestinian leaders will do in response to this emerging situation? Give reasons for your views."

- **Personalizing:** Ask students to make personal connections to a text or issue. For example, "Type II diabetes among U.S. children is now front-page news. In writing, express what you see as the main causes of this problem."

- **Defining:** Have students create definitions based upon their discussion, reading, or inquiry. For example, "Now that responses to your questionnaire are sorted, how would you define 'Good English'? Create a definition."

- **Applying:** Invite students to apply what they have learned. For example, "Now that you've participated in today's activity, take 10 minutes to jot down the key points you need to remember for tomorrow's quiz and next week's project."

- **Summarizing:** Ask students to paraphrase, translate, or summarize a text or discussion. For example, "Write a letter to a good friend who was not in class today that sums up the key points of the lesson on osmosis."

- **Analyzing:** Direct students to think analytically about a text or their own writing. For example, "Now that you've read the policy statements of the candidates, create a Venn diagram that shows points of agreement and disagreement."

- **Evaluating:** Encourage students to make judgments about the worth or beauty of a text or event. For example, "Having heard the two composers, write about the one you regard as the better example of nineteenth century romanticism."

Imaginative formats help make thinking *fun*. For example, students in English might keep the diary of a character in a novel or play. Business students might write marketing material for their summer dream job (e.g., lawn-mowing, house-cleaning, window-washing, etc.). History students might imagine the fictional outcome of a major event. And students in other classes might create cartoons, prophecies, horoscopes, telegrams, obituaries and epitaphs, rap lyrics, posters, collages, mobiles, editorials, newspaper stories, email interchanges, memos, or historical "you-are-there" scenes.

Speaking of imagination, here's a neat little assignment designed by math teacher Brandon Nelson (personal communication, 2004) to help students appreciate "The Wonderful World of Numbers."

> Imagine you are an element in one of the sets of numbers we have discussed in class. To refresh your memory, the sets are Reals, Rationals, Irrationals, Whole Numbers, Integers, and Complex Numbers. Each set has its own special quality that separates it from the other sets.

> Write a letter to a friend who also belongs to your set. Some points you may consider including are these: How do you feel belonging to your set? How do you feel about the other sets? What makes you similar to, or different from, the elements of other sets? Relate a story that occurred involving an element (or elements) from a different set and you. Be creative!

Simply put, then, writing-to-learn exercises invite active knowledge construction. For example, if students assume the role of a historical figure—say, Harry Truman deciding whether to use atomic bombs in 1945—a moral dilemma will be viscerally experienced. Or if students write a letter from one literary character's viewpoint—say, Jim on Huckleberry Finn's raft—that character is certain to come alive. Or if kids assume the persona of "Dear Abby" or "Dr. Phil" to offer advice on solving a story problem in math, they are usually eager to share their chatty texts with one another.

Writing-to-Learn Samples

From the previous discussion, it's clear that writing-to-learn activities take many forms—and that a variety of formats, purposes, and audiences can help to keep such work from becoming routine.

For example, here is an in-class learning log response to the phrase *Great Depression* in the context of U.S. history. To prepare for the upcoming unit, the teacher wanted to assess what students already knew about this historical period and what questions they had.

> I think the Great Depression is about the stock market crash. Like when the stocks went down, people got really depressed because there money was wiped out. A lot of people lost there jobs, and that was depressing too. The thing I wonder is, what caused it and how they got over it.

Clearly, there's a foundation of background knowledge here—the stock market crash of 1929—but the student's understanding of the word *depression* needs to be expanded to include its economic meaning. The questions provide a hook for teaching.

And here's a brief writing-to-learn entry from a typical student in middle school mathematics who was asked to find the volume of an irregular three-dimensional figure in a "problem of the week" activity. The teacher's directions were to copy a geometric figure onto another sheet of paper, show math calculations in solving the problem, and then explain (in writing) the method used. The student's writing follows:

> I split the figure into three sections A, B, and C. Then I calculated the volume for section A by using the volume formula (length × width × height). Again, I found the volume for section B, then C. Afterwards, I added up all the volumes of sections A, B, and C. My answer is 26 cm.

Although students can easily fake their math calculations by copying, written accounts like this one provide a window into their real thinking and reasoning process.

A different type of writing-to-learn entry occurred in a general science class, where students chose from an array of natural objects including—among others—a sperm whale tooth, sheep jawbone, obsidian, sugar pine cone, insect gall, topaz crystals, gypsum, fossilized coral, chestnut, beard lichen, and bog peat. Capitalizing on the students' curiosity, the teacher asked students to make a series of "close scientific observations" on a single object, carefully describing its texture, composition, colors, patterns, or special characteristics. Here's one such entry:

> The abalone shell is about five inches long and sort of oval shaped. Its gleaming inner part is called mother of pearl. It's surface has colors like silvery white, green, gray, pink, blue and lavender, they are all blended together. Mother of pearl feels smooth and hard, like enamel paint. Little holes are found along the shell's outer rim.

The teacher then had students think about converting the literal description of science into the "language of wonder." After students thought about their object in its natural habitat, they read a few model poems and transformed their log entries into similarly styled free verse. An example follows.

> *Dreaming of*
> *milk-white surf*
>
> *an abalone shell*
> *on a brown desktop*
>
> *its smooth curve*
> *gleams with*
> *ocean pastels*
> *blended by*
> *lavender light*
> *mother of pearl*
> *from our mother*
> *the sea*

Finally, in a high school psychology class, students learned about brain waves linked to various psychological states. They watched a video concerning laboratory work with brain waves and discussed meditation techniques used to induce alpha waves. To help the class consider the pros and cons of biofeedback technology, the teacher asked student groups to create an advertisement for a biofeedback machine. Here's one example:

> Model XR 2100
> The Ultimate in Biofeedback
>
> Color feedback and digital audio! Ten screens for biofeedback entertaining and family fun! Plus all the dependability you've come to expect from Psychotek, the leader in meditation aids!

The XR 2100 helps you reach deeper into inner space than you ever thought possible! Our patented Bio-Hold Tuner tracks your optimal alpha, beta, or theta frequencies. And all our machines include a bedroom Med-i-Sleep hookup for oceans of deep, relaxing sleep!

Don't be satisfied with old-fashioned biofeedback. You and your loved ones deserve the Ultimate Quality Experience from Psychotek.

As these examples suggest, expressive writing connects students with the content under study. An imagined dialogue differs from a letter to the editor, which in turn differs from a summary of key points—but all have writing-to-learn potential. Such tasks are limited only by our creative thinking.

Thinking Outside the Box

This chapter's headnote—"First we shape our institutions, and then they shape us"—suggests that traditions have momentum. In education, most of us tend to teach as we've been taught. Thinking outside the box is rare, and rarer still is taking action outside the box.

Put another way: The basic structures of schools resist change. Although we now have whiteboards (both conventional and electronic) rather than chalkboards, hand-held calculators as opposed to slide rules, and movable desks instead of desks with wooden runners, such changes are cosmetic. The desks often remain in rows, just as they did in yesteryear. And today's drill-and-practice software packages, though delivered on sleek high-tech computers, are much like the workbooks used by earlier generations.

The same holds true for grades and tests. Of course, some academic writing *is* a test, and tests matter. The stakes are high in today's tense environment of performance standards. And recognizing that students need to be savvy about essay exams, many of us teach to the test, advising students to use five-paragraph formats. However, if we *restrict* writing to such mindless scaffolds, and insist that students always "keep it simple," we may also communicate a darker message: that form matters more than content and that school writing aims only to prove to some dim-witted reader that one can make three perfunctory points framed by a boilerplate introduction and conclusion.

In this chapter, we considered the insidious effects of the hidden curriculum. Most of us are well-schooled in its lessons. Indeed, Kim's story may remind us of our own student days—reluctant to confront our ignorance, uncertain about our skills. Like Kim, haven't we all asked the "what-do-you-want" question? Yes, our geography report may have been copied from a musty encyclopedia rather than downloaded, but how *meaningful* was the writing? And how about the patchwork of quotations we hastily submitted when a research paper came due?

As we've seen, it's easy to think of grades as a "given condition," a little like the air we breathe. Like Kim, we may even believe that grades are "the whole point of school, the only reason students show up." Some of us rationalize that ungraded writing may lead to mistakes and that we don't want our students practicing mistakes; others of us worry, based on past experience, that students will ignore our ungraded tasks. The possible loss of control may make us shudder.

But if the desks are in rows rather than a student-friendly U-shape, it may be because we doubt our own powers to shape the environment for productive dialogue. And if we refuse to consider ungraded writing-to-learn activities like the ones in this chapter, it may be because we're reluctant to question our own practice or muster the energy for forward-thinking ideas. After all, it takes courage to teach—the kind voiced by math teacher Amy Jensen (personal communication, 2003) in a learning log *about* learning logs:

> As an educator, it is important to remember that students understand and remember more when they are required to talk or write about the material. I think having students explain algorithms, etc. to one another, having them bring it to a verbal level, will increase their learning. When you teach someone else, you must clearly understand it first. . . . After students are involved in this way, they will achieve higher levels of learning.

My hope is that as we forego *some* of our grading in favor of the kind of learning described by Amy—using frequent writing-to-learn activities—we'll discover a powerful antidote to the mind-numbing effects of writing's hidden curriculum. Chapter 3 extends this outside-the-box thinking.

Write-for-Insight Activity

Imagine yourself in the faculty lounge at the school where you teach. When a colleague asks what you've been up to lately, you mention *Coaching Writing in Content Areas,* the little methods book you've been reading. Your colleague rolls his eyes.

"You've got to be kidding."

"Just finished Chapter 2."

"Let me guess," your colleague says. "Now we get to circle all the spelling and punctuation mistakes besides teaching our subject."

"Well, not exactly. It's really about a different approach—ungraded writing."

"Come again?"

"You know, having kids write to learn, sharing with each other—"

"And you believe in the Tooth Fairy, right?"

"Let's say it just got me thinking."

"About what?"

Team up with a partner to role-play this scenario. Use it as a springboard to improvise an oral dialogue about the ideas in Chapter 2. Keep the dialogue going for five minutes or so—and then switch roles. In the second dialogue, try to clarify your understanding of the chapter and raise questions about it. (Heads up: Your instructor or workshop leader may ask you to share your improvisation with the class!) Afterwards, write an email message to an imagined colleague, expressing your insights. For example, are there specific points of the hidden curriculum that resonate with your experience? Are there points you want to challenge? Share this text with your instructor or workshop leader.

3

Exploring Expressive Writing

The point of a notebook is to jump-start the mind.
—John Gregory Dunne

Windows to the Heart

There's no shortage of critics for secondary schools. In fact, to qualify as a self-appointed education expert, all one really needs is school attendance. With such credentials, one can rail endlessly in letters to the editor and school board meetings. But it's on appropriation committees of the state legislature that folks with an ax to grind achieve "critical mass."

Despite this reality, great teachers like Launa Moser provide reason to take heart. A 30-year teaching veteran, with expertise in health education, health occupations, physical conditioning, and coaching, Ms. Moser works at Preston High School in southern Idaho. Her smile is open and welcoming, like the surrounding ranchland, but her school could easily be a flagship for rural poverty. With the lowest per pupil funding in Idaho—plus the dubious distinction of being third lowest in the nation—teachers in Preston have a "tough row to hoe." So what keeps this teacher in teaching? You guessed it: the kids.

For Launa Moser, "Words are windows to the heart." That's why her health education students write expressively every other day. That's why she uses role-playing scenarios when introducing units to "get kids to buy in first." And that's why her "*Stop the Tears!*" hallway board stops students in their tracks outside Room 222. This board, depicted in Figure 3.1, has dozens of short, anonymous teardrop narratives about drug and alcohol abuse. Ms. Moser's teaching is viewed by colleagues as "simply amazing" for all these reasons—but also for coaching students to *five* state championships in volleyball.

My aim in this chapter is to sample the richness of writing-to-learn assignments across content areas—and then to explore a few expressive strategies in more depth. Like the activities in Chapter 2, these have the potential to engage the imagination and serve as wake-up calls to somnambulant students. Also, these ideas are easy to manage—as long as you're comfortable with laughter and lively interchange before, during, or after a discussion, lecture, or lab activity.

Figure 3.1

"Stop the Tears!" Hallway Board

My aunt & uncles were both on drugs. They were raising 2 kids. My uncle died & now my two favorite cousins are living with their mom who is addicted to meth & who knows what else. She was drunk & got pregnant so now she has another kid. They don't even have real beds to sleep in. She is constantly coming to us for money & now I'm worried my cousins are drinking & smoking too.

I was at my baseball game & my friend's father came to the field high. He began yelling how terrible my friend was. His mom tried to stop him but nothing worked. He got really out of hand & had to be escorted by the police. I saw my friend and his mom hold back tears. Some of the other people at the game found it funny & made fun of him and his family. It really hurt him & his father's relationship.

My sister went to college 4 yrs ago. Her 2nd year she had to be taken to the hospital. She was never much of a partier, but one night, she thought she couldn't handle it anymore. She just wanted to ease the hurt she felt. She drank a lot. Her friends would talk to her & she wouldn't respond at all, they rushed her to the hospital to try & help her. She is okay now, but that one night I remember my mom went hysterical. She was crying all night long because we were hours away from my sister. So much pain for one night of forgetting? It's not worth it.

When I was little, my sister & I were playing, and my mom was drunk and went to sleep. My sister (7 yrs old) and I went outside and were trying to cross the Boise highway. We got to the middle of it and just stayed there. My dad was on his way home and stopped and got us. When he went to the house, he found my mom asleep and he got my sister's things and mine and brought us to Preston. (The rest is too personal.) My mom is now a stranger to me because of how she ruined the family. Now my dad won't let me see my mom.

My grandpa started smoking when he was 11. He's 64 now and has emphysema. He goes through a pack every day, and it used to be so bad that my mom never took me to visit my grandparents. My grandma had to come over separately to see all my siblings and me. I go over now that I'm older but my grandma no longer lets him smoke inside & he doesn't light up as much when the grandkids come over. He is one of the kindest, generous people I know. It's just sad to see his health decrease and for him to miss out on a lot of things in our family because of his addiction.

Some teachers have students date and number entries in a learning log—either a real notebook or a digital weblog—with total entries contributing to a semester's letter grade. Others ask students to flag their three *best* entries for spot-checks. Still others use a weekly "check mark" system to keep students honest with daily writing. Students earn a check mark for good-faith participation or a "check plus" whenever they do especially well—and these marks can easily be converted to points.

Over time, the vast majority of secondary learners succumb to the appeal of prompts focused on discovery, particularly if you set them up well. But let me reiterate the important idea that most writing-to-learn activities are *ungraded* in the traditional sense. Their real aim is to hook students into content area thinking. "If students see the relevance," Launa Moser says, "they learn."

Opening Expressive Windows

It's old news that school structures tend to suppress—or sometimes crush—the playful impulses of childhood. Teachers are hardly pernicious, but the reality of managing large groups of high-activity learners means that order and conformity get emphasized. Of course, in learning to sit still, listen, and follow directions, many students also shut down their curiosity. Lessons continue in secondary schools. As drill-and-practice and quiz-show discussions conspire against genuine inquiry, far too many students voice the groaning question of adolescence: "Do we *have* to?"

On the other hand, "students will float to the mark you set," as Mike Rose (1989, p. 26) has shrewdly observed. This means that writing-to-learn activities can become part of academic routines and culture, as in Launa Moser's classes. Figure 3.2 lists some of the writing formats (or genre) in which students can exercise imaginative impulses beyond the constraints of a five-paragraph theme. Of course, these formats can also lead to more involved process writing activities, such as those described in Chapters 6 to 10.

Let's briefly consider the work of Diana Mitchell (1996), who recommends many different formats for expressive writing across the content areas. Some ideas generate **Quick-Writes**, whereas others may invite more development. The point here is to open the window of writing possibilities.

What If . . . ?

This activity encourages hypothetical thinking about "absences" in a content area. As higher-order thinking is prompted by good "What If" questions, students may want to explore new writing formats.

What if George had not killed Lennie in *Of Mice and Men*?

What if there had been no Abe Lincoln?

What if people didn't sweat during and after exercise?

What would music sound like if there were no major modes?

(Mitchell, 1996, p. 94)

Figure 3.2

Formats for Writing

Advertisements	Eulogies	Posters
Advice letters	Feature articles	Prescriptions
Advocacy letters	Flyers (all kinds)	Press releases
Anecdotes	Game directions	Profiles
Announcements	Greeting cards	Prophecies
Applications	Historical fiction	Protest letters
Autobiographies	How-to manuals	Recipes
Awards	Information forms	Recommendations
Ballads/Songs	Interviews	Requests
Biographies	Journals (real, imagined)	Research reports
Bookmarks	Lab reports	Responses/Rebuttals
Brochures	Laws/Regulations	Resumes
Cartoon strips	Letters (all kinds)	Reviews (books, etc.)
Case studies	Memoirs	Science fiction texts
Certificates (birth, death)	Memos (business)	Scripts (plays, movies)
Children's books	Monographs	Sermons
Collages/Mobiles	Monologues	Song lyrics
Complaint letters	Mottos/Slogans	Sports reports
Concert notes	Multimedia scripts	Stories (all kinds)
Cover letters (portfolios)	Newsletters	Summaries
Current event reports	News reports	Survey results
Debates	Obituaries	Tall tales
Demonstrations	Observation notes	Technical reports
Dialogues	Op-ed pieces	Telegram
Diary entries	Oral histories	"Top Ten" listings
Dictionary entries	Pamphlets	Tributes
Editorials	Parodies/Satires	TV commercials
Essays (all kinds)	Poems (all kinds)	Utopias
Eyewitness accounts	Police reports	

Three Words

In this activity, students first choose three words that best describe some content topic—for example, a character, historical era, or chapter assignment. Then students write about why their three words capture the essence of what was read or studied.

What three words describe the problems in the American diet?

What three words best describe the Bill of Rights?

What three words best describe the mossy stage of a climax community?

(Mitchell, 1996, p. 95)

Take a Stand

As the name suggests, students can't sit on the fence with this activity. They debate issues relevant to a content area, taking positions for or against a proposition. Writing may either precede discussion or follow it.

> Gerrymandering other than by geographic location should be prohibited.
>
> Genetic testing should be required of all potential parents.
>
> Predictions of the earth being overpopulated by 2020 are/are not supported by mathematical projections.

(Mitchell, 1996, p. 95)

Letters

The activity of letter writing seems to have broad appeal across the content areas. By its very nature, letter writing invites playful impulses, even among older students. Of course, letters can be personal (apology, congratulations, love, sympathy, thanks) or related to business (application, complaint, inquiry, permission) or public (advice letter, letter to editor, public letter).

> Write a letter from Mozart to you at the time he is writing his final Mass.
>
> Write a letter explaining to next year's students what they can expect from this class.

(Mitchell, 1996, p. 96)

"You Are There" Scenes

This activity offers a practical alternative to traditional reports. Students inhabit a scene as reporters, eyewitnesses, or interviewers. As we'll see later, students can get imaginatively as well as cognitively involved.

> You are there when the existence of black holes is confirmed. Describe who was there, how they determined what a black hole was, how others reacted.
>
> You are there in Piccaso's studio when he is in his "blue" period. Describe what is happening.

(Mitchell, 1996, p. 96)

Now let's further explore five easy-to-use strategies to enhance content learning: **quotation prompts**, **guided imagery**, **dramatic scenarios**, **role-playing**, and **dialogues**. As we examine these approaches, remember that expressive writing can also prompt talk about serious or controversial topics that arouse powerful emotions and deep insights.

Quotation Prompts

Social studies teachers emphasize *character education*, and so does Launa Moser in her health education class for sophomores. Class meetings often open with a learning log activity focused on a specific quotation, each loosely tied to a unit being studied. In this way Ms. Moser aims to personalize curriculum concepts.

The semester-long curriculum—a graduation requirement—includes all the expected topics of mental health and suicide prevention; tobacco, alcohol, and drugs; CPR training and first aid; coping with loss and death; reproduction; and nutrition basics. Students keep dated responses to quotations in a spiral-bound notebook, with no more than three entries per page. Students copy each quote and Moser's prompt into their notebooks; then they respond with (at least) a three-sentence paragraph.

Each completed activity earns points. Periodically, students are paired up to read each other's logs and tally total points, and two parent volunteers enter these into a grading program. Not surprisingly, most students earn full credit for their participation—and in the process reflect *personally* on what they're studying.

Here are a few quotations used as writing springboards by Ms. Moser:

> Don't put the key to your happiness in someone else's pocket. Keep it in your own.
>
> If you get up in the morning expecting to have a bad day, you'll rarely disappoint yourself.
>
> Life is like a grindstone. Whether it wears you down or polishes you up depends on what you're made of.
>
> Holding a grudge is like drinking poison and waiting for the other person to die.

Each quote has a prompting nudge. For example, in the unit on tobacco, alcohol, and drugs, Ms. Moser put this quotation on her whiteboard: *Alcohol irrigates problems.* And here's her prompt: *How can alcohol make problems grow?* The responses of two typical (anonymous) students follow:

> Drinking will make you feel better at the time, but later you will have bigger problems. You will drift away from your family, blow all your money on booze, & have poor health. Alcohol will <u>NOT</u> solve your problems, they will still be there when you sober up.
>
> Alcohol makes problems grow because it interfeares with life. It makes people do dumb things that they most likely will regret in the future, those things may also be big problem causers. Stay away from alcohol and keep problems low.

Of course, brief entries like these can often provide a bridge to discussion, just as we saw with the **admit slip** activity in Chapter 2.

Guided Imagery

The technique of guided mental imagery asks students to imagine a scene or situation and to *use* that involvement in discussion and writing-to-learn activities. Done well, a guided imagery exercise can be emotionally powerful and intellectually productive.

That's why coaches and sports psychologists routinely train Olympic competitors and professional athletes to use imagery as part of their workout routines. The effects of such training are well documented. "Not only can mental imagery improve specific motor skills," writes Annie Plessinger, "but it also seems to enhance motivation, mental toughness, and confidence, all of which will help elevate the level of play" (2004, p. 5).

Basically, guided imagery is a story that you narrate to students, a kind of "mind journey." Students close their eyes to focus mental attention. To set up the activity the first time, try an introduction like this one:

> Today let's apply the concepts we've learned about [topic]. Your task is to imagine what I describe. Try to see the situation or scene in your mind's eye. Imagine the sounds, the smells, and the feel of things. Let yourself feel the emotions of this mind journey. See if you can concentrate only on this experience and ignore everything else. If you're ready now, here we go.

So if you're a history teacher, why not use guided imagery to transport students back to the Revolutionary War setting of the novel *Johnny Tremain* or the Battle of the Little Big Horn or some other event? If you're a biology teacher, why not take students on a "fantastic voyage" through the life cycle of king salmon? If you're a health teacher dealing with the risks of cigarette smoking, why not use an activity like "Cancer Sticks":

> I want you to be able to visualize smoke going into your lungs. Assume that on an experimental basis you elected to take one draw on a cigarette. There is a machine that is hooked up to your chest; it looks like an x-ray machine, but instead it projects a magnified picture of your respiratory system on a large screen. Visualize taking a large puff on the cigarette and holding it in. (pause) On the screen you can see the smoke rush down the trachea; the smoke appears dark gray on the screen; you can see the cilia in the trachea get covered with smoke, and their movements slow down. Imagine smoke pouring down the lung. You can see little black spots being deposited along the side of the brachioles; you know that is tar. As the smoke arrives at the alveoli, the screen magnifies the smoke and analyzes it. On the side of the screen you see a list of different poisons within the smoke. (pause) Examine the oxygen exchange. You can see at the pulmonary capillaries the carbon dioxide coming off the red blood cells, and instead of oxygen grabbing onto the sites of the red blood cells, the carbon monoxide poison attaches. (pause) Imagine now expelling the smoke, leaving behind some grayish color.
>
>   (Richardson, 1982, p. 116)

When teaching high school English, I often used guided imagery to set the scene for poems and stories. For example, in advance of Archibald MacLeish's "Lines for an Interment," my students mentally visited a graveyard in Belgium, where MacLeish speaks to his brother, killed 15 years earlier. In advance of Matthew Arnold's "Dover Beach," my students took a night journey to the white cliffs of Dover, where I wove in the debate of religion versus evolutionary theory in the mid-nineteenth century.

When linked with brief writing prompts, guided imagery can make curriculum content unforgettable. For example, here are two interesting prompts—one in math, one in science—that could easily follow a guided imagery activity.

Imagine that your whole family has been turned into geometric shapes: write a story explaining what shape each person is and how that works to his/her disadvantage as they interact with other family members.

Create a story in which you pretend you are an atom of hydrogen in a water molecule. Describe in detail how you would feel and what would happen to you if you went through two different types of changes—physical and chemical.

(Mitchell, 1996, p. 94)

Guided imagery feels *different* from regular school routines. And that's why this easy-to-use writing strategy is worth a try, especially as a prereading activity.

Dramatic Scenarios (Cases)

Closely linked to guided imagery is the technique of dramatic scenarios or "cases"—an imaginative prompt that puts students in an unresolved situation. Often the scenario presents a problem or conflict related to skills or knowledge currently being studied. In order to solve the problem or resolve the conflict, students must discuss or write or engage in other productive activities.

When some teachers first hear about scenarios, they dismiss the idea as educational "fluff." Real education, they say, is all about getting students to knuckle down and do their reading. So why is it, one might ask, that Harvard University has long used case-based teaching (extended dramatic scenarios) to train the nation's top business executives, administrators, and lawyers? After all, Harvard is hardly a place where professors cut corners when it comes to intellectual rigor. And why have many medical schools and engineering programs also adopted case-based teaching?

The answer, of course, is that the method works. The case (or scenario) gives learners a context in which to apply what they are learning. Moreover, the dramatic scenario forces students to think through the competing claims and issues embedded in the problem—which is what they must do in the real world. In other words, they must *actively* bring knowledge to bear on the given problem and *actively* organize their responses into coherent language that reveals their thinking.

Of course, to be engaging, scenarios don't have to be as elaborate and detailed as those used at Harvard or elsewhere. Here's an example of a compelling little scenario that might spark lively discussion in a government or history class. Of course, to respond to this case, students must review the historical context and the facts:

You are on the jury of the Sacco and Vanzetti case in the 1920s trial. Of the 12 jurors, you are the only one who thinks they are innocent. Write a letter convincing the other 11 of their innocence.

(Mitchell, 1996, p. 95)

A more detailed scenario was developed by physics teacher F. D. Lee (Bean, Drenk, & Lee, 1982) as part of an imaginative series of "quandary-posing" cases involving velocity, acceleration, and other physics concepts. In these exercises, Lee restricted student writing to a **microtheme** format of a single 5 × 8 card. Of course, this constraint forced students to get to the point, using clear, specific language.

Suppose that you are Dr. Science, the question-and-answer person for a popular magazine called *Practical Science*. Readers of your magazine are invited to submit letters to Dr. Science, who answers them in "Dear Abby" style in a special section of the magazine. One day you receive the following letter:

Dear Dr. Science:

You've got to help me settle this argument I am having with my girlfriend. We were watching a baseball game several weeks ago when this guy hit a pop-up straight over the catcher's head. When it finally came down, the catcher caught it standing on home plate. Well, my girlfriend told me that when the ball stopped in midair just before it started back down, its velocity was zero, but acceleration was not zero. I said she was stupid. If something isn't moving at all, how could it have any acceleration? Ever since then she has been making a big deal out of this and won't let me kiss her. I love her, but I don't think we can get back together until we settle this argument. We checked some physics books, but they weren't very clear. We agreed that I would write to you and let you settle the argument. But, Dr. Science, don't just tell us the answer. You've got to explain it so we both understand, because my girlfriend is really dogmatic. She said she wouldn't even trust Einstein unless he could explain himself clearly.

Sincerely,

Baseball Blues

Can This Relationship Be Saved?

Your task is to write an answer to Baseball Blues. Because space in your magazine is limited, restrict your answer to what you can put on a single 5 × 8 card. Don't confuse Baseball and his girlfriend by using any special physics terms unless you clearly explain what they mean. If you think diagrams would help, include them on a separate sheet.

(p. 35)

If you're interested in the case method applied to science and mathematics, check out two websites. The award-winning National Center for Case Study Teaching in Science (http://ublib.buffalo.edu/libraries/projects/cases/case.html) has developed terrific material for both science and math. Also, the Far West Educational Laboratory (http://www.wested.org) has an extensive collection of cases for math education. High-quality materials like these have great potential as discussion and writing springboards.

Role-Playing

Any teacher faced with classroom chatter knows how much kids love to talk. We'll next examine an approach that invites students to give voice, literally, to their imaginations. Role-playing can offer a welcome break from the traditional routines of read, recite, and review—and harness energy toward productive ends.

The idea of role-playing is to have students *imagine* their way into content area situations. To accomplish this end, role-playing asks students to talk and write from an imagined perspective, adopting the voice of someone other than themselves. Eventually, of course, the talk leads to writing.

For example, in a government class, they might study a problem scenario—for instance, the issue of how to handle national security while also protecting civil rights—and write from the viewpoint of a presidential advisor. In industrial arts, they might adopt the role of shop foreman and explain a welding process to apprentices. In literature, they might write a diary entry from a character's viewpoint, like Esperanza in *The House on Mango Street* by Sandra Cisneros. In a marketing class, they might take on the role of an advertising firm, planning a campaign to create awareness of a new product.

Also, you can have students imagine themselves as members of an organization and then write from an institutional viewpoint. Here are three prompts posed by Mitchell (1996) for biology, literature, and the arts:

What would People for Ethical Treatment of Animals say about pig dissections?

What would the National Organization of Women say about the works of Ernest Hemingway?

What would members of the National Endowment for the Arts say to school board members who think that music and art are "frills"?

(p. 96)

In Launa Moser's health classes, students divide into groups of six for a one-minute role-play focused on the harsh realities of aging. Each student gets a different situation. One has to tie shoelaces without the use of thumbs. Another has to stand with unbent knees and walk without bending his or her knees, ankles, and toes to simulate leg braces. A third has earplugs but must follow everything being said. A fourth has eyeglasses smeared with petroleum jelly. A fifth must pick up paper clips using a single heavily gloved hand. A sixth has to walk around the room with a knotted 18-inch string placed around the ankles.

Afterwards, in small groups, students briefly share experiences to prepare for writing. Then each student writes for a few minutes about his or her particular affliction—specifically, its likely effects on emotions and day-to-day behavior. These brief texts provide a good foundation for large-group discussion.

The key to managing a role-playing exercise is preparation. Students need to know why the activity is worth doing, what it requires of them, and how it is to be accomplished. For example, in a speech or human relations class studying "conflicts with authority," the topic is *oral negotiation*. The purpose of role-playing, you'd explain, is to help students test their skills of communicating respectfully and clearly—but without arguing. You'd explain that each student is paired with a partner and that all pairs role-play simultaneously. Depending on the class, you might model your expectations or write directions on the board. After a few minutes of practice in small groups, you'd ask selected pairs of students to perform their role-play as a focus for large-group discussion or follow-up writing.

Here is a simple set of role-playing situations.

Problem A
Characters: Teacher, student.
Scene: After school in a classroom.
Situation: The teacher needs to have the semester's grades in tomorrow. The student has not completed the class. Without the course credit, the student will be ineligible to participate in a special school event.

Problem B
Characters: Parent, teenager.
Scene: Dinner on Friday evening.
Situation: The teenager wants to go to a dance on Saturday night but has not met the parent's curfew rules from the weekend before. The penalty for breaking the rules is being "grounded."

Problem C
Characters: Employer, employee.
Scene: The employer's office.
Situation: The employee wants a raise in pay from minimum wage. The employee has missed several days of work recently and sometimes seems rude to customers.

Problem D
Characters: Coach, basketball player.
Scene: Hallway near the gym.
Situation: The coach has demanded that all players have their hair trimmed to a "reasonable" length. The players want to wear longer hair.

Role-playing may seem like a management nightmare, but it often pays big dividends in student involvement. For example, science teacher Chris Gooch worked with eighth graders studying rock classifications. Based on three types of rock (igneous, sedimentary, and metamorphic), he divided his class into small groups and had them compose "group essays." Gooch told students that aliens from Mars were threatening to attack and that the aliens worshiped rocks. If the groups could convince the aliens that Earth had "cool rocks," the attack would be averted; if not, Earth was doomed. Each group had to describe at least three rocks, discuss their classification, and say a little about their geologic history.

Gooch (personal communication, March 2003) was "pleasantly surprised at how engaged the students were." The groups presented their short essays to the class, and the class in turn played the role of aliens, voting on whether Earth was doomed based on each short essay. Of course, voting had nothing to do with each student's grade in the activity. Such exercises lead easily to dialogue writing, our next topic.

Dialogue Writing

Like other activities in this chapter, dialogue writing involves imagination. That is, instead of taking quizzes or doing reports, students have to invent language that meets the dramatic constraints of given situations. Typically, such activities are regarded as "fun," because they're a break from routine and because they're mentally stimulating. Dialogues serve as a reminder, as if one were needed, that learning feels good.

Art teacher Priscilla Zimmerman (1985) used dialogues in an art appreciation course. Aiming to enhance understanding of concepts being studied—namely, lines and shapes as well as principles of unity, contrast, and variation—she asked students to list and describe the elements in a reproduced painting, then analyze its principles. Afterwards, they wrote a dialogue that incorporated their analysis. Following initial drafting, she challenged students to revise their dialogues, focusing on clarity. Her prompt required students to use two voices—an art gallery owner and a potential customer. She provided this opening line for student-created dialogues: "How on earth can this be worth $100,000?" (p. 38).

Here's one example of what students produced, a portion of a longer dialogue:

Visitor: How on earth can this be worth $100,000?

Owner: Now, sir, please don't be so irrational, note its extraordinary qualities.

Visitor: What qualities? You mean a few multiple colored oil paints slapped on a piece of canvas?

Owner: Sir, please note the artist's use of contrast, repetition, and variation.

Visitor: What do you mean? What's contrast?

Owner: Contrast is just one of the three principles of art I just mentioned. Contrast is defined as a strong difference, for example, dark versus light, or big versus small.

Visitor: Okay, I see the darker colors of the painting are contrasting with the light ones as are the large triangles and squares to the smaller ones.

Owner: That's right. Now you're catching on. Shapes can contrast as well as color and shades of value.

Visitor: And what do those other two principles mean that you mentioned? Repetition and variation.

Owner: Repetition means to repeat the same shape over and over, but the artist doesn't just stop there, he also uses variation in the shapes. Variation means a slight difference, a slight change from shape to shape. The two combined create unity. Otherwise the painting would be very dull.

Visitor: I see, so without repetition and variation working together, the design would be missing something, right?

Owner: Right, because unity brings together all the principles and elements of art to create a sense of oneness to make the perfect design.

Visitor: Boy, without contrast, repetition, variation, and especially unity, art would be worthless. I can see now how designs are valued at such high prices.

Owner: By Jove, I think you've got it. So would you like to purchase this particular painting?

(pp. 39–40)

What do you think? Did the students have fun in creating witty dialogues and sharing them? Of course. But, equally important, did students actively rehearse the target concepts of the art class, the ones in Zimmerman's unit plan? Yes again. Good writing-to-learn activities invite active integration—active processing—of ideas.

Here are several more ideas, drawn from Mitchell (1996), for dialogue writing in other content areas:

Construct a food chain conversation between a mouse and a hawk.

Construct a conversation between a negative number and a positive number showing some similarities and differences.

Write a conversation between Booker T. Washington and W. E. B. DuBois.

Write a conversation between potential and chemical energy.

Write a conversation between the bench press and pectoral muscles.

Write a conversation between a musician and his/her instrument.

(p. 94)

Dialogue is psychologically interesting, because it enables the human mind to stimulate and teach itself. The tension between the two voices propels the dialogue forward. The technique is especially interesting when students "invent" the author of a text they're reading and begin a conversation. Can you imagine students interacting with Shakespeare or with the authors of their biology text? What would students have to say? What answers would the authors give?

Finally—and on a more personal note—can you imagine a dialogue between you as reader and me as writer?

A Reader/Writer Dialogue

Your eyebrows arch like twin question marks as you cross your arms. "Look, what I'm really worried about is the *workload*—all that grading."

"Maybe writing for insight doesn't always need a grade. It's just a thought."

You laugh. "A crazy one."

"Why is that?"

"Because teachers make writing assignments and then grade them."

"Maybe that's the crazy idea. Since when do athletic coaches or music teachers or drama coaches grade the practice efforts? Maybe practice doesn't *need* a grade."

You laugh again. "But kids *expect* grades."

I hesitate. "So they're running the show?"

Now you shrug. "Sometimes I'm not sure."

"Well, give it a try without grades. Let kids earn points for expressive writing and a zero if they don't write. Let the drawing and creative written work occasionally earn small prizes like penny candy. Let writing be the 'gateway' or 'ticket' to fun activities or follow-up discussion. Make writing—in all its forms—a way of participating."

"Okay, but the idea of 'insight' still puzzles me. How do I explain that?"

"Think about the punch line of a joke and that split-second of understanding when you can't help but laugh. When your circuits light up—*that's* insight. Or think about childhood stories. Each made some point that you took away and thought about."

"Like seeing things from another viewpoint."

"Exactly," I reply. "Understanding doesn't happen in a vacuum. When you truly *know* something, it becomes part of you—and writing can tell your story."

"But sometimes I don't know what I know. It's just a muddle."

"Writing helps with that, too. You name what you don't understand. Just naming the problem sometimes helps you deal with it."

You smirk. "When I'm doing math problems, sometimes I make a drawing—or jot down key information. I'll talk to myself—make notes—"

"That's the tool function of writing. And when you solve it—how does that feel?"

"It's like—hey, no problem—what took me so long? It feels good."

"So put it all together."

You nail the thought. "The insights kids have—that's what they take away, what they *really* remember. Writing helps them track what they know and don't know."

"Okay, let's build on that. Let's say you're trying to understand something new—and reading your own words. What's that like?"

You pause. "I *see* my own ideas—and sort of hear them."

"Think about that."

"So writing puts me in control. I can see my gaps in understanding—"

"And therefore?"

"I've got the power. I can build on what's there, change it, whatever."

"And what if you share your writing with others? And read what they've written?"

You hesitate. "Okay, I learn from them, and they learn from me."

"Right. Insights come from within but also from working with others. And if nothing else, you know where learners are, what they're thinking. That's pretty useful."

"Hmmm," you reply. "This sounds too good to be true."

Write-for-Insight Activity

If you're a teacher at heart, you know why I used a dialogue between us. It was a device to surprise and entertain you—but also to clarify the concept of insight. The perils of such an approach are many, but I hoped to engage both your imagination and intellect.

Plato used the same approach over two thousand years ago in his famous Socratic dialogues. If we're lucky, you'll recall the issues in my reader/writer dialogue whenever you overhear spirited talk about writing in the teachers' lounge. Because vivid narratives and dialogues are easily remembered, religions the world over have long used them to teach. Stories engage us imaginatively.

Let's extend the reader/writer dialogue. *Give voice to your questions, and then try to answer those questions in my voice, the voice of this text.* In doing so, you'll discover what's on your mind—and perhaps what's on mine as well!

To get into the spirit of expressive writing, I suggest teaming up with a friendly colleague in oral role-playing. In the exercise, you pose an honest question to your partner, who will valiantly attempt to respond as the "author." For example, you might ask, "Okay, so how might I use dialogue writing in my health education class?"

Stick with oral role-playing for five minutes or so—at least long enough to get past the laughter and awkwardness of not knowing what to say. Then switch roles. Your partner will voice his or her questions, and you'll try to respond as the "author."

After this oral warm-up, you're ready to write. Put down your honest questions and generate what you see as my responses. Of course, don't pose softball questions or soft-headed answers! After you develop your dialogue, share a copy of it with your instructor. Then reflect (in writing, of course!) on what the dialogue exercise taught you about this chapter's focus—expressive, imaginative writing.

Tapping the Power of Metaphor

> *Creativity is continual surprise.*
> —Ray Bradbury

Valentine's Day

Outside my office window, snow falls in dreamlike blossoms. I'm finishing two small poems for the Saturday mail: one to a daughter in San Jose, the other to a son in Seattle. Each will be paired with a photo from a long-ago beach trip. In one, my 10-year-old daughter grins up at me in her orange two-piece suit, with water droplets glistening. In the other, my 7-year-old son sprawls on his beach towel, arms and legs akimbo, like a young John Travolta practicing a disco move. My Valentine's Day deadline is near.

The twelve lines of "Stones" will go to my daughter.

The winter ice is gone.
You shiver in the turquoise glare,
Lapis lapping ankles and calves,
Sun warming your goosebumps.
You are bony shoulders, skinned knees,
Toes burrowing the sandy gravel.

The flat round stones you find
Are poems flung from the summer heart,
Leaping like love across the lake—
Skitter, bounce, and splash.
We follow their wild, wordless arc,
Know the moments of in-between.

And the twelve lines of "Chestnuts" will go to my son.

As a boy, years ago,
You brought chestnuts to my desk,
Each one burnished brown,

A smooth perfection in your hands.
Your gesture said it all,
You with chestnut eyes.

Words get in the way sometimes.
Love, perhaps, is like a chestnut,
Whose eloquence is known by touch—
Polished, buttery, warmed by sun.
Time will return the favor,
Wordless as chestnuts.

So what prompts an aging dad to fuss with valentines? Surely, a greeting card would accomplish the same goal—reminding adult children, with kids of their own, of family ties. Yet I'm trying hard to please a reader within, one who keeps whispering, "Try again."

Maybe my motivation lies in the fact that chestnuts and stones are **metaphors** to express matters of the human heart. Metaphor helps me connect one thing (like parental love) to another (like stones or chestnuts). Such thinking is an attentive state of mind.

So far, we've considered narrative as a tool for knowledge construction, explored learning logs, and discussed the possibilities of expressive, imaginative writing. Let's now tap the power of metaphorical thinking.

The Power of Metaphor

Metaphorical thinking draws upon our *image-making* ability as human beings. It's the discovery of seeing things in surprising new ways. In fact, metaphor is absolutely essential to good teaching—and writing—because it helps us understand and explain big ideas.

Am I arguing that "poetic" language should replace the no-nonsense language that gets the world's work done? Am I discounting the need for clear, logical language in academic work? Of course not. I'm simply saying that metaphor *also* plays a vital role—and that logical language, for all its virtues, is sometimes too crude an instrument for expressing subtle, complicated ideas. Metaphor also works hard.

For example, suppose you're a middle school science teacher, and today's topic is the atom. To help students visualize the atom and have some basis for understanding, you're almost forced to resort to metaphor. Notice how Deepak Chopra uses this type of visual language in the explanation that follows:

> An atom has a little nucleus with a large cloud of electrons around it. To visualize this, imagine a peanut in the middle of a football stadium. The peanut represents the nucleus, and the stadium represents the size of the electron cloud around the nucleus. When we touch an object, we perceive solidity when the clouds of electrons meet.

(2003, p. 40)

Or suppose you're a U.S. history teacher whose class is studying the Civil War. You focus on the "house-divided-against-itself" metaphor used by Lincoln in June, 1858, in accepting the nomination for U.S. Senate. Then, too, there's the Underground

Railroad metaphor, an informal network of halfway houses used by Frederick Douglass and other fugitive slaves to escape bondage. In describing the war's political context, you'd want students to consider the metaphors of the eminent historian Bruce Catton:

> Slavery poisoned the whole situation. It was the issue that could not be compromised. It put a cutting edge on all arguments. It was not the only cause of the Civil War, but it was unquestionably the one cause without which the war would not have taken place.

(1996, p. 7)

Or suppose you're a physical education teacher who believes that "every game is composed of two parts, an outer game and an inner game," and that the inner game "takes place in the mind of the player . . . against such obstacles as lapses in concentration, nervousness, self-doubt and self-condemnation" (Gallwey, 1997, p. xix). In class you create a whiteboard illustration—a metaphor—showing how Self 1 (the "teller") and Self 2 (the "doer") are often at odds until one masters the inner game.

> The player of the inner game comes to value the art of relaxed concentration above all skills; he discovers the true basis for self-confidence; and he learns that the secret to winning any game lies in not trying too hard. He aims at the kind of spontaneous performance which only occurs when the mind is calm and seems at one with the body, which finds its own surprising ways to surpass its own limits again and again. Moreover, while overcoming hang-ups of competition, the player of the inner game uncovers a will to win which unlocks all his energy and which is never discouraged by losing.

(Gallwey, 1997, p. xix)

Or maybe you're a business teacher who wants students to understand that economic policies involve political tradeoffs. To do so, you might use an extended metaphor provided by award-winning economists Robert Heilbroner and Lester Thurow:

> [The] engine of an economy is different from the engine of a car in one vital respect: Its parts are people. A mechanic may be able to fix a badly working engine by disconnecting or reconnecting things or by discarding worn-out parts for new ones. But when you fix an economic engine, you are disconnecting or reconnecting *people*—to work, money, opportunity. When you throw old parts of the engine aside and put in new ones, you are consigning industries, regions, cities, to hardship or good fortune. Thus an economist can never fix an economy the way a mechanic may fix a car. No matter whether he assures you that the economy will run faster and farther and more smoothly after his repairs than before, there are always human costs as well as human benefits involved. Changes in the economic machinery never lift everyone evenly, like boats on an incoming tide.

(1981, p. x)

Which brings us back to the poems. In "Stones," when I refer to "poems flung from the summer heart," I point to the memory of father and daughter skipping rocks at the lake. When I describe stones as "leaping like love" in a "wild, wordless arc," I suggest, without saying so, that some memories transcend language. In "Chestnuts," when I describe my son's gift as a "smooth perfection in your hands," I acknowledge, imaginatively, the love they signify. When I refer to "you with chestnut eyes," I hint at more than eye color. Clearly, metaphorical thinking has its own special power.

Exercising Metaphor

Let's turn now to practical issues—various ways to stimulate metaphorical thinking and writing. This chapter offers an array of ideas for helping middle school and high school students get imaginatively engaged in content learning.

To get started, we return to the teaching of Bob Tierney, whose work with learning logs was discussed in Chapter 2. Understanding that biology students can drown in technical terms and abstractions, Bob decided to make the ideas of his discipline both visual and dramatic with stimulating assignments. He created a list of "concept triggers" (see Appendix B) that could be used repeatedly to stimulate metaphorical thinking.

When studying cell energy, for example, one group of students might be asked to think about the cell as an electric guitar, another group to consider it as a lightning bolt, and so on. Of course, metaphors "work" when they are internally consistent—that is, when parts of the central image integrate the concept or process being visualized. In small groups, students worked to *transform* their understandings of the cell into drawings of an electric guitar or a lightning bolt—or whatever metaphor they chose or were assigned.

Drawings were posted on classroom walls and became props for oral presentations and follow-up writing about cell energy. Through these **Wall Texts** (Meeks & Austin, 2003), students constructed their own meanings, came to understand the drawings of other groups, and developed vivid core concepts in biology. Figure 4.1, for example, shows a typical student drawing that depicts plant photosynthesis.

Using a factory metaphor, the drawing shows how plant leaves receive light and water, and how the cells convert these into chlorophyll, which in turn mixes with carbon dioxide from the atmosphere to produce sugar water, a nutrient that is taken to other parts of the plant to sustain life. Notice how photosynthesis releases oxygen back into the atmosphere as a friendly by-product. Since "a picture is worth a thousand words," you should now better appreciate the power of metaphor—as well as the power of Wall Texts. For more on Wall Texts, see Chapter 5.

To further your understanding, let me offer a brief demonstration, focusing not on biology but on *writing,* the subject of this book. My demonstration begins as I turn to Appendix B, close my eyes, and let my index finger fall randomly on one of the "trigger concept" words. As it turns out, fate has selected the word *army* as my writing focus. So let's see what I can do in just five minutes of nonstop **freewriting**, without any preliminary thinking. The idea of freewriting is to keep moving. So here goes:

> The writing process is like an army because writing works from the top down. Just as an army must have a commanding general, a person to plot strategy and give direc- tions, a writer has to have a controlling idea. Also, just as an army is well organized, with different jobs for different people, so writing has different "jobs" for its different paragraphs. Some paragraphs are like the bold soldiers who establish a position, or thesis; other paragraphs follow to provide support and develop the campaign; and

Figure 4.1

Student Photosynthesis Drawing

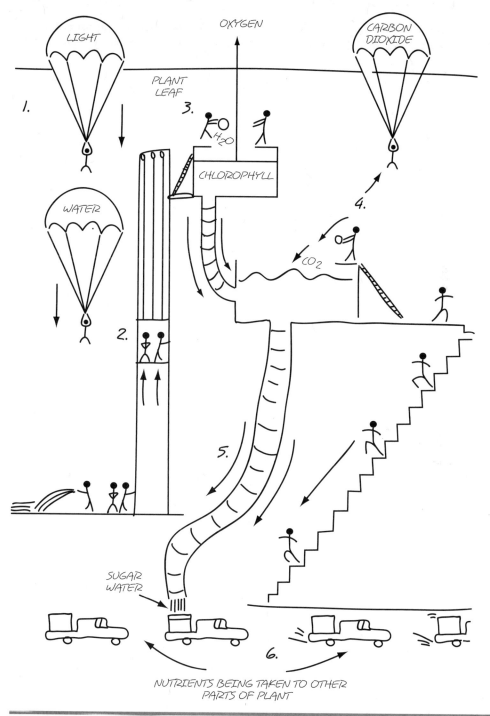

finally come the paragraphs that secure the position and protect the flank from counterattack. The secret to success in any army is discipline, organization, and a battle plan; the same is true for writing.

Looking back at my "army" paragraph, I feel okay about it. It won't win a Pulitzer Prize, but I'm pleasantly surprised with my sentence about the commanding general, which is linked to the notion of "controlling idea." I discovered this small insight in the process of writing—and I'll probably use it the next time I teach this topic to beginning writers.

In fact, I'm so encouraged by my army paragraph that I've again turned back to Appendix B to see if I can make lightning strike twice. The randomly selected word is *wedge*. So how is writing like a wedge? Good question!

> Writing is like a wedge because it enables me to analyze, or "split," ideas. Right now, for example, I am splitting the broad idea of writing into parts through the wedge of analysis. There is writer and audience, content and form, message and style—a series of splits. But the writing process can also be split into behaviors, or stages. We can think of a generating stage, a drafting stage, a rewriting stage, and a publication stage. Each of these stages can, in turn, be split into different parts. In rewriting, for example, there is revision (reworking content) and editing (reworking form). Using writing as a wedge, I can better understand the complexity of ideas that I encounter. This analytic function of writing seems essential for rational thought. Thus, writing is like a wedge.

For some reason, I'm less enthusiastic as I reread my "wedge" paragraph. It's logical, I suppose, but the insights here don't interest me as much. On the other hand, the wedge metaphor is vivid in my mind as I glance back at the paragraph. I like to picture a writer splitting ideas cleanly apart, like white pine logs on a cold winter day.

Working with trigger concepts is easy and fun. This expressive activity is easily adaptable to all content areas as students focus on key concepts of a discipline—and then share their metaphoric insights in pairs and small groups.

More about Metaphor

"Wait a minute," you may be thinking. "What if my students resist metaphorical thinking? Or what if they don't have a clue about metaphor?"

The following sequence, adapted from *Bridging: A Teacher's Guide to Metaphorical Thinking* (Pugh, Hicks, Davis, & Venstra, 1992), offers a flexible, creative plan for introducing metaphor in a hands-on way to secondary students. For this lesson, you'll need a box of familiar items, such as an American flag, lightbulb, candle, valentine, photograph, mirror, key, scissors, hammer, paper clip, eyeglasses, package of seeds, measuring tape, banana, sponge, cup, diskette, and rubber band. Whatever's handy will work fine. Just make sure you have enough items for each of your students, plus extra items for demonstration purposes. Of course, if you can get students to contribute junk drawer items to the "metaphor box," so much the better.

To begin the lesson, choose an item with familiar metaphorical comparisons—a valentine or an American flag, or perhaps a lightbulb or candle. The idea is for students to think about the "associations" such objects have—the valentine with *love*, the flag with *freedom,* the lightbulb with *bright idea,* the candle with *life.* The lesson gets interesting as you invite the class to discuss comparisons between a single object and concept—for example, between a sponge and the mind/brain:

Sponge	*Mind/Brain*
absorbs liquid	absorbs knowledge
holds liquid	holds knowledge
can be rinsed	can be washed (brainwashed)
dries up when not used	dries up when not used

(Pugh et al., 1992, p. 6)

Once students understand the general idea of metaphor, try displaying the objects and then announcing a target concept such as "human memory." Students then begin to examine the objects for their metaphoric properties. For example, one student might point to a diskette as a metaphor for human memory—but another student might suggest a photograph. The fun comes in exploring comparisons.

Diskette	*Human Memory*
holds information	holds information
can be searched	can be retrieved
can be written over	can be changed
can be damaged	can be damaged
must have input	must have experience

Photograph	*Human Memory*
contains an image	contains images
captures experience	captures experience
can fade over time	can fade over time
conversation starter	conversation starter

With just a little hands-on practice, students can begin to appreciate the subtlety and power of metaphor. Suppose, for example, that your target concept is "knowledge." Many students will gravitate to familiar metaphors—the key or candle, for example—but with a discussion, they can be encouraged to stretch their thinking.

> For example, a student might decide that knowledge is a pair of scissors because it can cut through confusion. The context for this metaphor would be the student's knowledge of how scissors work. The salient feature would be the common idea of cutting edges; the relationships might be the progressive cutting action and the notion of individual control of this action. The connection would be in the physical feel of having the right knowledge with which to address a problem.

(Pugh et al., 1992, p. 6)

A follow-up activity, for either individuals or small groups, is to provide a list of several concepts, ask students to choose one, and then have them select an object for doing the metaphorical comparison that was modeled previously. An even more engaging activity is to prepare a list of "metaphor starters" on slips of paper that students draw, sight unseen, to go with their chosen object. (For a typical class, you'd want to have each metaphor starter on three slips of paper so that students can form small groups.) Metaphor starters like these will work well.

Hope is a _____.	Joy is a _____.
Friendship is a _____.	Beauty is a _____.
Learning is a _____.	Authority is a _____.
Procrastination is a _____.	Illness is a _____.
Loneliness is a _____.	Uncertainty is a _____.
Inspiration is a _____.	Excellence is a _____.

After students individually list the ways that their object is like—and unlike—a given concept, they join with others who have drawn the same concept. Their task, as a group, is to decide which metaphors they like best and share these with the class. Interesting comparisons are put on the board in the large-group sharing process.

Finally, of course, students can be asked to *apply* metaphorical thinking by finding their own objects, selecting a new concept, and creating extended metaphors to be shared (in writing) with the class. Of course, it's the background of scaffolded teaching that prepares students to use metaphors in content area writing.

Using Semantic Charts

Now that you've got students producing metaphors, consider using a semantic chart to solidify their understanding. Using a broad concept like those listed earlier, you could ask students to help you generate a list of metaphorical words and phrases. Or you could follow the lead of Pugh et al. (1992, p. 75) and use *school* as the concept word as shown here. Your students will have lots to say about this topic!

School is. . . .

a joke	a social club
a factory to prepare you for life	a war zone
a game or contest	a prison
a way out of the ghetto	a warehouse for kids
a construction site for learning	a fantasy island

In the next step of the process, have students choose two or three metaphors as the focus for brainstorming. The idea is to develop a list of random characteristics.

School is. . . .

Game or Contest	**Prison**
competition to get grades	teachers like wardens
recognition for winning	students forced to be there
students against teachers	highly regimented
teachers like coaches	students sometimes riot
cheating frowned upon	punishment for misbehavior
self-discipline matters	forced labor
teamwork helps	students get released sometimes

Having given students a *method* for generating extended metaphors, it now makes sense to turn to some of the key concepts of your discipline. What are some of those "big ideas" that make up your content area? As students are encouraged to transform these ideas into meaningful and coherent metaphors, their comprehension is constructed from the inside out.

Using Pattern Poems

Now let's look at some practical ideas for using metaphors, focusing on simple pattern poems that help students rehearse curriculum content or respond to their in-class reading.

Ruth Morgan, a world history teacher at Mount Crest High School in northern Utah, used the **limerick** as an assessment strategy. It's no small feat to condense historical information into a 36-syllable form, but here is one of three clever limericks produced by a student—this focused on the English monarch, King James II:

There once was a King James II
Who welcomed great power when it beckoned.
　　He ignored the Test Act,
　　His Catholic friends he did back
With the wrath of Parliament he reckoned.

(Meeks & Austin, 2003, p. 143)

A pattern poem used by social studies teacher Brendan Smith is the **cinquain** (Topping & McManus, 2002, p. 113). Smith asked middle school students to use key words from their unit on westward expansion—words such as *steel, plow, reaper, national road, Erie Canal, steamboat,* and *steam locomotive*—to compose poems in the cinquain format, with numbers referring to lines.

1. One noun (or noun phrase)

2. Two adjectives describing the noun

3. Three words that describe action

4. Four words that express feeling

5. A synonym for the noun in the first line

Of course, the point of such expressive writing isn't to produce deathless poetry, but instead to awaken and motivate students. Here's a nice student example:

> *Reaper*
> *Large, sharp*
> *Moves, slashes, throws*
> *Scary, threatening, ominous, replacement*
> *Machine*

(Topping & McManus, 2002, p. 114)

Another easy format for students is the **diamante** (or "diamond-shaped" poem). Interestingly, as Topping and McManus point out, this form helps students use terms or concepts that have opposite meanings (2002, p. 114). The first half of the diamante deals with one concept while the second half deals with its opposite. Here is the diamante formula.

1. One noun (subject)

2. Two adjectives that describe line 1

3. Three verbs ending in -*ing* or -*ed* that describe line 1

4. Four nouns (first two relate to line 1; next two relate to line 7)

5. Three verbs ending in -*ing* or -*ed* that describe line 7

6. Two adjectives that describe line 7

7. One noun (subject, opposite of line 1)

Here's a diamante example that deals with the water cycle opposites of *condensation* and *evaporation*. In order to process such concepts poetically, students have to think about them, not just memorize textbook definitions. It's in this process that they can construct personal insights about major concepts.

> *Condensation*
> *Unpleasant, soggy*
> *Dropped, pelted, soaked*
> *Rain, snow, sunshine, heat*
> *Dried, aired, disappeared*
> *Pleasant, welcome*
> *Evaporation*

(Topping & McManus, 2002, p. 114)

In the same vein, biology teacher Patricia Johnston (1985) reasoned that "unless the student can explain the concept or experiment clearly to someone else, he or she does not, in fact, understand the concept or the research project very well" (p. 95). She therefore had students compose simple **biocrostic poems** early in the year, either as unit summaries or as a break from regular routines, stipulating that each line "must begin with the first letter of sequence in the spelled animal's name" (p. 93). To do this task, students had to understand content and work within constraints. Points were given for correct use of vocabulary words. Here's a sample of student writing, a small gem of adolescent imagination:

Phylum Mollusca *SQUIDS*

S hells are VESTICLE and we call them a "pen"
Q uick is the movement that caves them again
U nder their suckers is a toothed horny nail
I nk sacs protect them by making "smoke screen"
D eep sea kinds are LUMINOUSLY seen
S trong vicious jaws make them not like a snail.

(Gere, 1985, p. 93)

Another type of pattern poem used for self-expressive writing—or for the imagined diary entry of a literary or historical figure—is the widely used **"I Am" formula**:

I AM

I am (two special characteristics you have)
I wonder (something you are actually curious about)
I hear (an imaginary sound)
I see (an imaginary sight)
I want (an actual desire)
I am (the first line of the poem repeated)

I pretend (something you actually pretend to do)
I feel (a feeling about something imaginary)
I touch (an imaginary touch)
I worry (something that makes you worry)
I cry (something that makes you very sad)
I am (the first line of the poem repeated)

I understand (something you know is true)
I say (something you believe in)
I dream (something you actually dream about)
I try (something you really make an effort about)
I hope (something you actually hope for)
I am (the first line of the poem repeated)

A related format is the popular **biopoem**. This pattern can also be used to write about a literary character, historical figure, celebrity in the news, or oneself. As Gere points out, "Biopoems enable students to synthesize learning because they must select precise language to fit into this form" (1985, p. 222).

Biopoem

Line 1   First name

Line 2   Four traits that describe character

Line 3   Relative ("brother," "sister," "daughter," etc.) of _____

Line 4   Lover of _____ (list three things or people)

Line 5   Who feels _____ (three items)

Line 6   Who needs _____ (three items)

Line 7   Who fears _____ (three items)

Line 8   Who gives _____ (three items)

Line 9   Who would like to see _____ (three items)

Line 10   Resident of _____

Line 11   Last name

(Gere, 1985, p. 222)

Teacher Jessie Yoshida (1985) adapted the biopoem to help students better understand the character of the Grand Inquisitor in Dostoyevski's *The Brothers Karamazov*. She noted that while many students analyze character in literal terms, one student achieved more through his use of metaphor and imagery. By painting "an unflinchingly cold portrait" of the Grand Inquisitor, to use Yoshida's words, the student "takes the thinking process a step higher and fuses it with imagination."

> *Inquisitor,*
> *Cynical, bold, all knowing, and fearless.*
> *Friend of no one, peer of few.*
> *Lover of self, wisdom, and unconquerable knowledge.*
> *Who feels neither pity nor compassion nor the love of God.*
> *Who needs no man, save for himself.*
> *Who fears the kiss that warms the heart.*
> *And the coming tide that will not retreat.*
> *Who radiates cold shafts of broken glass*
> *And who fits all mankind with collar and chain.*
> *Who would like to see the deceivers burned*
> *And Christ to be humbled before him.*
> *Resident of ages past.*
> *The Grand Inquisitor.*

(Gere, 1985, p. 124)

After reading such student work, you better understand what "writing with metaphorical power"—the focus for this chapter—is all about. It's writing that amplifies the voice of students, reminding us that good solid teaching is still worth the effort.

Metaphors in Prose

While the previous examples emphasize metaphors in poetry, note that metaphors also occur in prose, and that these metaphors can be developed, or extended, through analogies or other means. I still recall trying to explain transcendentalism to high school juniors—and how Emerson's cryptic statement, "Every heart vibrates to that iron string," inspired glazed looks across the room. And so it was that I borrowed tuning forks from the physics lab to show how striking one fork causes others of the same frequency to vibrate and emit a musical note. Suddenly, Emerson's metaphor made sense.

John Bean (1996) gives these examples that might serve as writing starters in music, world history, and psychology:

- Baroque music is like _____, but romantic music is like _____.
- Napoleon is to the French Revolution as _____ is to _____.
- How does the weather change as you go from Freud's view of the personality to B. F. Skinner's?

(p. 111)

A special type of extended metaphor is **personification**. Using personification, students "become" an object and write expressively from that frame of reference. Here are several prompts for personification in different content areas (Mitchell, 1996):

- I am a muscle, and I'll tell you what I like and don't like about my life.
- I am a decimal point. Here's what my life is like.
- I am an electron. Come with me as I describe my journey through the GM cranking circuit all the way back to the battery.
- I am an irregular verb. I will explain the advantage to being this kind of verb.

(p. 95)

Encouraging students to develop extended metaphors can help you assess their understanding of key ideas. For example, in my teacher education course, focused on content area reading and writing, I ask students to personalize—and visualize—what they've learned and then share these in papers and projects. What matters, I emphasize, is what makes sense to them personally, the knowledge they construct.

Of course, not everyone welcomes such invitations. Schooling is "way easier," some students contend, if expectations and activities are laid out step-by-step. I point out the possible confusion between *schooling* (what one does to earn credits and get a grade) and *learning* (what one truly takes away in terms of insights, changes in attitude, or new behaviors). I am all for clear goals and scaffolded expectations, but I also believe there's plenty of room to personalize learning.

"Surprise me," I sometimes urge. "Have some fun with this assignment."

So imagine it's late in the semester, and you're reading the take-home section of exams. You've challenged students to create some way of visualizing (and organizing) whatever they've learned. And then you come to a paper written by agriculture education teacher Melanie Peterson (personal communication, 2003):

> **Lint and Language: Using Words to Learn**
> I pull out the metal lint screen in the dryer. Then I peel the strip of bluish-colored velvet off the screen, pondering the idea that is lint. Lint is a fluffy smorgasbord of bits of thread and ravelings from yarn or cloth. Lint does not just come from one source. Lint comes from blue jeans, white t-shirts, and even the red hat your grandmother knitted you for Christmas. The lint from each of these items is sucked into the dryer screen to make one continuous lint sheet that you pull out and discard after each cycle. Lint, clothes, and dryer remind me of language and this course.
>
> I think of the individual methods I've learned in this course like lint, the categories I place each of these methods in as items of clothing, and the way in which I organize them all together in my mind like the lint sheet. How do the pieces of information (lint) get arranged in your head in the nice lint sheet? Let me explain. In order to get to the lint strip, you need a mechanism, which in this case is a dryer. Likewise, in order to arrange information (each of the pieces of "lint") in your head, you need some kind of mechanism. This course has taught me that the mechanism for organizing information, and creating a lint strip in your head, is language.
>
> Language can be used to create the lint sheet in students' heads and help them to learn from five big ideas. In this course Prereading, Talking, Writing, Graphic Representations, and Study Skills are the big ideas that help students to learn from language. Each of these ideas has its own methods.

As Melanie's teacher, did I want to read on? Of course! Drawing upon her real-world laundry experience, Melanie had created a compelling personal metaphor for sharing her insights. Her three-page essay went on to identify some of the methods that she regarded as interesting and useful, thus satisfying my goals for the assessment.

By encouraging extended metaphors like this one, I believe that we shift the dynamics of traditional instruction. The students become our teachers, if only for a few moments. As I enjoyed Melanie's paper, I scrawled a note in the margin about being "forever changed by your analogy"—and I think I spoke the truth.

Metaphors of Teaching

Finally, I want to clarify the concept of extended metaphor by offering examples from the world of teaching to make the point that metaphor is really an important everyday event, not an esoteric or "poetic" one.

Take, for example, the many "construction" metaphors used in this book. It's no accident that I've characterized writing as a learning *tool,* or expressive writing as a *foundation* for tasks in the *upper domains,* or *scaffolded instruction* as the means for students to *build* knowledge. Clearly, all of these related metaphors grow out of my "constructivist" philosophy of instruction, one that regards individual students as active *meaning-makers* and their teachers as engaged *on-site facilitators.*

Other examples of educational metaphor will be familiar to you. You've no doubt heard teachers use "photography" as a metaphor, explaining how they *focus* attention, *expose* learners to ideas, and *develop* appreciation of the *big picture.* Or perhaps you've heard colleagues use "medical" metaphors to describe how they *diagnose* problems in order to *remediate, correct,* or *prescribe therapy* for the learning *deficits* of students. Or perhaps you've heard "gardening" metaphors that involve *enriching* the environment, *planting seeds* for the future, and *nurturing growth,* as students engage in a *field of study.* Or perhaps you've heard policymakers use "factory" metaphors to urge greater *accountability* for a *world-class product* through *frequent testing, outcomes-based planning,* and *time on task.*

While all of these metaphors are common currency, the most pervasive one, as Frank Smith points out, is the "military" metaphor for schooling:

> We talk of the *deployment* of resources, the *recruitment* of teachers and students, *advancing* or *withdrawing* students, *promotion* to higher grades, *drills* for learners, *strategies* for teachers, *batteries* of tests, word *attack* skills, attainment *targets, reinforcement, cohorts, campaigns* for achievement in mathematics and *wars* against illiteracy. The fact that this language seems natural to us, that we have become so accustomed to it, perfectly illustrates the insidious infiltration of militaristic thinking in education.

> (1998, p. 47)

Adding to Smith's points, I'll observe that popular methods of *discipline* include *proximity control* and *divide-and-conquer*—and that teachers who complain of *being on the front lines* or *in the trenches* often suffer symptoms of *battle fatigue* and *burnout.*

So the bottom line is this: Having students use extended metaphors to write about curriculum content encourages them to process that information both visually and cognitively. And when *that* happens, something called learning occurs.

Write-for-Insight Activity

In this chapter you saw how **freewriting** could lead to unexpected results with Bob Tierney's "trigger words" in Appendix B. The idea was to write fast so the process itself pushed metaphorical thinking. As your students practice freewriting, you'll discover increases in idea fluency and sentence fluency. Try upbeat music in the background.

Let's review how the process works. First, you let serendipity choose one of the trigger concepts. Then you challenge yourself to keep the writing going for five minutes or so, remembering that less fluent writers will probably take more time to get rolling. It's very effective to model freewriting on an overhead projector, because most students are fascinated with the unfolding language. Some teachers like to say the words as they write in a kind of "think aloud" modeling. If you make mistakes or misspell words, so much the better. Simply emphasize that freewriting is about fluency, not correctness! Editing can come later.

Of course, the concepts you'll use relate to the key ideas of your course. If you're a biologist, the concept might be "photosynthesis"; if you're a history teacher, it might be "tariffs"; if you're a mathematician, it might be "prime numbers"; and if you're an English teacher, the concept might be "writing." Here's one more brief example, written in a five-minute learning log exercise.

> Writing is like a cauldron. Sometimes words just boil up unexpectedly from the heated ideas bubbling in my brain. It's terrific because I don't have to worry about how to write—it's just there, cooking away, and I can dip into the cauldron, ladling the material into paragraphs that fill up right before my eyes, hot and steaming, just the way I like them. Later, after the writing has cooled, I'll go back and work the surface of the warm material, smoothing its form.

The follow-up strategy, if you're courageous, is to have a partner select a "golden line," a phrase or sentence that really works, from your freewriting. As the writer, you then use that golden line as the starting point for **focused freewriting**, which presses you to make further discoveries. Some students groan, but bright ones often love the challenge of this double-barreled activity, because they surprise themselves with new insights.

Your write-for-insight activity has five simple parts. First, find a familiar concept in your content area and use the "serendipity method" to select a trigger word in Appendix B. Second, do a freewrite for a full five minutes (ten is better), pushing yourself to discover new ideas. Third, get a partner to read your paragraph and have that person select a favorite golden line, one that's especially interesting, clever, or insightful. Fourth, as an option, do a focused freewrite for another five minutes, using the golden line as your launching pad. Fifth, reflect on the process: Was it fun? Was it interesting or surprising? Would it work with students?

Share this written work with others and with your instructor or workshop leader.

Helping Basic Writers Succeed

I never wrote a word that I didn't hear as I read.
—Eudora Welty

Basics of Good Teaching

Macie Wolfe is the teacher you'd want for your own children. Focused and friendly, with the management skills of a true pro, she welcomes students of all abilities at Mt. Ogden Junior High in northern Utah, a school that prides itself on a "diverse and dynamic population." To visitors, it comes as no surprise that Ms. Wolfe was Utah's Teacher of the Year in 2003—or that she now coaches 23 other teachers as part of her work day.

Her science classroom is alive with writing. Huge student-created charts, authored by small teams, cover the walls. Individual journals are stacked on lab tables. Each day—*every day*—opens with a six-minute Quick-Write followed by four minutes of team sharing. This activity often segues into brief, but orchestrated, large-group discussion—what Wolfe calls her "numbered heads" (or "pop-up") activity.

Each student has an assigned number within a team of four. Thus, when Ms. Wolfe calls for "Number 2 pop-ups," all students with this number are ready, literally, to "stand and deliver," sharing their team's best thinking. Sometimes the pop-up is a 30-second report, and sometimes students read aloud in strong voices. "Your writing is coming along," Ms. Wolfe reminds them. "I'm impressed."

She calls her approach **flexible teaming**. It's flexible because she reassigns the teams periodically and because teams sometimes collaborate. She's especially alert to the needs of students with skill deficiencies—resource kids, slow readers, and English language learners—all of whom need encouraging support from better-skilled peers. Here's what one student, Maria, had to say about Ms. Wolfe's approach to teaching:

> At first I was scared to death to pop up, but then I realized it didn't matter if I was wrong because my team and I had come up with our explanation together. And other teams might have different or better ideas. That's a cool way to do it!

(Wolfe, Personal Communication, 2010)

Each student notebook has a running table of contents—a dated (and numbered) listing of all Quick-Writes and in-class activities, including quizzes, homework assignments, and class handouts, which are taped onto black pages. A rubric establishes the points possible for each occasion that notebooks are "officially" checked—about once a month. In between the monthly assessments, students color-code their Quick-Write entries with *traffic lights*. A green dot signals that learning is on track; a yellow dot signals that further explanation would be helpful; and a red dot signals *stop—please re-teach this concept*!

In a Nature of Science unit, for example, small teams read children's biographies with science content—books such as *Starry Messenger: Galileo Galilei* by Peter Sis (1997), *The Librarian Who Measured the Earth* by Kathryn Lasky (1994), and *Snowflake Bentley* by Jacqueline Martin (1998). Afterwards, larger teams create poster-sized charts, or **Wall Text** (Meeks & Austin, 2003), for presentation to the entire class (see Figure 5.1).

Each Wall Text is organized under the headings of *Personal Qualities*, *Processes and Methods*, and *Science Skills*. Students already know that their culminating unit paper will focus on the Nature of Science, so they actively take notes on the three categories. In this way they apply what they've learned about careful observation and note-taking—the part of the discipline that leads to good science writing.

Figure 5.1

Starry Messenger Wall Text

Starry Messenger: Galileo Galilei		
Personal Qualities	*Processes & Methods*	*Science Skills*
• Dedicated • Intelligent • Questioning • Curious • Was argumentive & wanted to know the facts • Loves to learn • Perservearant • Shy • Observant • Wondered • Afraid • Hardworking	• Observed the nature of the milky way • Followed scientific method • Night after night, he studied stars to know more • Used his telescope to study the stars • Drew detailed copies of the moon • Did many experiments • Went against the church because of his beliefs	• Good at observing • Invented the telescope • Telescope gazing • Became a Profecer in mathmatics • Knew many languages • Good at creating expiraments • Wrote down everything he observed • Good at making hypothesis

Wall Text Basics

Like earlier chapters, this one emphasizes **writing fluency** as a factor in content learning. What's different here are the levels of support, or scaffolding, to help learners with special needs approach (and then achieve) our academic expectations.

Color-coding on each team's Wall Text ensures participation from *all* students. Each student contributes to the chart with a felt marker of a different color. The back of each Wall Text provides the "authorship key" to the colors of individuals. Also, all team members must copy the product of working together into their *own* notebooks to earn credit. No learning log entry, no credit. Finally, as we saw in Chapter 4, Wall Texts can be reviewed or "toured" repeatedly to keep students engaged.

Wolfe's "Paper Towel Wars" offers another example of student engagement. Following discussion of TV advertisements for paper towels, seventh-grade teams designed experiments that tested claims about "the quicker picker-upper"—and were challenged to report their procedures, data, and conclusions in clear scientific language. Unlike "cookbook" science, in which students follow someone else's recipe, the teams had to decide how to control the variables in experiments and how to report their results in Wall Text posters. Such an activity engaged students of all abilities—but proved especially helpful for basic writers, because their spelling and language use was "coached" by more-able peers. Figure 5.2 shows a typical team effort.

As for the outcome of the Paper Towel Wars, it turns out that other teams—experimenting with other towels in other ways—reported different results. So, the research goes on!

Wolfe also uses a "cubing" strategy (see Appendix C for details) to help struggling writers (and others) with writing fluency and content learning. In one unit, for example, each team received a different object from the sea—for example, clam shell, starfish, sand dollar, conch shell—for close description, discussion, and research. The cubing strategy calls for students to consider their object in six different ways. Using this approach, teams worked up Wall Texts to share with the class and generated lots of written language. Appendix C provides a sample Wall Text on sea urchins.

Clearly, Wall Text helps basic writers learn new content. That's why it's such a flexible, powerful strategy in across-the-curriculum applications. As previously noted, when a team works on a charting or lab task, all students must transcribe content information into their *own* notebooks to earn academic credit. This too is part of fluency development.

Back to Human Basics

In this chapter we'll also consider the skill of **transcribing** as well as other basic writing tasks—for example, **summarizing** and **paraphrasing**—so critical to school learning. We'll focus attention on **spelling** and **vocabulary**. And finally we'll see how skill-building work such as **fact sheets** and **sentence combining** can teach academic content.

Figure 5.2

Paper Towel Experiment—Wall Text

Problem: *Is Bounty the quicker-picker-upper?*

Hypothesis: *We think Bounty will be the quicker-picker-upper because of its claims.*

Materials: *Graduated cylinder, beaker, water, paper towels (four types), stopwatch.*

Controls: *Independent Variable—type of paper towel; Dependent Variable—the amount of time it takes to absorb the water; Controlled Variables—how long the paper towel is in the water; how deep the paper towel is placed in the water.*

Procedure:

1. *Prepare the work space.*
2. *Fill the graduated cylinder with 5 ml of water.*
3. *Cut the paper towels to 2 cm width.*
4. *Slowly lower the paper towel into the graduated cylinder.*
5. *When the paper towel comes in contact with the water, start the timer.*
6. *Take the paper towel out of the graduated cylinder.*
7. *Record the amount of time that the paper towel took to absorb all of the water.*

Data Table:

Tests	Bounty	Western Family	Kirkland	Generic
1st Test	12	22	19	20
2nd Test	20	23	22	32
3rd Test	18	32	32	27
Average	16.7	25.7	24.3	26.3

Conclusion:

We found that our hypothesis was supported by our data. Bounty used far less time.

If you're a veteran teacher, you know the low-performing kids who struggle in school. Teaching them is a challenge—and, no, you can't fix their poverty, or give them pills for language skills, or wish away a bleak academic history. All you can do is teach well. It makes little difference whether the audience is English language learners or mainstreamed, special education kids in need of extra coaching. With common sense adaptations, what works with one kind of student often works with the other.

Imagine yourself as a basic writer and ask how you'd like to be treated. You'd like to be respected, of course; you'd like to know *what* you're doing in class and *why*; and you'd like to feel you're learning every day. And what's your recourse if these needs *aren't* met? You telegraph your alienation in dress, language, and behavior.

LITERACY CLUB

Pants dey baggy, an' mouth be cruel;
Our sneer hidin' hurt from dey ridicule.
Caps flip back—we lookin' so bored—
Ignorin' dey word 'cause we be ignored.
Dey say we lazy—an' say we rude—
But maybe we learnin' dey attitude.

(Strong, 2001, p. 10)

So, will we equip this voice with strategies for success? Or will we consign it to the margins of our classroom, where it can sleep unnoticed? The work produced by such students isn't "bad writing" any more than walking is "bad running." In skill development, it's helpful to think of basic writers as "novices"—those needing instructive experience.

My premise is that clear, well-organized teaching and daily practice enables most basic writers to transcend their identities as academic throwaways. Helping such students find daily success is critical because small, incremental steps motivate ongoing learning. But to teach skills effectively, we have to know what we're doing and why. That means knowing how to motivate discouraged students who are afraid to take risks—and how to sustain their attention over the long haul of learning.

So, let's say you've shared a rationale for writing fluency, but students resist working in learning logs. Try a simple demonstration. After a well-taught content lesson, ask them to summarize its main idea into a single sentence, *which they hold silently in their heads.* Have them raise their hands to signal that they've got their sentence figured out. Then pull a surprise: *Have them switch pens or pencils to the opposite writing hand and transcribe the sentence.* After the groans and laughter subside, the single-sentence writing will take a minute or two.

Afterward, discuss the point that writing with the opposite hand makes us focus on handwriting rather than on the *content* of our thinking. It saps mental energy. And that's why it's so important to develop writing fluency with daily practice in learning logs. Fluency releases brain power, giving us access to the good ideas between our ears.

Another way to sell fluency development is to have students consider the skills they've *already* learned—for example, riding a bike, playing the guitar, skateboarding, shooting baskets, surfing the Internet, driving a car, and so on. Challenge them to think about the small steps—and practice—that moved them from novice learning to some level of proficiency. Learning to drive is nerve-racking at first, but becomes automatic with practice.

Finally, there's the story of George "Shotgun" Shuba, one of baseball's greatest home run hitters. Shuba was legendary for his incredibly "natural swing," the utterly "fluid power" of his batting. But what no one knew was Shuba's evening routine from adolescence on. Every evening—day after day, week after week, year after year—he descended the basement stairs; picked up a heavy, weighted bat; and swung it 600 times. A fluid swing indeed!

Developing Transcribing Skill

In this chapter's head note, the legendary writer Eudora Welty confesses, "I never wrote a word that I didn't hear as I read." And C. S. Lewis offers advice for anyone willing to pay attention, including basic writers and their teachers:

> Always write (and read) with the ear, not the eye. You should hear every sentence you write as if it was being read aloud or spoken.

> (in Murray, 1990, p. 134)

Unfortunately, many students don't understand that the ear is an organ to be trusted. Instead, they believe what they've been taught—that good writing results from adherence to abstract grammar rules. As a result, novice writers shift their focus from making sense of their half-formed ideas to an anxious fixation on "writing correctly" or "doing the assignment right." They are blocked before they even begin.

Another issue for basic writers is their conception of writing. Students usually don't understand that easy reading (the kind that anticipates our needs and respects us) is *difficult* to write—and that hard reading (the kind that leaves us confused and shaking our heads) is *easy* to write. Basic writers believe that good writing arrives magically if a person has a writing "gift" or "talent." And because writing is so hard for them, they conclude (incorrectly) that they are "just dumb"—and they shrug and give up.

It's important to reprogram the thinking of basic writers, but it's equally important to provide practice that develops skills, step-by-step. Begin by posting the C. S. Lewis admonition. Invite students to talk about it so they understand the need to *hear* written language. Then explain why you want to conduct a series of brief in-class activities to develop the skill of **transcribing**, the most basic of basic skills.

Transcribing underlies the ability to put down words while others are held in short-term memory or rising in consciousness. Without this ability, it's impossible to write. Moreover, if students are trying to figure out spelling and punctuation conventions, there's really no way they can attend to the *meaning* of words. The human brain is awesomely efficient, but it doesn't like overload. Tell students the truth: Multi-tasking makes you stupid.

Motivation matters—so students need to know what they'll be doing and why. As they begin hearing (and holding) language in their heads in content-centered dictation practice, they should also commit themselves to developing fluency through free-writing practice in learning logs. Why? Because fluency helps make writing fun—or less of a chore—and because it frees them up to consider *what* they're saying and *how* it might be revised.

The developmental sequence for basic writers is easy to articulate, but hard to implement: First we focus on fluency, then on form and content, then correctness. Help students understand that if they "keep the faith" and work *with* you, their writing skills and content learning will improve simultaneously.

Using Content-Based Dictation

Oral dictation exercises—two or three sentences at first—will help basic writers develop transcribing skill. Choose content-related material from your field, but make sure the vocabulary is accessible and the sentences are not too long. I recommend two oral readings of the selection, "chunking" the phrases so students can hold them in short-term memory. With practice, students will hold increasingly long chunks of language in memory, and dictation can be speeded up. However, five or ten minutes of dictation practice each day is plenty.

After oral dictation, put the source material on an overhead projector. You (or a student) should read it aloud again. Let students compare their versions to the originals, checking spelling, punctuation, and capital letters. Of course, repeated practice—like calisthenics—strengthens the connection between oral and written language. Simply paying attention helps students acquire skill in marking sentence boundaries.

In the dictation practice material, students should pay attention to contractions, question marks, and semicolons. In the dictation follow-up, you might point out that semicolons are "stronger" than commas for linking two closely related sentences.

"Oh," some students will say to themselves. "I get it."

After modeling dictation over several days, you can make the practice more student-centered in short skill-building drills. Pair students up and have one student read two or three key sentences from the textbook aloud to his or her partner, who takes down the dictation. Then the partners switch roles, and a second brief passage is read aloud. Finally, have students put their heads together over the textbook to check their transcribing accuracy. As partners, they are now ready to participate in your content-related discussion or other activity.

Having encouraged practice in transcribing, you can also use dictation as a response to content material—whether a brief lecture, video, or problem scenario. This activity can be done in pairs or small groups. It involves *oral* response to a stimulus, one that partners transcribe word for word. The speaker says one sentence and allows time for transcription. The speaker says another related sentence, and transcription continues. Finally, a third sentence is spoken to complete the dictation. Afterwards, the speaker and transcriber huddle over the text, which is read aloud as a paragraph. This content-focused interchange sounds simple, but it demands real focus for both the speaker and transcribers.

As noted previously, such activities help basic students develop the capacity to write expressively in learning logs. Of course, writing skills develop slowly, and it's unreasonable to expect overnight miracles.

Summarizing and Paraphrasing

Let's pause here to consider the comprehension skills you're using as you read this book. If someone challenged you to summarize the preceding section, you'd probably say (or write) something like this:

> The section explains how to set up and use brief oral dictations in content-based teaching. A teacher can use the textbook or other content material to give basic writers daily practice in holding sentences in short-term memory and then transcribing them. Afterwards, students check their transcribed sentences against the originals. Teacher modeling is followed by paired dictation practice and by oral (transcribed) responses to regular content lessons. The aim of these activities is to teach content and basic writing skills at the same time. Such work helps basic writers increase their writing fluency.

Our ability to summarize what we've read—to reconstruct its gist—is a skill we've acquired through academic practice. But although it's mostly automatic for us, it's often a mystery to our students. Therefore, we shouldn't be too surprised that low-performing students tend to ignore academic tasks focused on summarizing. It's tough to respond when no one shows you how.

One way to teach this skill is through "given language" exercises. Here's an activity prepared by special education teacher Dave Nielsen (Strong, 1986, p. 39) that helps students develop paraphrasing skills.

Planning an Essay Answer

1. You are taking an essay exam.
2. You should set aside a few moments.
3. You should plan your answer in advance.
4. You should make a list of key points.
5. You intend to cover them in your answer.
6. You can get distracted under pressure.
7. You may leave out important ideas.
8. You know the ideas well.
9. You will refer to your basic list.
10. You will often remember more details.
11. These details will give your essay depth.
12. They will also improve its organization.

The task is to put this information into fewer sentences. Doing so will force students to engage in mental activities basic to paraphrasing. After showing what's expected on the first few sentences, turn students loose to work on the problem. Here's one outcome.

(1) If you are taking an essay exam, you should set aside a few moments and plan your answer in advance. (2) Make a list of key points that you intend to cover in your answer. (3) You can get distracted under pressure, leaving out important ideas that you know well. (4) As you refer to your list, you will often remember more details. (5) These details will give your essay depth and improve its organization.

(Strong, 1986, p. 39)

Notice that this activity not only teaches the skill of paraphrasing but also imparts useful information about writing.

A related activity is the fact sheet, drawn from content material. According to Nielsen, "fact sheets can be written in minutes and used in many ways—to introduce a topic, reinforce learning, or increase comprehension while helping to improve writing skill" (Strong, 1986, p. 39). A typical fact-generating scenario is a unit review, with students working in small groups, and teachers listing student ideas on an overhead transparency. Figure 5.3 shows a fact sheet on whales.

And how is such an activity used? As Nielsen puts it, "the student's first task is to select phrases that make sense together. Then the phrases are combined to form sentences. Finally, the sentences are arranged into a paragraph" (Strong, 1986, p. 39). The "levels" listed by Nielsen challenge students to stretch themselves. For example, the following short paragraph uses five facts in no more than four sentences (level A), but students can then move up the ladder by writing more information.

Whales are mammals. Ranging from 4 feet to 100 feet, they live in all of the world's oceans. These mammals are among the most intelligent animals. This social animal may become extinct.

(Strong, 1986, p. 39)

Moving beyond such activities, have learners find the topic in sentences, paragraphs, and sections of content area material. Of course, "topic" refers to what the material is about. Teacher-led demos should be followed by paired student practice, first in sentence contexts, then in short paragraphs. Practice material comes directly from the content area—usually the textbook or class handouts—so students learn key ideas and skills simultaneously.

After students have developed skill in finding topics, they can write one-sentence summaries (called "headlines" by some teachers) for paragraph-length content material. Again, this process needs to be modeled, so learners know what they're doing and why. Put a content paragraph on the overhead projector and show how to first find a topic and then draw from the paragraph's ideas something to say about it. Do a **think-aloud** demonstration so students can hear the process of your thinking. Verbalize your one-sentence summary aloud, transcribing it (and tinkering with it) on a transparency before the class.

Afterwards, use another content paragraph and repeat the process, inviting students to help develop a one-sentence summary. Ask them to find the main topic and to volunteer ideas that say something about the topic. Prompt them to pair up and generate ideas. Pass

Figure 5.3

Fact Sheet: Whales

are among the most intelligent animals
have no ears
use sound signals to communicate
use sound signals to navigate
are the largest living creatures
strain plankton from the seawater
are mammals
can sometimes be found in fresh water
have voices
may become extinct
have teeth
eat fish
have fishlike bodies
have paddle-shaped flippers
range in size from the porpoise to the blue whale
can hold their breath up to two hours
are insulated by a layer of blubber, or fat
are aquatic animals
have lungs, not gills
have horizontal tail fins, unlike fish
are different from fish
have thick, smooth skin
can dive to depths of 4,800 feet
do not see very well
range from 4 feet to 100 feet in length
are social animals
may weigh as much as 150 tons
cannot smell
have nose openings, or blow holes, atop their heads
are hunted for oils in their bodies
live in all of the world's oceans

At level	Students are able to
A	use five facts in no more than four sentences
B	use ten facts in no more than six sentences
C	use fifteen facts in no more than eight sentences
D	use twenty facts in no more than ten sentences
E	use twenty-five facts in no more than twelve sentences

around acetate sheets and water-soluble pens, so student teams can transcribe one-sentence summaries. Then project the transparencies, inviting discussion. Finally, provide several content paragraphs for individual or paired practice.

Such a teaching sequence shows kids *how* to do what you expect them to do. It's later, of course, that you use the same process of modeling and paired practice to help students summarize multiple-paragraph selections in their own words, which is a much more challenging task. The point is to build skills, step by step. Once skills are learned, you can use graphic organizers to assist student note-taking.

Nine graphic organizers in Appendix D provide frameworks for summarizing and note-taking. Like the Venn diagram that invites comparison/contrast thinking and the double-entry journal discussed in Chapter 2, these organizers serve as scaffolds. The visual cues offered by such organizers are helpful for all students—and especially so for basic writers.

Teaching Basics Strategically

In *Strategies for Struggling Writers,* James Collins lays out a four-step plan for teaching basic skills effectively:

- Identifying a strategy worth teaching
- Introducing the strategy by modeling it
- Helping the students try the strategy out with workshop-style teacher guidance
- Helping students work toward independent mastery of the strategy through repeated practice and reinforcement

(1998, p. 65)

With these steps as context, let's briefly consider the issue of **spelling**, one of the most vexing problems for skill-deficient students. We'll assume you're trying to help basic writers learn key vocabulary words in your content area.

Many basic writers have serious spelling problems because they don't read very much (spelling is a visual memory skill, mostly learned through reading) and because they have few strategies for learning to spell. So how do we approach spelling in a way that informs them about what will happen and why, invites involvement, and assures day-to-day progress?

First, pull target words from content lessons and demonstrate how visual memory works. Have students attend to each word's shape and syllables, saying it slowly, and then tracing (or writing) it—first while looking at it, then while covering it up. I like to model large-scale "air writing" (visualizing the letters as they are whispered), but students can also close their eyes and do finger tracings on their arms. Some learners try tactile surfaces—silky fabric, fur, or sandpaper—to improve their memory of words. Kids can be amazingly inventive when they take on the challenge of learning to spell.

Next, model how learning logs can be used for personal word lists—not only misspellings but also of "words worth knowing and using." Many of these will be content-related words, as well as words of general interest. Personal lists provide the basis for spelling quizzes, with students paired up to quiz each other: You give me your list, and I'll give you mine. As for the misspelled words drawn from writing tasks, students should organize their target words into three columns: *Misspelling* (with the correction indicated); the *Corrected Word* in its proper form; and a *Reminder or Rule* generated by the student (Strong, 2001).

Try giving your students a targeted list. Type "high-frequency words" into your web browser, and you should find Fry's list of the 300 most common words, which "make up about 65 percent of all written material" (Fry, Kress, & Fountoukidis, 1993, p. 23). While you're at it, type "spelling demons" into your browser, and you'll find useful short lists of tricky words for students to master.

"Think about it," you say to your classes. "Learn these words, and you're two-thirds of the way to becoming a good speller!"

For practice, put basic writers in pairs and let them quiz each other, with one point for each correct spelling. Missed words go on each student's personal list.

And finally, preview the key concept words in advance of reading assignments. Putting new words in a list is useful, but it's often better to present them within a graphic organizer that shows their relationships to each other. For example, here's a simple three-part overview for the topic "Rocks" in a geology unit:

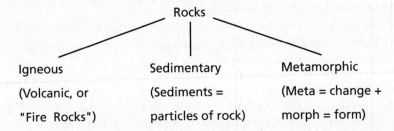

As students copy the organizer into their notes, use think-aloud modeling to focus on synonyms, encourage guesses about meanings, and highlight structural clues. For example, the word *metamorphosis* is made up of two parts—*meta* (change) and *morph* (form)—which combine to mean a "change in form." For fun, students can visualize the metamorphosis of Spiderman or the Incredible Hulk as they break the word into two parts for easy spelling. Now, as other earth science words are added to the organizer, encourage students to use the visualizing strategy, sharing ideas aloud. Eventually, you can erase (or cover up) parts of the graphic organizer and ask students to visualize its missing elements.

Under "igneous rocks," for example, you might contrast intrusive cooling and extrusive cooling and then invite guesses about where such cooling occurs. You'd explain that the slow cooling of magma ("molten rock") beneath Earth's surface leads to large crystals in rock, whereas surface cooling leads to fine-grained rock. You'd have both kinds of rock for students to handle, and you'd add the two processes as well as the specific rock names to the graphic organizer. Working in this way, you'd build background for your reading assignment and for expressive writing follow-up.

All of these ideas encourage students to adopt an active, strategic approach to learning. No longer are they victims of past teaching or their own laziness. This move to engaged, attentive learning represents a real psychological shift for basic writers.

Sentence-Combining Basics

Transcribing practice, coupled with summarizing practice, help to develop skills that support writing fluency. But how do we further enhance skills? How can we help basic writers pay attention to language and reduce the frequency of garbled sentences?

Enter **sentence combining**—or SC, for short. SC exercises are made up of short, "kernel" sentences—the simple, unmodified units of meaning that seem to underlie more complex constructions. Short sentences, all focused on the same topic, are organized into clusters, and each cluster represents a potential new sentence. Thus, each cluster presents its own sentence-combining challenge—and sometimes multiple challenges.

As students work with these activities, they draw upon their existing knowledge of language and also discover new ways of solving the SC problems. Typically, the combined, or transformed, sentences result in a coherent paragraph or short essay. Of course, such exercises can also serve as springboards for follow-up writing.

To help you understand what a typical SC exercise looks like—and how it can promote skill development while also imparting curriculum content—consider the following activity for social studies:

Opposite Views

When it comes to culture, most of us see our own way as "normal." But maybe our own way is all we know. Is ignorance bliss?

1.1 Most Americans go about their daily business.
1.2 Most Japanese go about their daily business.
1.3 They are unaware of striking contrasts.
1.4 The contrasts are in their cultural behavior.

2.1 Americans always mount horses from the left.
2.2 Japanese approach them from the right.
2.3 The approach is habitual.
2.4 The approach is successful.

3.1 Black is the color of mourning in the United States.
3.2 The color is traditional.
3.3 The Japanese wear white.
3.4 A loved one dies.

4.1 Americans use terms like *northwest* for locations.
4.2 Americans use terms like *southeast* for locations.
4.3 The same direction in Japan would be *westnorth*.
4.4 The same direction in Japan would be *eastsouth*.

5.1 Rowing teams in the United States use a backward motion.
5.2 The motion is for oar strokes.
5.3 Teams in Japan row in a forward direction.

6.1 An American host fills glasses to the rim.
6.2 This is to signal hospitality.
6.3 The same gesture in Japan is rude.
6.4 The same gesture in Japan is impolite.

7.1 American children count.
7.2 They start with a closed fist.
7.3 They extend their fingers in succession.
7.4 Japanese children start with an open hand.
7.5 They bend fingers inward to count.

8.1 Americans sit on toilets.
8.2 Their backs are to the water tanks.
8.3 Japanese usually take the opposite approach.
8.4 They face the back of the toilet.

Invitation: Is there a need for more tolerance among ethnic groups? Make your case in writing, using personal experience.

Source: Strong, W. (1996). *Writer's toolbox: A sentence combining workshop.* New York: McGraw-Hill. © 1996 The McGraw-Hill Companies, Inc.

Notice that the exercise has eight clusters of kernel (and near-kernel) sentences. In modeling expectations, I emphasize that each cluster has multiple right answers rather than a single "correct" solution. I also say that the goal isn't to make long sentences but instead to make good ones. I tell students that it's okay to occasionally leave a cluster uncombined—or to break up a cluster into two shorter sentences.

What's important is that students hear different ways of solving the combining problems—and then choose the best-sounding sentences. I pair students so they can read sentences aloud, figure out the options, and transcribe their solutions independently. But sometimes I have pairs (or small groups) use water-soluble pens to put combined sentences onto acetate transparencies. I can then project these to the class, and we can discuss what students are doing well. Here's one way to combine the given sentences:

Opposite Views

As most Americans and most Japanese go about their daily business, they are unaware of striking contrasts in their cultural behavior. Americans always mount horses from the left, but Japanese habitually and successfully approach them from the right. Black is the traditional color of mourning in the United States, but Japanese wear white when a loved one dies. Americans use terms like *northwest* and *southeast* for locations, whereas the same direction in Japan would be *westnorth* and *eastsouth*. Rowing teams in the United States use a backward motion for oar strokes, but teams in Japan row in a forward direction. An American host fills glasses to the rim to signal hospitality, whereas the same gesture in Japan is rude or impolite. When American children count, they start with a closed fist, but Japanese children start with an open hand and bend fingers inward to count. And although Americans sit on toilets with their back to the water tank, Japanese usually take the opposite approach, facing the back of the toilet.

This exercise may be too hard for some basic writers, especially English as a second language (ESL) learners. But this SC exercise—or any other—can be adjusted in difficulty simply by changing its vocabulary and shortening the clusters for combining. Moreover, this exercise— or any other—can be made more accessible by adding "closure clues." I put such clues on transparencies and project them to the class. The closure clues provide key words to assist learners in making a target sentence. Students "fill in the blanks" mentally as they transcribe sentences on their own or work with partners. For example, here's a simple closure clue for cluster 1.

Going _____,
most _____.

Sentence-combining practice invites students to solve basic problems of written expression in a positive, nonthreatening way—and without resorting to grammar terms. Students work together, bringing their oral language to the table and strengthening their transcribing skills. Also, the exercises can introduce, expand, or reinforce key ideas from a content area. And finally they can set the stage for in-class workshops that reduce the frequency of errors.

Workshop-Style Teaching

Let's say you've divided writers in a social studies class into eight groups, with each group assigned to tackle one of the "Opposite Views" clusters without the help of closure clues. You've told students that you want them to do their best, but that it's okay to make mistakes. And you've also reminded them that no one can make fun of another person's effort—and no points are lost for errors. "Our aim," you emphasize, "is to *learn* from mistakes!"

Each of the eight groups puts its sentence-combining solution on a transparency, which is projected to the class. Within the set of transparencies is this sentence, written by a small group of struggling writers in response to cluster 3 of "Opposite Views":

3. Black is a traditional Morning color, its white in Japan because a loved One dies.

A sentence like this shows a lot about your students' developmental levels. You see the missing endings on words—and missing words. You see the misspelling, the absence of apostrophes, and the comma splice. But you also see what students *can* do—for example, use capital letters at the opening of the sentence and on proper nouns, and use end punctuation. So is the glass half-full or half-empty?

"What's *good* about this sentence?" you ask.

"Capital letters," Jason responds.

"It's got all the information," Tonya adds.

"Commas," says Carlos. "It's got them, plus a period."

You nod at Carlos. "Yes, we're going to talk about the commas. So does anybody spot a problem, something we can learn from?"

And so it goes. As the collective intelligence of the class focuses on careless errors such as dropped endings, missing words, and misspellings, students learn how to proofread their own writing, and you show how to fix errors. And if students don't see the sentence boundary errors, you have the perfect opportunity to teach what kids need to learn—in context, on the spot. And you then move on.

Teaching skills in mini-lessons works for three reasons: First, students are not defensive about the content of their writing (the content is provided); second, the class setup emphasizes what students are doing well in addition to what they need to learn; and third, there's absolutely no risk (or penalty) for making mistakes.

And what about source material for SC exercises? My textbooks, listed in this book's references, contain many exercises for use in secondary content areas. Here are a few titles from *Sentence Combining: A Composing Book* (Strong, 1994) and the relevant disciplines in which they might be used:

Exercise Title	Content Area
Value Judgment	English/Language Arts
Hispanic Movement	Government
Bait and Switch	Economics/Personal Living
Hurricane Behavior	Earth Science
Gambling Fever	Social Studies
Alcohol Facts	Health Education
Nuclear Waste	Environmental Science
Karate Explained	Physical Education
Black Music	Music Education
Hypnotic Trance	Psychology
Genetic Counseling	Biology
World Population	Mathematics
Black Death	World History
First Settlers	U.S. History
The Potter	Art Education
Black Holes	Physics

In addition to commercially prepared SC exercises, don't overlook the idea of teaming up with other teachers to develop short, interesting activities for your classes. Focus on a curriculum topic—say, the Civil War—and team up with your U.S. history colleagues to create (and swap) good materials. The exercises are fun to create and often provide a welcome diversion from routine in-class activities.

But do SC exercises help students write better? On this point, George Hillocks (1986) conducted a meta-analysis of empirical studies in writing instruction. As one of the nation's top writing researchers, Hillocks examined the best studies, pooled the data statistically, and computed "effect sizes" for various teaching methods. His conclusions follow:

> The practice of building more complex sentences from simpler ones has been shown to be effective in a large number of experimental studies. This research shows sentence combining, on the average, to be more than twice as effective as free writing as a means of enhancing the quality of student writing.

(Hillocks, 1986, p. 249)

Hillocks' findings have been reconfirmed in a subsequent meta-analysis (Graham & Perin, 2007), which is discussed in the "Revisiting Insight" Epilogue of this book. Clearly, SC exercises offer a research-proven tool, one that gives students hands-on and risk-free practice in putting phrases, clauses, and sentences together in meaningful ways.

A Bridge to Literacy

Let me call him Eddie.

Wearing glasses with thick plastic frames, he sat in front and gazed at me with shy, questioning eyes. His arms were thin, and he wore hand-me-down shirts. He was almost invisible among his classmates in downtown Honolulu, this brown-skinned seventh-grader with close-cropped black hair. Congenial and compliant, he liked to doodle in a blue denim notebook, making sketches of fire-breathing dragons and ninja warriors.

At first I thought he was lazy. "Come on, Eddie. Let's get to it, okay?"

Later I thought the problem was motivation. I told him how interesting he'd find the reading if he'd just get started—and I emphasized upcoming quizzes and grades.

Nothing was working. As Eddie ducked his head in discussions and handed in two-sentence papers, I began to wonder how much his home background compromised his school work. He struggled in reading and writing—and I was failing to develop those skills.

So one morning, while the class worked, I pulled him aside for a little talk, "a chance to know you better." I learned about his extended family and interests.

"What's hard about reading?" I finally asked.

Eddie hesitated. "Uh, like to understand the words?"

Eddie didn't qualify for pull-out reading instruction because his decoding skills were surprisingly good. The problem, I surmised, was weaknesses in vocabulary. In other words, his oral language didn't yet support the academic demands of seventh grade.

Eddie grinned when I pulled a ninja comic book from my desk drawer.

His comic book reading was halting, but he managed to decode the simple text. After two or three minutes, I asked some basic questions, and he handled them without much trouble, glancing at pictures as he talked.

"That's good reading," I said. "How about our textbook?"

"Hard words."

"So, what if I preview the hard words for the class?"

He hesitated. "What's *preview*?" he asked.

"You've seen video previews of new ninja movies. You know, like what's next? We could have word previews."

Still eyeing the comic book, Eddie was eager to get off the hook.

"Tell you what," I continued. "You're a smart kid, but we need to strengthen your word knowledge. That okay?"

Eddie shrugged, maybe unsure about the question.

"But if we're working together," I added, "I need your help."

"Like what?" he asked.

"Eddie, I can't preview all the hard words. So in your notebook, keep a list of them and discuss them with your study buddy each day."

"Copy them?"

"Right—copy the ones you can't figure out as you read. Do this all week, okay?"

Now he looked worried. "Do something wrong?"

"No," I said. "You haven't done anything wrong. You're helping me teach you. Keep that word list so you can get help learning them, okay?"

Eddie nodded assent.

"And one other thing about writing," I added. "Maybe you need help with spelling during writing time. Just raise your hand and I'll put words on the board for you."

"Like *preview*?" he asked.

"Exactly," I nodded. "Whatever word you need, just raise your hand."

We shook hands on the deal: I'd preview hard words before in-class reading, and he'd keep track of hard words to discuss with a study buddy; and when it came to writing, all he had to do was raise a hand to get help with spelling.

What I didn't tell Eddie was that other hands besides his would go up during in-class writing—or that the board would sometimes be *covered* with new words, ones he'd first hear and then find himself using. Nor did I mention that I'd ask able readers to do read-alouds in a small group that included him. I reasoned that hearing and seeing the text would help Eddie comprehend more as it developed his skills. He still eyed the comic book.

"At the end of the week, if you work hard, you get the comic book. Fair enough?"

"I'll draw you a picture," he replied.

"Cool," I said.

Write-for-Insight Activity

Look back at James Collins' four-step plan for basic writers earlier in the chapter. Now think about a concept or skill in your content area that you want to teach. How might activities in this chapter help you teach this concept or skill to basic writers? For example, can you visualize how you might use Macie Wolfe's flexible teaming approach, or other ideas like dictation, summarizing, or sentence-combining? Develop a brief lesson plan that identifies a concept or skill and includes at least one strategy to help basic writers. As you do so, reflect on your personal philosophy of working with skill-deficient or unmotivated learners. In your opinion, what attitudes must you project to be successful? What moves do you need to make to help most students most of the time? Be ready to share your discipline-specific application and your personal reflection with colleagues and your instructor or workshop leader.

Designing Assignments and Rubrics

The ultimate confrontation is with that blank sheet of paper.

—John McPhee

Darth Vader in Action

Let's imagine a movie script with a *Star Wars* theme—one featuring Darth Vader, that helmeted, heavy-breathing figure of sinister intent, the archetypal villain we love to hate. Vader's purpose is *mind control*. It's darkness versus light, ignorance versus insight, in the nation's middle school and high school classrooms. Imagine that the powers of the Evil Empire have gained control of what goes on in the name of writing instruction.

In Scenario 1, we see middle school kids at computer terminals, hard at work. A camera monitors time-on-task for the school's nine-step Assessment Support System ("ASS-in-Nine," for short). Each young face is bright-eyed, well-scrubbed, eager-to-please. Then we hear Darth Vader's evil, chilling voice in an ominous voice-over.

"Observe," he whispers, "our program in action."

The camera focuses on a computer-monitored worksheet. It's a multiple-choice list for writing process steps. A student completes her drill on terminology, then moves on to matching items that deal with outlining.

"Busywork," Vader murmurs. "We avoid any writing about curriculum content."

A boy looks up, his brow furrowed, as Vader continues. "By making students *fearful* of errors, both real and imagined, we choke motivation. Over time, our lessons in *fear* become beliefs. That's one secret to our success—undermining the child's early beliefs that writing is power. We teach the opposite."

The camera picks up off-task behavior, and an Instructional Manager swoops into action, her voice shrill. Two students head for the principal's office, but not before they're assigned to write a theme for punishment.

Vader's raspy voice trembles with enthusiasm. "Using writing to discipline students is a *wonderful* approach," he intones. "Coupling punishment with fear, we can *guarantee* non-writers later on!"

Abruptly, in Scenario 2, the camera shifts to a high school classroom, where students take objective exams—true/false and multiple-guess questions. Is this science, math, social studies, health, business, or another content area? It's hard to tell.

"Writing *must* be removed from content teaching," Vader continues. "We ask for single-word answers, a phrase at most. Our aim is to constrict thinking, not expand it."

Students have finished their tests. The camera swings to an assignment on the board: *Research reports due Friday.*

"How long?" one student asks.

"How many sources?" another wonders aloud.

"How much is it worth?" comes the classroom chorus.

The Instructional Manager distributes assigned topics as students roll their eyes and groan, then march sullenly toward the Media Center.

Again we hear Vader's throaty whisper. "Academic reports keep up appearances. We don't allow choice or coach students in research. By keeping expectations murky, we help them see plagiarism as a smart approach to busywork."

A boy leafs aimlessly through reference books. Meanwhile, a girl downloads material, pastes it into a document, and types her name at the top. When two students propose collaboration, the Instructional Manager kills the idea.

Vader hisses with dark enthusiasm. "Teamwork is dangerous—because that's how work in the real world gets done. Forcing students to work alone, we keep them from developing or sharing any interest in learning."

In Scenario 3, high school seniors are slumped at their desks, their faces slack, eyes opaque. An Instructional Manager looks angry and weary, glancing at the clock where 40 minutes remain. "Take out a sheet of paper," he barks.

A topic is scrawled across the board. As one student secretly sends a text message, saying "scul suks," others stare at their desktops, waiting for release.

"Writing as time-filler," Vader says. "Students have zero interest in the task, or skill for accomplishing it—and teachers now have to correct the pathetic, scribbled lines ripped from notebooks."

Suddenly and dramatically, Vader's blank, black gaze fills the screen. "What is writing?" he hisses, letting the question hang. "Writing is a *laser*—a tool for thinking and learning. By disarming future citizens of the searing laser light called writing, the conquest of darkness is *inevitable*. Wouldn't *you* agree?"

Assignments by Design

As Scenario 3 in the previous example makes clear, it's all too easy to pull dreadful academic assignments out of thin air, especially when our planning is less-than-professional or we're frustrated. But what makes a *good* writing assignment? That's the basic question we'll consider in this chapter, which builds on earlier chapters on expressive writing.

Our aim here is to consider academic tasks that deal with substantive content topics. As such, these "public writing" assignments typically ask students to write in narrative, informative, and persuasive domains, as outlined in the Preface (Figure I.1, p. xv). Of course, the activity that engages one class may inspire yawns from another. But basic principles of assignment design are worth considering as we think professionally about content area writing prompts.

In Chapter 5 you saw how Macie Wolfe prepared seventh graders for a "Nature of Science" writing assignment. Teams read biographies of famous scientists and then created Wall Texts to share information about each individual's life story. The Wall Texts had parallel frameworks, enabling students to aggregate information. Students took notes *actively* as oral reports were presented, knowing they'd use the notes for a culminating writing task—an important one for their teacher.

Afterwards, Ms. Wolfe helped kids think about a possible format for their essay. Yes, she'd be one audience, but who else might read it? What kind of language should they strive for? How might they integrate key science concepts from the year's work? And—oh, yes—how would this work get graded? Table 6.1 shows Macie Wolfe's grading rubric, which is

Table 6.1   Nature of Science Grading Rubric

	Excellent (25 Points)	Fair (15 Points)	Needs Improvement (10 Points)
Science Content	Accurate: Connected to big ideas in science.	Mostly accurate: Connections to big ideas are not clear.	Inaccurate: Not connected to big ideas in science.
Organization & Presentation	Main ideas are clearly presented; ideas are presented in an appropriate order; ideas are supported by information and logic. Appropriate conclusions are based upon evidence presented.	Main ideas are presented to some extent; ideas are not presented in an order that adds clarity; some ideas are supported by information and logic. Conclusions do not follow from ideas presented.	No main ideas are presented; ideas are presented in an order that distracts from clear communication; ideas are not supported by information and are illogical. Inappropriate conclusions are presented.
Conventions	Generally error free in regard to sentence structure, punctuation, capitalization, spelling, and standard usage.	Sentence structure, punctuation, capitalization, spelling, and standard usage errors are noticeable, but do not impair readability.	Errors in sentence structure, punctuation, capitalization, spelling, and standard usage impair readability.
Use of Science Language	Consistent use of appropriate science language and terminology.	Partial use of appropriate science language and terminology.	Inaccurate use of science language and terminology.

available (along with her Nature of Science lesson plan) at the Utah Education Network website [http://www.uen.org].

This is great teaching. Why? Because students generate a notebook full of prewriting ideas, receive strategic instruction on academic writing, and understand the grading standards that their teacher will use. See Figure 6.1 for a nifty five-paragraph essay written by one of Ms. Wolfe's seventh-graders, Aleisha Keller (Wolfe, personal communication, 2010). Using the rubric, how would you score this paper?

Assignments to Motivate

Let's now read three assignments from an upper-grades perspective, asking whether they would motivate high school students. This task, drawn from the work of John Bean, is for a psychology class:

> In the morning, when Professor Catlove opens a new can of cat food, his cats run into the kitchen purring and meowing and rubbing their backs against his legs. What examples, if any, of classical conditioning, operant conditioning, and social learning are at work in this brief scene? Note that both the cats and professor might be exhibiting conditioned behavior here.

> (1996, p. 80)

The follow-up directions define a study-group situation in which "you are convinced that the other members of the group are confused about the concepts." The prompt asks students to write a "one- to two-page essay that sets them straight" (p. 80). Here we have a situational problem, a focus on application of key concepts, and directions that specify a purpose and audience beyond the teacher.

The following math writing prompt is also from John Bean's work:

> In class yesterday, 80 percent of you agreed with this statement: "The maximum speed of sailboat occurs when the boat is sailing in the same direction as the wind." However, that intuitive answer is wrong. Sailboats can actually go much faster when they sail across the wind. How so? Using what you have been learning in vector algebra, explain why sailboats can sail faster when the wind blows sideways to their direction rather than from directly behind them. Make your explanation clear enough for the general public to understand. You can use diagrams if that helps.

> (1996, p. 27)

I contend that this assignment works for three reasons. First, it creates cognitive dissonance as students are situated in a problem they helped create. Second, the task asks them to *use* recently acquired knowledge to resolve a dilemma. Third, the assignment specifies an audience and invites drawing to support the writing.

Unlike a traditional assignment—where the main problem is to guess what is expected and then "please" the teacher—the sailboat assignment encourages students to think critically about an issue, apply their math skills, and communicate their results within certain constraints.

Figure 6.1

Nature of Science Essay by Aleisha Keller

Science is based on observable evidence and problem solving. Scientists are a part of the nature of science because they are the ones who follow the scientific method, do experiments, and make conclusions that help us understand science today. There are many great scientists who contributed facts to science and made discoveries which helped add to the nature of science.

Galileo Galilei was a great scientist who played a major role in the scientific revolution. He made great discoveries in science. He learned many things about the planets and our solar system, and he observed sunspots. Galileo is known as, "The Father of Science, and The Father of Modern Science." That title means that Galileo did much for the nature of science today. One of the most well known acts Galileo has done was inventing the telescope. With the telescope, Galileo made many discoveries about space. With our current knowledge now and improved telescopes, we have even more knowledge than before. This happened because Galileo studied and worked to invent the telescope.

Wilson "Snowflake" Bentley wasn't one of the most well-known scientists, but he did a lot for science and the nature of science. Snowflake Bentley was one of the first photographers to photograph a snowflake before it melted or evaporated. When Bentley was experimenting for the right way to capture snowflakes, he tried many different methods to see which one worked best. Bentley was very patient when he was working and if the experiment he was trying didn't work, he didn't get discouraged. He just kept trying until he had it right. Bentley made sure that on every experiment he tried, he did his best work. Bentley was very smart and learned fast without much schooling. Snowflake Bentley was a great scientist who helped us understand the nature of snowflakes and science better.

Eratosthenes was one of the greatest scientists ever known. He was the first person to ever use the word geography and understand it. Without Eratosthenes, our maps today would look a lot different than they do. Eratosthenes made the system of longitude and latitude that we use today. He was the first person ever to calculate the circumference of the earth and with great accuracy. During his lifetime he did this by using the length of stadiums. He also measured the tilt of the Earth's axis with great accuracy. He measured the distance from the earth to the sun as well. Those who lived in the same time period as Eratosthenes nicknamed him "Beta" (from the second letter of the Greek alphabet) because he supposedly proved himself to be the second best in the world in almost any field of knowledge. With his knowledge he also created a map of the world. Eratosthenes was a superb scientist who formed the basis of what we know about the earth. Today scientists keep adding more information to what Eratosthenes discovered.

These three scientists contributed much of the information about science that we have today. The world is much better off because of their knowledge. These are only a few of the many scientists in the world who have added much information about the nature of science. These scientists are a big part of the nature of science and how we understand it today.

Finally, here's my assignment for Ray Bradbury's *Fahrenheit 451,* a perennial choice in literature classes because of its high-quality writing and relevance to contemporary life. The novel depicts a future world where reading is censored—indeed, the job of firemen is to burn books—and where big-screen reality TV occupies society's center stage.

> The editor of our local newspaper is planning a special issue focused on "School Life." She has invited selected community leaders and students to develop interesting feature articles dealing with topics of their choice. Her suggested topics include, but are not limited to, the following:
>
> ■ Television and School Life Today
> ■ Censorship Versus the Student's Right to Read
> ■ How Democracy Depends on Books
>
> If you have a better topic for your article, feel free to use it. Of course, make sure to use *Farenheit 451* as support for whatever points you choose to make. Also, remember to title your newspaper article and to develop a "lead" that will hook busy adult readers (and other students) in our community.

Notice that this writing-about-literature assignment provides a *context* for writing, a *role* for the student writer, an *audience* beyond the teacher, a feature article *format,* and a choice of *topics.* There are real academic expectations here, but there's also room for students to exercise creativity in their responses.

In my opinion, such tasks help us dismantle the hidden curriculum discussed in Chapter 2. So let's consider the basic principles of assignment design in more detail.

Ten Design Principles

Although the following principles are separated for ease of reading, they really depend on each other. Think of them as a set of interrelated recommendations.

1. Create topics that invite *inventive* thinking; conversely, avoid topics that invite clichés or a straight listing of facts. Since the usual purpose of a process writing assignment is to integrate content knowledge, keep the assignment focused. A vague assignment with confusing directions invites dull, vacuous responses.

2. Choose topics with *purpose.* Ask, "What kind of writing do I want from students? Would *I* be interested in doing this sort of task?" The more purposeful the assignment in students' eyes, the more likely you are to accomplish your teaching aims. In other words, have a reason for your assignment and communicate it.

3. Make sure your topics are *meaningful* within students' experience. Design topics that allow students to use their own experience, or the semester's work, for examples and support. Skilled teachers often build in prewriting activities that help students explore personal connections to the topic or writing task.

4. Design topics to elicit *specific, immediate responses* from students, not vague, abstract ones. Compare the assignment to "discuss freedom" with this one: "List the freedoms you enjoy and freedoms you are denied. What is the reason for the denials? To what extent do you accept the reasons? Write an essay on the subject."

5. If you use a *hypothetical situation,* make it interesting. Assignments may ask students to use voices other than their own, to use formats other than traditional essay, and to use imaginative problem-solving. Such forms of writing can demand thinking skills that range from basic reports to high-level analysis and persuasion.

6. Use *specific terms* (such as *define, illustrate, persuade, compare, contrast, analyze, evaluate,* or *invent*) as precise signposts of your expectations. Talk to students about what these terms mean. Specify the steps you want students to follow—particularly prewriting steps such as discussing, interviewing, listing, researching, and so on.

7. Use *creative formats* for some assignments. Why not a letter from Mendel to a colleague explaining a genetic principle? Or an editorial arguing for (or against) a piece of legislation in our nation's past? Or a response to a "Dear Abby" math problem? Or a report on nutrition written by a Martian visitor? Such formats can be fun for students.

8. Think of *CRAFT* when designing assignments. That is, does the task specify a Context? A Role for the writer? An Audience? A Format? A Topic? By using CRAFT as a mental checklist, you can improve lackluster writing tasks. Of course, not all assignments need to contain all the CRAFT elements. The acronym is a guide, not a straitjacket.

9. Whenever possible, allow for *choice* in writing assignments. Most students like choice—and a chosen topic is usually more motivating than a forced one. Offering students a choice of topics isn't always possible, but sometimes it's the best way to accommodate the vast range of abilities in your content area classroom.

10. Define the *grading criteria* you'll use. The more explicit and public your criteria, the more likely it is that students will meet your expectations. Explicit criteria can actually free students to be thoughtful and creative. Most students like to know what's expected, so why not share (and thoroughly discuss) these criteria in advance?

Context + RAFT = CRAFT

As previously noted, CRAFT is an acronym for assignment design. Good teachers have long used the RAFT formula with success, helping their students visualize a writing *role,* an *audience,* a text *format,* and writing *topic.* (For a quick review of the formats for writing, see Figure 3.2, p. 33.) Table 6.2 shows a layout of RAFT assignments across secondary content areas. Notice that even the informational tasks invite creativity.

In my opinion, most middle school and high school students *hunger* for context. That's why I suggest adding the important element of *context* to the RAFT layout in Table 6.2. The point, of course, is to situate writing prompts dramatically.

Table 6.2 Examples of RAFT Assignments

Role	Audience	Format	Topic
Stem cell researcher	Aldous Huxley	Letter	Response to *Brave New World*
Vincent Van Gogh	Self	Diary	Painting of "Starry, Starry Night"
Sojourner Truth	Abolitionists	Fund-raising solicitation	Needs of black volunteers in 1863
Tiger Woods	Weight Watchers	Motivational talk	Lifelong exercise
Editorial writer	General public	Newspaper editorial	Analysis of recent political trends
Archimedes	Hiero, king of Syracuse	Report of field test on gold crown	Law of buoyancy and law of the lever
Possessive apostrophe	Young writers	Complaint	How it's left out or misused
Willy Loman	Family members	Last will and testament	*Death of a Salesman* story
Sequoia tree	Sun	Poem	Photosynthesis
Bill Gates	Microsoft shareholders	Annual report	The future of computers
Grand Inquisitor	Galileo	Church edict for imprisonment	Grave suspicion of heresy
Square root	Whole number	Love letter	Explaining our relationship
Physician	Young newlyweds	Informational talk	Fetal Alcohol Syndrome
Osama bin Laden	Nations of the West	Public letter	Motivation for terrorist activity
Martha Stewart	Business executives	*Fortune* magazine article	Importance of personal integrity
Newspaper reporter	Readers in 1859	Obituary	Hanging of John Brown
Space alien	Intergalactic commander	Analysis of crowd psychology	Holiday shopping
Hermit	Self	Diary	Personal hygiene
Lungs	Tobacco products	Complaint	Effects of smoking
Lawyer	U.S. Supreme Court	Appeal speech	"Separate but equal" decision of 1892

continued

Table 6.2 Examples of RAFT Assignments *Continued*

Role	Audience	Format	Topic
Harry Truman	Dear Abby	Advice column	Decision to drop atomic bomb
Meriwether Lewis and William Clark	Sacajawea	Letter of appreciation	Service to the expedition
Emeril Lagasse	Gourmet cooks	Newsletter	Fun in the kitchen
Citizen	U.S. senator	Persuasive letter	Control of assault weapons
Mountain man	Self	Diary	Relationships with Native Americans
Ophelia	Hamlet	Personal letter	A woman's view of *Hamlet*
Newswriter	Public	News release	Global warming
Shop foreman	Welders	Safety poster	List of reminders for welding safety
Repeating decimal	Set of rational numbers	Petition	Proving you belong to the set
U.S. Department of Health	TV audience	Public service announcement	Vegetables in the diet
Black Elk	White settlers	Meditation	The westward expansion
Potato chip	Other chips	Travel guide	Journey through digestive system
Adolf Hitler	Anne Frank	Letter	Response to *Diary of Anne Frank*
Brook trout	Self	Diary	Effects of acid rain

For example, in middle school geometry, Sarah Gale (personal communication, 2003) developed a prompt from the RAFT formula. Students were asked to take on the role of rectangle and to imagine the Council of Parallelograms as their audience. The specified writing format was a letter, and the topic involved proving that the rectangle should be included in the set of all parallelograms. With the basics in place, Sarah then added context—namely, the rectangle's desire to "gain admission" to the Council of Parallelograms, an elite group.

Sarah encouraged students to be creative and have fun with the assignment. They were also directed to write a minimum of 10 sentences in correct letter form and to include key definitions, pictures of themselves, and so on.

Taking on the role of "Rhonda Rhombus, Council President," Sarah did more than check spelling errors. She developed a clever form letter to respond to students whose writing didn't quite hit the mark. Notice Sarah's open-ended, invitational tone:

Dear Madam or Sir:

Thank you for your letter to the Council of Parallelograms. We have reviewed your case and decided, based on the information you have given us, that there is insufficient evidence to warrant a membership for you in our council. You did not specify one or more of the following:

• Opposite sides are parallel.

• Opposite sides are congruent.

• Opposite angles are congruent.

• Diagonals bisect each other.

Please feel free to contact us again.

Sincerely,

Rhonda Rhombus, Council President

Of course, upon receiving the student's "revised" application, the Council President immediately responded with a congratulatory letter—one that apologized "for any pain or grief we may have caused due to your previous exclusion from our group."

Fun? Absolutely. But it also served to motivate learning. In fact, Sarah had a two-word summary for her little writing prompt: "Extremely successful."

Case Study of an Assignment

Now that you've been introduced to the principles of assignment design, let's look at two illustrative tasks, related to earth science and, more specifically, to volcanos, a topic that fascinates many adolescents. Thanks to "Krakatoa," a *Nova* special on giant waves, called "tsunamis," I became interested in volcanos as a possible generator of such waves. What I found were amazing Internet resources on volcanos, and a story of a potential disaster looming in the future.

Of course, in the aftermath of December 26, 2004 (southeast Asia) and March 11, 2011 (Japan), we now understand the power of tsunamis. These catastrophic waves unleashed trillions of tons of sea water, taking many thousands of lives. No longer do we visualize such waves as the product of special effects, as in movies like *The Day After Tomorrow*. The power of tsunamis is documented by video footage of houses, buses, and people swept away by terrible walls of water.

My research focused on the island of La Palma, part of the Canary Islands off the coast of West Africa. On October 4, 2000, the BBC published an article titled "Giant

Wave Could Threaten U.S." (http://news.bbc.co.uk/1/hi/sci/tech/956280.stm). Then on August 29, 2001, the BBC published a second report, titled "Giant Wave Devastation Feared" (http://news.bbc.co.uk/1/hi/sci/tech/1513342.stm), authored by Alex Kirby. Both reports referred to the instability of the Cumbre Vieja volcano on La Palma. While nobody predicted an imminent collapse, the articles warned that the volcano's eruption could trigger a landslide of enormous magnitude—500 billion tons of earth—creating the biggest tidal wave in recorded history. In fact, "the energy released by the collapse would equal the entire U.S. electricity consumption for six months."

The BBC articles are based on papers developed by Dr. Steven Ward, University of California, and Dr. Simon Day, University College, London—papers that scientifically estimate the tsunami size and speed: "The dome of water it caused would be 900 metres (2,950 feet) high, and the resulting tsunami . . . would travel outwards, reaching speeds of 800 km an hour (500 mph)." According to Dr. Day, "It's entirely possible you'd see 50-metre [164 foot] waves coming ashore in Florida, New York, Boston, all the way up to Greenland, and in some cases reaching up to 10 kilometres [about 6 miles]."

Because the Internet resources related to La Palma are so remarkable—and because the story itself is so compelling, especially from a geology perspective—this topic seemed like an excellent springboard for a process writing assignment. To illustrate the CRAFT principles listed earlier, I developed two writing tasks. See what you think:

CRAFT Assignment 1 Recent geologic activity on the island of La Palma, off the west coast of Africa, has begun to raise fears along the eastern seaboard of the United States that the "unthinkable" might happen in the future. Imagine yourself as part of a team that will design and produce an information brochure as part of a campaign on disaster preparation. The brochure's purpose is to help the citizens develop their *own* advance plans for coping with a possible general evacuation from eastern cities and low-lying areas. However, it is very important not to spread panic about the prospect of a giant tidal wave. Also, you must use clear, direct language, because many citizens (up to 20% of adults) read at very basic levels. As a writer, you will need to understand giant tidal waves (tsunamis) and La Palma geology. Also, you will need to inform yourself about basic civil defense strategy by doing Internet research (e.g., FEMA, USGS, and other websites). Finally, you will need to choose a city or region and study Internet maps to plan exit routes. National Civil Defense planners have established broad guidelines—for example, that almost all highways along the eastern seaboard will be converted to one-way traffic headed west. Work as a team to gather information, take notes, and report back to your team members; then work as a group to decide on the approach your brochure will take.

Context:	Development of a Civil Defense booklet/brochure
Role:	Researcher and writer of the booklet/brochure
Audience:	General public
Format:	Booklet/Brochure (with graphics)
Topic:	Disaster preparation (mega-wave)

CRAFT Assignment 2 Imagine yourself as a real estate developer and resort property manager on the island of La Palma. Because of concerns about a giant wave at some unspecified point in the future, your business has fallen sharply in recent years, as have prices of the island's resort property. You are interested in developing an advertising brochure about the many attractions of La Palma that will entice people to plan vacations there and to invest in resort property such as condos. From past experience in real estate sales and condo management, you know that wealthier and better-educated individuals represent your target audience. Some of these are young, upwardly mobile professionals; others are successful persons who have retired or soon plan to retire. It will therefore be important to communicate in a way that appeals to them. What are the attractions of climate, geography, and lifestyle that make La Palma so desirable? What appeals will you make to help possible investors overcome their concerns about personal safety or the possibility of their investment sliding into the ocean? Learn all you can about giant waves caused by volcanos. Also, do Internet research on La Palma to learn more about its geography, geology, culture, and many attractions. Using information and graphics from such resources—but your own language—develop these into a booklet/brochure.

Context:	Sales booklet/brochure
Role:	Real estate developer/Property manager
Audience:	Upscale, affluent audience
Format:	Booklet/Brochure (with graphics)
Topic:	Many natural attractions of La Palma

Of course, the brochures developed by students for such assignments will be quite different. One will be *informational/functional writing* (emergency preparation), the other *argumentative/persuasive writing* (marketing of real estate). Yet both will require content knowledge, research skills, collaboration with others, and thoughtful writing. I contend that such work holds far more instructional promise than a dreary multiple-choice test drawn from a publisher's test manual.

As for evaluation rubrics—the checklists that students use when composing or meeting in response groups—I recommend keeping them simple. Here, for example, are five basic questions that could provide direction for students.

La Palma Brochure Checklist
- Is it *scientifically accurate* with respect to earth science?
- Is it clearly aimed at a *target audience?*
- Are *quotes and paraphrasing* used appropriately?
- Do *Internet graphics* support the message?
- Are *conventions* (spelling, usage, mechanics) correct?

Of course, a simple rating scale can be attached to these criteria for in-class use and for purposes of teacher evaluation. Providing such criteria to students, as shown here, helps clarify expectations. (Note that a five-point scale is used: 5 = excellent; 4 = strong; 3 = good; 2 = marginal; 1 = needs work.)

La Palma Brochure Grading Rubric

	1	2	3	4	5
Scientific Accuracy					
Audience Appeal					
Quotes and Paraphrasing					
Internet Graphics					
Grammar and Usage					

These criteria set broad parameters for the task but allow plenty of room for students to exercise creativity and imagination.

Content Area Writing Tasks

With the basic principles of assignment design in mind, let's now consider some other writing tasks that might appeal to middle school or high school students. What they have in common is the CRAFT approach. Several additional tasks featuring this approach are found in Appendix E.

Using a role-playing strategy, history teacher Natalie Burningham (personal communication, 2004) developed an assignment with built-in choice. Note that this prompt draws upon critical thinking (propaganda techniques) and that it includes Internet sites for student research.

Creating Propaganda

You are a newspaper columnist who works for one of the well-known papers in New England in 1775. You are new to the job, and your first assignment is to create a piece of propaganda either for or against a revolution from British rule. To spark the interest of colonial readers, you are to write your feature article in an obituary format, including a picture and caption to illustrate your statements. If you choose to be pro-war, you will write your obituary about the death of British values and rule. If you choose to be against the war, you will write your obituary about the death of the rising American independence and self-rule.

The first step in writing is to choose your side. Look in your textbook or on the Internet to research the situation if you are not sure which side to take. Here are a few Internet sites about America and Britain:

- http://revolution.h-net.msu.edu The American Revolution
- http://www.lib.jmu.edu/history/internet.html Research Guides: History
- http://www.spartacus.schoolnet.co.uk/Britain.html British History Page

Make sure to research three or more British or American values and to include them in your obituary along with supporting details. We'll use the following rubric when we discuss writing quality for this assignment.

	Keep Trying (1 point)	Good Work (2 points)	Excellent Work (3 points)
Accurate historical facts			
Three values and supporting details			
Picture and caption with text			
Use of propaganda techniques			
Spelling and grammar			

Physical education teacher Clark Funk (personal communication, 2004) wanted to use persuasive writing to prompt higher-order thinking, so he outlined a hypothetical problem and developed items for students to think about as they discussed the assigned issue and then got ready to write.

Notice how this assignment "scaffolds" expectations. For example, as students are asked to compare the benefits of Ultimate Frisbee with other sports, they move beyond a simple description of the game to an analysis of it. Handling such a task will probably require at least some revision, which can lead to insight.

Ultimate Frisbee

Imagine that during the past year you and some friends have gotten very involved with Ultimate Frisbee. You've enjoyed playing "pick-up" games together but have had trouble finding places to play without being disturbed. In the last month, you've been kicked off fields over a dozen times. Some of your friends are getting discouraged, and their numbers are starting to dwindle. You and your friends decide that now is the time to take action and seek help from the principal. You want to convince the principal that starting an intramural program for Ultimate Frisbee would be a good idea.

In your letter to the principal, describe the game of Ultimate Frisbee and explain its rules. Express your concern for what is happening to your group and try to persuade the principal of the need for an intramural program for your sport. Compare the benefits (physical, social, emotional, etc.) of Ultimate Frisbee to the other school-sponsored sports and explain the need for a reserved place to play. Give the principal your ideas of how Ultimate Frisbee could complement the other sports programs. Finally, to convince the principal that there is enough interest in the sport to justify it being included in the school's intramural program, describe the success you've had with your Ultimate Frisbee group.

Persuasive Letter Criteria (1 = low; 5 = high)	1	2	3	4	5
Ideas are clear and focused, with support for claims.					
Text organization is logical and easy to follow.					
Voice is confident and convincing in making a request.					
Sentences are correctly and effectively written.					

A very different kind of persuasive prompt was prepared by home economics teacher Amy Crosbie (personal communication, 2003) for her culinary cooking class. However, Amy's assignment was anything but a "cookbook" approach to writing. Students were put in a situation of choosing an entrée to submit to the president of a restaurant chain and persuading that individual to include it on the restaurant's new national menu. Amy framed the writing task so that students had to consider nutritional value, balance of chosen foods, plate presentation, and appropriateness for their restaurant. In Amy's words, it gave students "a situation in which they must apply the content they have learned and use the skills they have perfected in the lab." Look for the CRAFT elements in Amy's assignment.

"Healthy Choice" Meal Proposal

The Situation

You are Chief Chef in a restaurant for one of the large chains. The company president has sent a memo to all Chief Chefs inviting a proposal for a new entrée on next year's menu. The company seeks menu items that offer a healthy choice to customers. You have decided to submit a lunch or dinner entrée to be evaluated by the president, knowing that the winner will (1) receive a "meaty" bonus, (2) be featured in *Bon Appétit* magazine, and (3) have his or her entrée in the new menu.

Your Task

- Prepare a recipe, including a listing of all items (meat, starch, vegetable, etc.) that will be included in the meal. The recipe must be appropriate for the restaurant chosen and health-conscious.

- Submit a title and short, creative description of the meal to grab the customer's interest. Format it just as it would appear in the menu and include the number of fat grams for the meal. Also, design the logo that will indicate that the menu choice is health-conscious.

- Submit an analysis of the meal's nutritional value associated with the Food Guide Pyramid. Use the computer program "Computrition" in preparing your analysis.

- Write a two-page paper that proves why your entrée is an excellent healthy choice menu item. Include the analysis of the nutritional content and explain why it fits the existing menu, characteristics that will appeal to the customer, and balance of the meal in relation to taste, texture, aroma, color, and presentation. The goal is to persuade the president of the restaurant to choose your entrée; therefore, the proposal needs to be written in a confident and professional voice.

- Put the previous four items in a packet and complete by adding a brief cover letter written to the president. In half a page, introduce yourself, identify the location of your restaurant, and briefly mention your meal selection and why it would be a healthy and appropriate addition to the existing menu. If this cover letter is not carefully written, the president will likely not waste time looking at the rest of your proposal. Leave him or her eager to learn more about the menu item you submitted.

Summary

This project is an opportunity to showcase the content information learned this semester related to nutrition, plate presentation, menu writing, and appropriate meal choices. Be confident and creative as you persuade the president to choose your entrée, yet professional in the presentation.

Assignment Criteria for "Healthy Choice" Meal Proposal	Points Possible	Points Earned
Recipe is functional and appropriate for restaurant.	10	
Nutritional content relates to Food Guide Pyramid.	10	
Meal title and description reflect care and creativity.	05	
The proposal includes all assignment elements.	30	
The cover letter is professional and effective.	30	
Overall appearance and correctness of materials.	15	
TOTAL	100	

Finally, let's examine a business education task designed by teacher Sara Johnson (personal communication, 2004). Sara's goal was to link technology skills (such as the ability to create a website) with communication skills (such as the ability to develop and present a professional proposal). Interestingly, her assignment asked students to integrate many skills—research, technology, writing, and speaking—thus simulating real-world expectations. In the prompt that follows, notice how skillfully Sara weaves together the elements of context, role, audience, format, and topic.

Website Design Proposal

Context

Your group has been selected as a finalist for designing the school's new website. The website must be functional and visually appealing. Students, parents, teachers, administrators, and district representatives will all be using this site in the future.

Role

You will want to approach this assignment with a professional voice. Imagine your group as a company presenting the website report proposal to a prospective client.

Audience

The school board, administration, and student body officers each have a vote in selecting the winning website proposal. Consider each group's needs, concerns, and desires when compiling your proposal.

Format and Process

- Begin by doing an Internet search for other high school websites. Compile a list of strengths and weaknesses of the sites. Be sure to keep a log of URLs you visit for reference.

- Create a map of your proposed site. This map needs to show relationships between pages and the navigation options throughout the site (how a user can move from page to page or return to the home page).

- Create a professional report that details your group's vision of the new school website. Include a clear rationale for your design by addressing the (1) purpose of the website, (2) predicted users (who will be accessing the site), and (3) its technology.

- It is strongly recommended that you create an MS PowerPoint or other visual aid for your presentation to the selection committee. Revise your writing several times to ensure correct grammar and spelling.

- Finally, prepare a 10-minute oral presentation that summarizes key points about good high school websites and share your proposal.

Topic

You must consider two topics in completing this assignment. First, the purposes of the website are to provide current information on academic and extracurricular activities, to provide a directory of faculty and staff, and to display the school policy and procedures. The school board is open to your group's suggestions for additional features. Second, the purpose of your proposal is to thoroughly explain your website to the selection committee and persuade them to select it as the new, official school website. Remember, you do not have to create the website at this point. However, you must have a clear image of the site's design and be able to answer questions about it.

Proposal Grading Rubric (1 = low; 4 = high)	1	2	3	4
The writing contains all necessary elements: research notes, site map, report, and visual aid.				
The report clearly describes the purpose of the website, the predicted customers, and site technology.				
The ideas are creative, well organized, and structured in a professional, compelling manner.				
The report shows good word choice and sentence fluency, with no spelling or grammar errors.				

Darth Vader Revisited

This chapter began on a dark note, with Darth Vader threatening to extinguish *insight* with his diabolical plans for mind control. Vader pointed out, in his throatiest and blackest voice, that the conquest of darkness was inevitable—*if* he could disarm future citizens of the searing laser light called *writing*.

So what happens next? One possible scenario is quiet surrender. For example, we can continue to pretend that warehousing kids for standardized tests is the central goal of secondary education. On the other hand, we can marshal our collective wits against the Black Knight, adopting the guerilla tactics of good, hard-working teachers.

The camera zeros in on a classroom visited earlier—but now groups of students are brainstorming ideas for writing. Some set to work drawing maps, while others work on creative descriptions and factual information for their travel brochures.

"I love teaching like this," the teacher says. "There's interest and energy—and the students exercise their creativity. They do lots of research, plus they put their ideas in a real-world format, one that others can read."

The scene shifts to another class, where students are reviewing learning logs and highlighting the material they plan to use on tomorrow's in-class exam. This will be an "open notes" essay for which the teacher has provided a study guide.

"Cool," they say. "We get to use our logs."

"To *think* with," their teacher adds. "We're raising the bar here."

"So we can study together?" they ask.

Finally, the scene shifts to a high school classroom where small groups edit their final drafts and check them against a rubric. An earlier draft is stapled beneath the final copy to showcase each student's writing process. A quick glance at the drafts reveals changes in organization and mechanics. In this classroom, students earn one grade for evidence of revision and another grade for the quality of the final product.

"I was skeptical," one teacher says, "but writing *works*. You give good prompts and a few student models and a little advice—and what do you know? They learn by doing. There's no way I'd go back to the old approach of stand-and-deliver teaching."

And so it goes. Now that you understand the theory and practice of assignment design, check out several more model assignments and rubrics in Appendix E. Then try your hand at developing an assignment in your own content area. My "Writing Assignment to Construct a Writing Assignment" appears in the following text.

Write-for-Insight Activity

Let's imagine you're part of a Career Ladder Program focused on "Writing Across the Curriculum." This program asks teachers to design writing assignments to teach curriculum content and publishes the best tasks for other teachers. To be selected for publication means a library of paperback books for your classroom, plus leadership prestige!

Here are the criteria used by a teacher selection committee (chaired by your supervisor) for deciding upon top writing tasks. (Note that a five-point scale is used: 5 = excellent; 4 = strong; 3 = good; 2 = marginal; 1 = needs work.)

Committee Criteria for Process Writing Tasks					
1. Deals with a topic of *significant content value*.	1	2	3	4	5
2. Invites *imagination* and *problem-solving* skills.	1	2	3	4	5
3. Uses CRAFT to create a *context* for writing.	1	2	3	4	5
4. Provides clear *prewriting* guidelines or advice.	1	2	3	4	5
5. Outlines evaluation criteria in a rubric.	1	2	3	4	5
6. Uses correct language conventions.	1	2	3	4	5
7. Provides rationale for task in memo.	1	2	3	4	5

According to the committee's guidelines, this assignment should be a "major take-home or in-class assignment developed in stages." Therefore, your goals are (1) to develop a writing task of high quality, and (2) to develop a memo that explains the rationale for your assignment to your supervisor and the selection committee.

To accomplish these aims, first review the "Ten Design Principles" section of this chapter, paying special attention to the CRAFT suggestions. To begin, brainstorm the basic concepts or principles in your content area. Then consider using Internet resources to gather ideas for a writing task.

Your writing prompt will most likely consist of a task sheet that offers instruction, step-by-step activities for students, and other kinds of guidance (e.g., a timeline or resource reference). Of course, it's great if you can provide students with writing options so that they have some choice in writing tasks. After creating the writing assignment, create an accompanying grading rubric (like the one previously shown).

Then, write a clear professional memo to your supervisor—in this case, your course instructor or workshop leader—explaining your goals for the assignment, the intended grade level and context for writing, and teaching strategies that will support the task. Use a memo format and professional voice—and please make sure to use your spell checker!

Finally, share the writing task and memo with your instructor or workshop leader so that you can participate in follow-up discussion with your content area colleagues.

Managing the Writing Process

It's like driving a car at night. You never see further than your headlights, but you can make the whole trip that way.

—E. L. Doctorow

Coaching Writing

The computer lab hums with activity. Kids talk, keyboards click, and an ancient printer grinds out paperwork. Most students have notes or handwritten text, but some struggle to generate ideas. Like their teacher, I zigzag through the room, coaching individuals.

Rachel stares at her monitor as I drag up a chair. "So how's it going?" I ask.

"I don't know," she says. "This part doesn't sound good."

"Which part?"

She's looking at the screen again. "Do you think it's any good?"

"What are you trying to do?" I ask.

"Like we talked about: '*The bigger the issue, the smaller you write.*' That was cool."

"So you want a story opener for your essay?"

"Right. I just thought—oh, I don't know."

I let a couple of beats go by. "Okay, what's your focus?"

Now she looks at me. "Our assignment—you know, describing our writing process."

"Yes, but what do you want to *say* about it?"

"Getting started. How much trouble I have."

"That's a great idea to explore. Do you have it down in your notes?"

"Not yet."

"What interests you about the 'getting started' stage?"

She shakes her head. "Like if I can get started, it's not that bad, you know? But if I get stuck, it's, like, hopeless."

I'm wondering how much to lead. "I see. So you're thinking about how you *usually* approach a writing assignment—and what happens when you get stuck?"

"Right."

"I notice you don't have any notes to work from."

"Usually I just write it out."

"Are you stuck now?"

Rachel hesitates. "Pretty much."

"Hmmm. So the just-writing-it-out strategy isn't working, and some thoughts and feelings are stirred up. What are they?"

She laughs. "Like being frustrated? Wanting to quit?"

A hand goes up down the aisle. "I know the feeling. But let's say you make a list of those thoughts and feelings so you can get *unstuck*. What do you think?"

Rachel shrugs. "I guess."

"Give it a try, and I'll come back to see how you're doing." As I slip into the downstream current, Rachel flips open her notebook and wrinkles her nose again.

And so it goes. Conferences like this provide scaffolding for students as they struggle to generate ideas, organize texts, or make revisions based on peer feedback. In fact, for most teachers who help students with writing, mini-conferences are central to the game. Why? Because conferences reveal whether students are thinking about—or avoiding—the key issues in writing.

Although part of my conference with Rachel focused on content—her desire to write about the "getting started" part of writing—much of it dealt with process. Ironically, Rachel was still using a strategy that had not served her well in the past. So it seemed useful to encourage a substitute strategy of making a simple list.

Like someone who knows all about healthy lifestyles but strays from the path of regular exercise and good nutrition, Rachel already understood the value of prewriting tools, because they were part of her teacher's curriculum. All she needed was friendly encouragement to use what she had learned.

Visualizing the Writing Process

Our aim in this chapter is to consider the challenges faced by Rachel and her classmates—and understand how good teaching might support their learning. Like other chapters, this one assumes that **scaffolded instruction** enables learners to internalize new writing skills and achieve content area insights.

This chapter builds on earlier ideas about expressive writing, as well as the design of assignments and rubrics. As you know, writing-to-learn activities are often ungraded—the aim being to understand the concepts and issues in your field. Such writing promotes active learning—a rehearsal of ideas—that students draw upon when challenged with more complex tasks, as described in Chapter 6. Glancing back to the four writing domains (Figure I.1, p. xv) in the Preface, you'll recall that expressive writing supports the upper three domains—namely, (1) *narrative and poetic text*, (2) *informational and functional text*, and (3) *persuasive and argumentative text*.

In this chapter, we focus on helping students succeed with graded academic assignments. Here I'll share basic ideas about the writing process, a frame of reference for the key terms you can use with students. When you use terms like *prewriting* and *revising*—and such terms are also used by teachers in health, industrial arts, history, and other content areas—students take notice.

Figure 7.1 is a model of the **recursive writing process**. The term *recursive* means that to move *forward* in writing (improving the content or form) writers typically have to move *backward* to earlier steps. In other words, careful academic writing isn't usually a one-draft event. Generally, we have to do more research, or tinker with organization, or delete some words in favor of others. It's a kind of cognitive dance, and a physical one too.

As you study this illustration, notice that it depicts two "cycles" of activity—"shaping up" and "shipping out." The cycles are connected, but students need to consider them separately

Figure 7.1

How Writing Develops

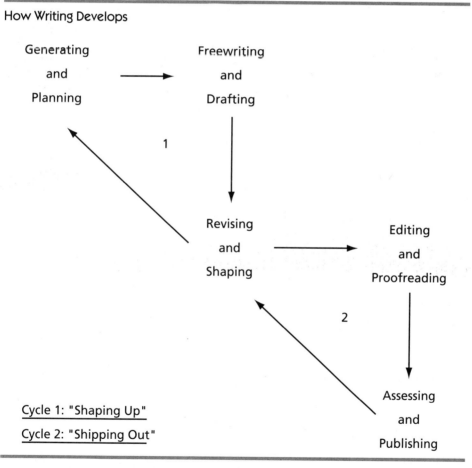

Generating
and
Planning

Freewriting
and
Drafting

1

Revising
and
Shaping

Editing
and
Proofreading

2

Assessing
and
Publishing

Cycle 1: "Shaping Up"

Cycle 2: "Shipping Out"

Source: Strong, W. (1996). *Writer's toolbox: A sentence-combining workshop.* New York: McGraw-Hill. © 1996 The McGraw-Hill Companies, Inc.

so that they see what to do first, second, third, and so on. Without such a map, it's easy to become overwhelmed and discouraged.

And what about those "backward pointing" arrows in the writing process model? These arrows emphasize, as Paul Valery once put it, that writing is "never finished, only abandoned" (Murray, 1990, p. 197). After all, what writer doesn't hope for another edition—a second chance to "get it right"? I got that opportunity with the book you're reading now.

In explaining Cycle 1 to students, point out that the work of developing solid content—something to say—is really "Job Number 1." Students often try to take shortcuts, just like Rachel in the opening scenario. But good content enables a writer to develop a draft, and the draft sets the stage for more content. That is, as writers read their drafts, often with the help of partners, they begin to see "holes" in their work—missing points that should be included. And that's where revision, the heart of the writing process, comes in.

In explaining Cycle 2, focus on the idea of *form* in writing. Explain that "form" refers to organization, the sequencing of paragraphs, or "idea flow." Note that good ideas, presented in a confused way, become muddled ideas. Encourage students to "preview" the organization of their reports in an introductory paragraph. Challenge them to move paragraphs around to improve readability. Explain why strong conclusions matter. Finally, have students focus on the basic mechanics of their papers—the spelling, usage, and conventions that are part of "good form." This, of course, is the editing step before "shipping out" the paper for teacher evaluation, or actual publication.

As you post such a model in your classroom, discuss it, and model a strategy or two, some students may say, "Hey, this isn't an English class."

"No, it isn't," you reply. "But I value good writing—and you should too. That's why I'm asking for your best revised work on our next assignment. Remember, *revision makes you smarter.*"

"You mean this writing counts on our grade?" someone will ask.

"You see? You're getting smarter already!"

Understanding the Model

With an overview of a two-stage model, let's now explore its details. As you read these descriptions of specific writing process strategies, think of your own writing and the extent to which you already use them. Also, think about how you might scaffold these strategies in the context of your own classroom teaching.

Prewriting techniques of **generating and planning** include, among others, listing ideas; clustering or "webbing" them; sketching, drawing, and doodling; talking to others, reading, and charting; asking and answering questions; outlining; and "cubing" (as discussed in Appendix C). Such activities help students discover a way into their topics.

Of course, it's one thing to assign writing, and another to teach it. Top-notch teachers prime the pump. For example, teachers can boost writing quality by demonstrating how to briefly outline an exam response before actually writing. They can also prompt students to revisit learning logs, or they can set up think-pair-share activities, or they can model

Venn diagrams for comparison/contrast writing. Finally, they can remind students that ungraded expressive writing can serve as useful *prewriting* for many graded tasks.

Another aspect of generating and planning is to prompt thought about purpose and audience before students invest a lot of time in drafting. To many students, writing means "pleasing the teacher." However, modeling a process of question-asking about broader aims and other audiences—and following this demo with work in small groups—helps make academic writing more meaningful and authentic.

Freewriting and drafting create direction for a text. You can compare drafting to riding a bike—and note that bike-riding requires momentum. Encourage students to relax and work fast, focusing first on *content*. Of course, some students will need a clear mental map before getting started, and perfectionists will equate drafting with "making mistakes." Make sure to discuss such points. As psychologist Howard Gardner (1982) has pointed out, Beethoven required many drafts to achieve his magnificent music. Mozart, on the other hand, planned so extensively in his head that his efforts seemed like brilliant first drafts:

> Like Mozart, Beethoven was a fluent and skillful improviser, but he composed only with much more overt difficulty. In addition to keeping a notebook replete with discarded themes and false starts, Beethoven would score a piece numerous times—revising, rejecting, crossing out in his impetuous and messy hand. While Mozart's rapidly produced scores seldom contained erased passages—and indeed were practically of "camera-ready" quality—Beethoven's sketchbooks chronicled painful, even tormented sieges of creation. Certainly Beethoven's agonies during the throes of creation—rather than Mozart's seemingly seamless composing activity—served as the model of the suffering romantic artist in his garret.

> (Gardner, 1982, pp. 359–360)

Since many students procrastinate, offer "process points" to get them started. Also, emphasize that drafts are the raw material for revision—and that after the draft is written, it always helps to put it aside for a day or two before revising. Finally, and importantly, resist the temptation to "grade" the rough drafts of your students. Such grading almost always reduces their motivation to revise.

In many ways, **shaping and revising** are the heart of the writing process. In revision, the emphasis is still on content—getting the ideas right—but organization and development are also high priorities. Of course, to improve logic or add examples, the writer often returns to basic questions: What's my message? Where am I going with this? How can I present it more clearly? The model of recursive writing presented earlier suggests that a writer may go back to the stage of generating and planning in order to draft additional text—providing illustrations for a theme, for example. Or the writer may move chunks of the text around, tweaking the "fit" of various paragraphs.

It's in the revising stage that **peer response** can be helpful. As the writer gives voice to intentions and shares a draft, well-trained peers can offer valid advice. Thus, revising becomes a collaborative effort, and candid feedback helps the novice writer see the text as having real effects on real readers. But as important as peer responders may be, the writer is always the "first reader" of the text, the one who must sort through advice, deciding what to act upon and what to ignore.

Although **editing and proofreading** can occur any time, it makes sense for novice writers to have such focus *after* their content and organization are solidly established. Editing refers to strategic decisions about word choice and sentence construction as well as the process of cleaning up errors in spelling, punctuation, and usage. Writing research suggests that "blocked" writers are preoccupied with editing at the early stages, when they should be thinking about finding, developing, and organizing ideas. A myopic focus on text details prevents them from attending to content and structure. For lazy writers—those who don't take the time to proofread—"expect more." Thus, you might give students a five-minute "reminder" lesson on sets of frequently confused words such as *its/it's, your/you're* and *there/their/they're*. This lesson can set the stage for focused proofreading.

Sharing good work with others completes the writing process. In the real world of writing, **assessing and publishing** are always intertwined. A letter to the editor, a job resume, an advertisement, an interoffice memo or company report, a dissertation proposal—all of these texts are shared with readers and assessed by them. In classroom writing assignments, the teacher serves as the main assessor, but there are many different levels of publication for student writing, ranging from an audience of one to an audience of many. As students' work is posted on classroom bulletin boards—or websites via the Internet—the opportunities for assessment multiply.

Guiding Cycle 1 Activities (Prewriting)

To help students get started with process writing tasks, try supporting their work with checklists. Simple checklists, given in advance of in-class workshops and conferences, are much like the grading rubrics in Chapter 6, except that students often help create them.

Let's say, for example, that your language arts class has been reading fables. Drawing from what students already understand about fables, you might list features of the fable genre at the board. Of course, these features define a fable writing task—and a corresponding checklist—for students.

A Fable for Today

1. The characters are animals with human qualities.
2. There is some kind of problem or conflict.
3. Animals may talk to one another in a fable.
4. Action grows out of the problem or conflict.
5. A clear "moral" comes at the end of the fable.

(Strong, 2001, p. 157)

Or let's say that your science class has been researching the causes and effects of global warming, and you've asked them to use a letter format to share findings with a broader audience. Students have the option of writing a personal letter, a letter to the editor (for a newspaper or magazine), or a business letter (to a specific corporation or government agency). You might have this kind of checklist:

A Global Warming Letter

1. The letter (personal, letter to the editor, business) is formatted correctly.

2. It makes a central point (thesis) about global warming.

3. At least three points of evidence (proof, reasons, examples) are given.

4. The letter has a clear beginning, middle, and end.

5. Words and ideas are appropriate for the chosen format.

Or let's imagine you're teaching general math, and you want students to analyze data sets. You post the nation's current nutrition guidelines, and then you give learners the data sets from several fast-food chains (available at local stores or via the Internet). In the computer lab, students work in teams, each researching a specific fast-food product (for example, chicken sandwiches, fries, or quarter-pound hamburgers). Products are compared on variables such as fat content, cholesterol, carbohydrates, and sodium, so that "consumer rankings" are developed on the class website. A checklist like this one would be helpful:

A Website Article (Your Contribution)

1. Develop a 2×2 matrix listing fast-food restaurants and nutrition variables.

2. Transfer all data for a single type of product to your matrix for analysis.

3. Now, rerank the restaurants from best to worst on your product's variables.

4. Explain your rank order in writing (some variables may conflict).

5. Submit your writing to the website editors, supported by your matrix.

Or let's say you're a history teacher who has teamed up with colleagues in the English department. As high school juniors read Mark Twain's *Huckleberry Finn* and Mildred Taylor's *Roll of Thunder, Hear My Cry,* you draw upon key ideas in American history and social studies. For example, in your assignment for Twain's novel, you ask students to imagine Huck and Jim as very old men in the twenty-first century, exchanging insights about race relations. You provide a checklist to further define the writing task:

A Dialogue between Huck and Jim

1. Create a setting and situation for your dialogue.

2. Weave modern historical facts (persons, events) into the dialogue.

3. Show how Huck and Jim see race relations in the twenty-first century.

4. Also show the present relationship between Huck and Jim.

5. Use correct writing conventions for dialogue (quotation marks).

Or let's suppose your psychology class has been studying Freud's theory of human personality, and you've asked students to describe a personal experience that they feel comfortable sharing (for example, whether to go to the mall with friends or study for a major exam) in which the constructs of the id and superego are in dynamic tension, attempting to influence the ego. Your checklist might look like this:

A Freudian Narrative

1. The narrative is based on a real event, not a fictional one.

2. A clear setting and situation are provided.

3. Two "inner voices" compete as the narrative develops.

4. One voice wins out, and a resulting action (consequence) is described.

5. A final paragraph reflects on the meaning of the story.

Clearly, checklists provide specific direction for students as they begin writing. But they also set the stage for productive talk in response groups, enabling students to get feedback from each other. Let's now examine how response groups can contribute to process writing activities.

Guiding Cycle 2 Activities (Revising)

The point of small response groups—three to five students—is to support and encourage revision. As a group offers helpful responses, the writer begins to see what's working in a text and what's not; then the writer gets ideas from others on how specific points might possibly be approached. Thus, good peer response takes the pressure off the teacher to be the sole judge and arbiter of writing quality.

Small response groups work best when each writer prepares photocopies of a draft. If this isn't possible in your classroom, organize students into groups of three, with the writer in the center and a peer responder on each side. It's vital that the responders actually read the text as it is read aloud by the writer. Here are some general guidelines for students:

How to Get Feedback on Writing

1. Read your work aloud twice.

2. Don't "defend" your work.

3. Take notes on what others tell you.

4. Ask questions to clarify what others say.

5. Thank people for their comments.

6. Never apologize for the piece you're going to read.

How to Give Feedback on Writing

1. Listen for the overall effect in the first reading.
2. Write notes and comments during the second reading.
3. Tell what you liked best about the writing.
4. Identify a place in the writing that may need work.
5. Comment on content and organization first, then mechanics.
6. Be specific by "pointing" to places on the actual page.

(Strong, 2001, pp. 138–39)

Before students work in response groups, it's vital to model the process and discuss these guidelines. Emphasize the value of *positive* feedback, because if students feel threatened by their groups, the process will be undermined immediately. By investing some time in training, you can avoid pitfalls.

To model the process, I recommend a "fishbowl" strategy. Set up a small response group as an inner circle and have students circle their desks to watch the action inside. Explain your purpose—to have live demonstrations of positive roles and negative roles. Then hand out role cards to response group players and "observation sheets" to students on the outside.

Fishbowl Observation Sheet

Directions: Name the four students in the inner circle, making sure to identify the writer. Then focus on what the three responders say and do. Take notes on their positive comments and behaviors—and also their negative ones. Use your notes in the debriefing session that follows. To earn points today, please hand in this sheet at the end of class.

Round 1

Mark	O O	Alisha
Sonia	O O	Carlos

Round 2

Laura	O O	Andy
Shauna	O O	Marcus

Round 3

Sam	O O	Michelle
Dana	O O	Will

As response group volunteers play roles in response to short pieces of anonymous writing from other classes, students on the outside take notes, usually with quiet intensity. Over several days, all students get to be "in" the fishbowl.

Role cards are fun to create. The positive ones include the Cheerleader (pointing to good points in the text), the Questioner (asking thoughtful open-ended questions), the Helper (offering specific useful tips for revision), the Encourager (expressing confidence that the writing is worth revising), and the Leader (keeping the group on task). Each positive role card should have general advice about being friendly, businesslike, and positive in verbal and nonverbal behaviors.

By contrast, the negative roles include ones like the Criticizer (naming all the weak parts of the text), the Dominator (monopolizing the feedback), the Mushmouth (rambling on, mostly incoherently), the Clown (fooling around, deflecting attention from response), the Detailer (focusing on nitpicky points, not ideas), and the Sleeper (self-explanatory). Students playing these roles are invited to frown, sneer, and make rude, belittling comments about the writing or the writer.

After about five or ten minutes of role-playing response, pause to debrief. The observers will point out "good," or helpful, comments and contrast these with "lame" responses. After a round of such training, students volunteer for the response group inner circle—and a chance to show off their acting skills. Of course, all students are "playing roles," so there's no cause for bruised egos.

Does role-playing encourage negative behaviors in real response groups? Not usually. Instead, your students internalize standards of good conduct from the *contrast* between positive and negative roles. As you challenge students to think about real response groups, you'll discuss your expectations and the fact that good response represents a pooling of intelligence. Students buy into the process when they see how honest, thoughtful collaboration helps everybody do better.

I encourage students to use this simple Common Code for marginal notes:

+ = Good (use more + signs as necessary)
✓ = Some kind of problem here ("check this")
? = Confusion for me at this point
= Expand, say more, elaborate

Afterwards, try modeling a real response group with help from volunteers. Once again the fishbowl strategy is used, but now students are being themselves. The outside observers pay close attention, using an observation guide that lists positive aspects of response. As the teacher, you lead the debriefing follow-up.

Response Group Training

Directions: Observe students in the fishbowl as they respond. Pay attention to *what* is said and *how* it is said (tone of voice, body language). Evaluate each person's feedback: 3 = very helpful; 2 = helpful; 1 = not so helpful.

Criteria for Effective Response	Jim	Sue	Joy	Ted
Faces the writer and seems interested				
Makes positive comments to support the writer				
Points to specific places in text with ideas				
Is friendly but businesslike with suggestions				
Asks questions and listens to the response				
Stays on task and doesn't get distracted				
Uses descriptive, nonjudgmental language				
Other:				

Source: Strong, 2001, p. 138

Following a few rounds of the second stage of training, students know what you expect, so now it's time to get to work. Cruise the room as small groups meet. Be alert to off-task behavior or insensitive criticism, and reinforce students for responding well to the work of others. Early on—and especially with difficult classes—have responders jot down key points before elaborating orally. Make sure to set time limits for group work (ten minutes of response for a one-page paper) and conclude the response group sessions by asking writers to *draft a revising plan.* Such closure makes the activity purposeful.

Students must understand that feedback sometimes confirms hunches and sometimes provides a challenge to content, organization, or writing style. It's after nondefensive "listening" that writers figure out what's best for their papers.

Prompting Self-Assessment

The book makes few absolute pronouncements, but this is one of them: *Self-assessment is the key to progress in writing.* In other words, once students get deeply involved in reading their own writing—and trying to improve it—we have the conditions for true insights. So, if our goal is to make self-assessment a habit of mind for young adults, how do we actually motivate and nurture such behavior?

To introduce the idea of "self-assessment," you might show several photographs of typical teenagers and ask students a few basic questions: How do they know what's "hot" and what's not? How much time do they spend each morning checking out how they look? Why do they do this?

You're leading toward a simple point—that the process of assessing that sexy, good-looking product in the bathroom mirror isn't all that different from slowly rereading a text that will go to one's peers and eventually to one's teacher. Many students wear cool outfits and fix their hair in special ways to make good impressions on their friends. They also check their writing with care because they value what others think—and because they don't want to look like fools.

Contrast a clearly developed student paragraph from your content area with a scrawled, inarticulate one, the kind students often rip from their notebooks. As you did with the photographs, ask students about their "first impressions." What judgments do they make (or inferences do they draw) about the authors of the two paragraphs? Do most of us make snap judgments about intelligence, level of education, and character based on first impressions? Of course we do.

This kind of lesson sets the stage for having students reflect on their own self-assessment strategies in writing. You might try an inventory like the following one.

Directions: Reflect on your attitudes toward writing and the approaches you usually take. Doing so will help you understand yourself as a learner. Keep this self-assessment on the inside cover of your working portfolio. Respond using this code: 1 = strongly agree; 2 = agree; 3 = disagree; 4 = strongly disagree.

1. __ I usually can write when I set my mind to it.
2. __ Figuring things out in writing is interesting to me.
3. __ When I write things down, I often learn more effectively.
4. __ I like to brainstorm lots of ideas before I begin to write.
5. __ I often jot down some kind of plan for my school writing.
6. __ I sometimes surprise myself with insights while writing.
7. __ I enjoy the feeling of sharing my writing with others.
8. __ I am willing to work hard at learning to write well.
9. __ Working with others helps me do my best writing.
10. __ I almost always know whether writing is good or not.
11. __ Having a quick conference with a teacher helps me write.
12. __ I generally know how to make my own writing better.
13. __ Rereading what I write is the way I improve my writing.
14. __ I whisper my writing to myself to check how it sounds.
15. __ I look forward to others' comments about my writing.
16. __ It's often fun to proofread and edit my own writing.
17. __ Learning to write is more important than the grade I get.
18. __ Even the best writers sometimes struggle with writing.
19. __ Writing well comes more from *doing* it than from inspiration.
20. __ Good writing skills will help me in my future life.

Source: Strong, 2001, p. 137.

After students discuss their responses to these items, try sharing these three self-assessment strategies, which can lead to dramatic improvements in writing quality.

Strategy 1 (Reading Aloud)

When professional writers offer writing advice, they inevitably mention reading aloud. This strategy, like standing in front of a mirror, is basic to self-assessment. To demonstrate this strategy for students, prepare an acetate transparency of a draft paragraph you've written and then "think aloud" about it, making changes and corrections. Such a demonstration may take only five minutes, but to many learners, it's "very cool." Point out how reading aloud not only reveals clunky sentences or gaps in logic, but also how it helps you catch small mistakes. As you show students how to do what you expect them to do, you build self-assessing skills.

Strategy 2 (Reading Imaginatively)

Skilled writers flip back and forth between the roles of "composer" and "reader." The imagined reader can be someone real, one or more persons known personally, but often it's an audience *invented* by the writer. The point is that imagined readers serve as co-creators of the text. To illustrate this idea, take the paragraph from your reading aloud demonstration and ask students to assume the role of voices in the writer's head. What questions do they have? What judgments are they making about the text? As these points are voiced, first take notes on them, and then tinker with the paragraph, making changes to the original. Students need to see how their imagined readers can help them revise.

Strategy 3 (Rereading with Care)

Although student writers might already read their writing aloud from an imagined reader's viewpoint, they sometimes don't reread with care. Such rereading involves letting the text "cool" for a day or two and then coming back to it. Typically, many students procrastinate until the last minute—a self-defeating strategy rather than a self-assessing one. In sharing the idea of careful rereading, you might compare it to an "appearance check" in the middle of a busy day—for example, making adjustments on hair style, deleting a gaudy fashion accessory, or adding a fresh cosmetic touch.

Bumps in Process Teaching

As we've already seen, checklists and rubrics assist assessment, especially when students help to define the standards. Another useful strategy is to use a few anonymous papers for discussion. As students look at model papers in relation to public criteria, they develop a more objective (less egocentric) frame of reference for self-assessment.

But let's be honest: Many students are so conditioned to traditional teacher and student roles that they resist such instruction. These are the students, like Kim in Chapter 2, who rush through writing tasks with little or no prewriting and who turn in papers with little or no revision. Given these realities, we shouldn't be too surprised when such students drag their feet during peer response and self-assessment. Expect such challenges, and don't be too discouraged by them. Just trust the process.

Change is as difficult for students as it is for us. If they're used to perfunctory assignments followed by top-down teacher grading, the dynamics of your teaching will feel incredibly *different* to them—and different can be scary. After all, you're asking for their real involvement, both intellectually and emotionally, and such a change requires a period of adjustment. Is this teacher for real? What are the risks here?

As a teacher, encourage self-assessment to your response. For example, after reading literacy autobiography drafts, I offer my students a process for preparing final papers. Specifically, I ask them to (1) monitor their responses to my comments and advice; (2) put the draft away for a day and then develop a revision plan; (3) go to work on revision; (4) compare their old paper and their new one, looking for areas of improvement; (5) fill out a self-assessment rubric (scoring guide); and (6) develop a self-assessment cover letter that tells the "inside story" of the revision process.

The cover letters are always fascinating. It's not unusual for students to resist my advice initially; but then, after a day or so, their feelings mellow. Still later, as they begin to revise, the writing usually becomes fun again, a process of rediscovery. By the time they compare the old draft with the final version, they're usually *proud* of the new product. And I've taught them the most important self-assessment lesson of all—what they *can* do.

Here's a typical self-assessment letter from science teacher Jeff Luke (personal communication, 2004):

> When I first read your evaluation of my [literacy autobiography] paper, I was a little disappointed. I thought that you would enjoy it more and critique it less. However, when I handed it in, I realized that it didn't fit the criteria for the assignment as well as it could. Seeing this, and also seeing the points you made in your cover letter to me, I decided to revise it.
>
> The first thing that I did was to think about my high school more (like you suggested). This got some ideas flowing which I actually jotted down on your cover sheet. This got me thinking about some college classes that influenced my attitudes as well (which I also jotted down).
>
> I thought a lot about how I was going to revise my paper. This thinking process spanned several days. I decided to add some of the things that I had jotted down and shorten the newspaper part of my paper. When I had actually done this, I realized that the "newspaper" theme did not really fit the rest of the paper. I tinkered with the opening and closing. Actually, I scrapped my old ones and did completely new ones. Although I am not sure how much I like the new ones, I feel they are better suited for the feel of my paper.
>
> It is hard to say how much thinking time went into revision, but total typing time was about three hours. I hope you like where the paper has gone.

This is the kind of clear, honest self-assessment that every teacher hopes for. With it, you get a pay-off for the time invested in coaching students. You'll learn more about responding to student work in Chapter 8, "Coaching and Judging Writing."

Managing Collaborative Writing

Visit real-world workplaces in a knowledge-driven economy, and you see people working in groups. Indeed, *teamwork* is probably the defining characteristic of today's corporate culture, whether in industry, finance, technology, government, or education. People have individual jobs, but they also participate in committees, task forces, and management groups to address issues relevant to their mutual survival.

And these teams write. They produce business plans, sales reports, engineering documents, and a bewildering array of other genre. If the teams are housed in schools, they produce grant proposals, accreditation materials, and Individual Education Plans, not to mention curriculum frameworks, web pages, and committee reports.

But aside from the fact that collaborative writing is required within the modern workplace, such work can also be justified on purely practical grounds—namely, that it *reduces* the paper load for secondary teachers. Typical secondary teachers may work with 150 (or more) students per day. However, if students are organized into writing teams of three, the reading load is suddenly reduced to 50 papers—still daunting, but at least within the bounds of reason.

With a good task, the written product reflects the best thinking of a group, and all students have some hand in actual writing. For example, students in a choral music class might prepare program notes for songs and composers in the annual Winter Solstice program. Students in an economics class might choose stocks and track their performance over a defined period, finally pooling their notes into a team-written paper. Spanish students might team up to assess the levels of computer literacy within the local Hispanic population, creating a report that is shared with the school board for community action.

Physics teacher George Hademenos designed an amazing year-long collaborative project for three classes of advanced students at Richardson High School in Richardson, Texas—and then teamed up with senior Julie McKinney to publish the results in *The Physics Teacher* (May, 2009). Small groups were assigned to write a 32-page book for students in upper elementary school grades (4–8) on randomly assigned physics topics such as "electrical circuits, electricity, energy, fluids, forces, light, magnetism, motion, optics, sound, temperature and heat, waves, and weather." Set up in three class periods, this ambitious project centered on the adventures of "Timothy T., a physics prodigy, and his always inquisitive sidekicks Earl and Pearl" (McKinney & Hademenos, 2009, p. 290).

Over the course of a year, teams did topic research, read children's books related to science, visited a children's book author and a science museum that featured hands-on demos, compiled activities, and identified website resources for their book's readers. Hademenos reasoned that "to write a successful science book geared toward elementary students, the physics students must demonstrate an in-depth understanding of the topic and a critical thought process" (McKinney & Hademenos, 2009, p. 294):

> The manuscripts were edited, formatted, and published through a self-publishing website (http://www.lulu.com). The books were published in black and white with a full-color cover and nominally priced so that the students, parents, and elementary teachers could easily afford to purchase copies of the books. Each book consisted of three chapters based on three concepts related to the topic, a Try It Yourself activity at the end of each chapter, and a Mission Possible project related to the overall topic of the book. . . .
>
> Magnet Communications students at our school . . . were assigned the goal of producing a video of the published books on forces, weather, and motion. The communications students identified their actors, adapted the stories into a screenplay, shot and edited the video with camera, and developed a soundtrack. These videos were completed and "premiered" at Science Fun Day [at the public library].
>
> (McKinney & Hademenos, 2009, pp. 293–294)

As a practical matter for such projects, Dale (1997) recommends that each co-authoring group name a "primary writer." This person takes notes, integrates revisions and corrections into a fresh draft, and makes copies for team members. Importantly, this role *rotates* during the semester. Dale also urges that "students not break the writing task into parts and parcel it out" (p. 45). Instead, the most productive groups write together and share in the big decisions of structure as well as the small details of phrasing and mechanics.

And what about grading? Dale suggests that the quality of the final co-authored product should be about 50% of the individual student's grade. The other 50% has to do with three kinds of assessments—moving among the groups and monitoring the contributions of individuals; reading students' learning logs and self-assessment forms; and collecting peer assessment forms. Such forms for classroom use are found in Dale's monograph *Co-Authoring in the Classroom* (1997).

While it's true that some students are adept at "faking it" in groups—hanging back and letting others do the work—it's equally true that competition for its own sake is hardly persuasive as an ultimate goal for education. Increasingly, individual success is linked to one's ability to work well with others—to cooperate and collaborate. Thus, collaborative writing makes sense as preparation for workplace realities and as a way to encourage self-assessment in writing. Keep collaboration in mind when you read Chapters 9 and 10.

Write-for-Insight Activity

You've developed several "Write for Insight" expressive pieces while reading this book. Our next task draws upon those efforts. To assist your revision of this piece, let's share it in a peer response group. Although this process may be new to you, don't worry. Others are probably just as nervous as you are. Here's the writing task:

> Imagine you're chairing the "Writing Across the Curriculum" committee for your middle school or high school. A colleague has this to say just before he storms out of the first committee

meeting: "Content area writing? Hey, give me a break! Kids learn handwriting in elementary school! I say you either know how to write or you don't—and the dummies need a special ed teacher, not me. And besides, isn't writing in the English department? I've got plenty to do teaching my subject, so don't add writing on *top!* Look, no offense, but I'm out of here!"

Write a crafted email letter to your colleague. Try to communicate respectfully while also broadening this teacher's perspective on writing. To set up this task, you may find it helpful to list your key points. Are there any analogies or personal examples you might use to address your colleague's "either/or" point-of-view? What tone will help you accomplish your aims? Following is a checklist you can use when sharing your text with others or assessing it on your own.

Email Letter to Colleague

1. The letter shows professional respect in its approach.
2. The letter summarizes the issue (or "problem") to be discussed.
3. The letter outlines alternative ways to think about the issue.
4. The letter invites further dialogue about the issue.
5. The letter demonstrates excellent control over writing mechanics.

Based on the response group feedback, revise and share your email letter with your instructor or workshop leader. Afterwards, discuss whether the process helped you improve your writing. If so, why? If not, why not?

8

Coaching and Judging Writing

The language must be careful and must appear effortless. It must not sweat.

—Toni Morrison

Responding to Writing

It's a Tuesday night after on-campus classes, school visits, and a hundred-mile trip to meet with a cohort of experienced teachers. Now, the emails are stacked like planes on final approach to Chicago's O'Hare airport.

Among them are several **microthemes**—part of my effort to monitor students' reading before each class. In these, I ask teachers-to-be to summarize key points and react personally. This task is my humble alternative to traditional quizzes, long used by teachers to motivate required reading. After quick responses to several microthemes, I know what students are thinking, and I use this information to prepare for class. Students never know whether any given microtheme will receive a response. All they know is that I keep electronic files—and no microtheme, no credit.

I click on an email from an affable young man who wants to teach English. So far this semester he's hung back a bit, with his arms folded across his chest. I see his potential, but his microtheme rocks me back in my chair.

> TRhe isue of grammar and the way in which it is to be taught is particularly perplexing to me. I have personaly found it discouraging that that the last "grammar" class I remember was taken in 7th grade taught by a large unbpleasant woman who told us that she became a teacher to exact revenge upon her teachers by punishing her inoccent and unsuspecting students. Fortunatly for me however, I must have been a member of the dominant culture of power because the language I learned at home enabled me to pass every grammar test ever thrust upon me. Still, I am unable to preform simple grammatical tasks. For instance, if I was asked to define what an adverb was my response whould be a talented display of "b.s." and evasion. For this ineptitude I find myself disturbed about teaching grammar. I am actualy not sure that anyone realy knows or can define correct grammar. This makes me both angry that I

was not taught more implicitly, and asking the question: "Why does it realy matter?" If you want an earfull about why it realy matters, I would be happy to elabortrate.

(Name withheld, 2003)

Rereading it, I hesitate. I know that email invites loose, off-the-top-of-the-head thinking. But do I respond only to the content of the message and ignore its lack of proofreading? What *is* its content exactly? Does this level of literacy define the kind of teacher I'd want working with *my* grandchildren? While my main interest is ideas, this writing seems to deserve fuller coaching. I finally conclude that I can't simply file it away, with an easy click. And so here's how I reply, addressing the student by name.

> OK, here's a challenge. Look back at your microtheme to see how many errors in grammar, usage, and spelling you can find. I want to help you answer the question of "Why does it realy [sic] matter?"
>
> Your question is important, and answering it will help you see some reason for studying and applying language principles and, equally important, encouraging your students to get involved in such study. Otherwise, you risk going down the same path as the teacher you criticize—and giving kids negative views about language. I'd be surprised if you wanted THAT outcome!
>
> In short, I DO want you to elaborate, but I hope the elaboration might result in REAL conversation, one that involves respect for the person receiving your email. By "respect," I don't mean a deferential, brown-nosing attitude. I simply mean exercising a bit more care in communication!
>
> After all, your words say who you are and signal your attitudes toward the reader— whether a student, parent, or professor. You asked, "Why does it really matter?" I hope my honest response helps you think about your question.

Tough feedback? Yes. Are there risks here? Of course. But maybe there's a point when teachers have to resist acquiescing to "anything goes" conventions in written language. Maybe it's a disservice to students when we quietly abdicate standards of communication, the so-called "basic skills" of writing.

Of course, as professional teachers—not just assessors—we have to support our stance with age-appropriate coaching. For many students, such coaching means patient feedback on skills and some friendly encouragement to "hang in there." But for others—like this student, I think—it may mean a gentle kick in the butt.

I'm pleased to report a happy ending to the story. On the student's very next microtheme there was a dramatic turnaround—clear, interesting, thoughtful writing about the teaching of poetry. It wasn't perfect prose, but it showed a good-faith effort to summarize and react to textbook reading. And now I felt eager to respond to him.

> Great job! You're into this chapter, and you're seeing yourself in the classroom, dealing with kids. This raises a question in my mind: What do you think about poetry memori- zation and poetry performance? Are you for it or against it?

This student's answer to my question was almost immediate, a full page of detailed response. Now he was interested in working with *me,* and I was glad to know that.

Thinking about Assessment

This story focuses attention on **coaching** and **judging** activities—the oral and written feedback to student work. In this book, I've contended that expressive writing should often go ungraded, though we may need to reinforce it with points, smiley faces, or sticky notes—or by having students *use* such writing in their formalized public writing, the kind described in Chapters 6 and 7. So it's in the context of *graded* assignments that students generally need feedback about their writing skills. Let's explore this idea further.

Rhoda Maxwell conceptualizes school writing in three levels, arguing that each level dictates a different style of response. Level 1 is personal and expressive, its aim being to generate ideas and organize thoughts through journal writing, note-taking, and so on. If evaluation occurs, the focus will be on content only. Level 2—like my microtheme assignment—is more formal and organized, its aim being to explain thoughts or inform others through homework, reports, and exams. Therefore, response focuses on both content and form, with skills addressed in relation to readability. Level 3, the most formalized (and infrequent) of school writing tasks, requires high-quality texts in forms such as poetry, letters to the editor, job resumes, and research papers. Our standards are exacting, revision is the norm, and in-class publication (or posting) is common. Most school writing should be at Level 1 or Level 2, Maxwell says, in order to have maximum instructional benefit. In her view, Level 3 is reserved for "only occasional use" (Maxwell, 1996, p. 44).

Maxwell's point about tailoring response to the level of the task makes practical sense. At Level 1, writing-to-learn tasks need only cursory reading, and sometimes not even that; at Level 2, the focus is mainly content accuracy, but with some attention to form and conventions; and at Level 3, there are explicit content standards, plus high standards for writing quality, which are usually accomplished through revision. It's only as we verbalize our *goals* for student writing that we can figure out how to respond usefully.

If you're a harried content teacher with plenty to do, giving feedback on writing may seem like a black hole for your instructional energy. Relax. No one expects you to take up the English teacher's workload. Instead, this chapter outlines practical methods of response for times when you do have breathing room for assessment—or for occasions when parent volunteers can be mobilized to give you a hand. Believe it or not, many school districts have great "lay reader" programs to assist content area teachers. Typically, these programs are staffed by adult volunteers and trained by district personnel to help with the paper load.

Coaching versus Judging

When it comes to writing, we can serve either as **coaches** or as **judges**. Of course, the traditional role is the teacher-as-examiner, the adult who passes judgment on the quality of student work and "grades" it. A trickier role is the teacher-as-coach, the mentor who helps learners achieve their full potential through dialogue and revision. Students get confused when we send mixed signals about these roles.

In my opinion, it's silly to characterize one role as "good" and the other as "bad." Teachers frequently serve as judges as they assess students' knowledge or skills at the end of a semester. Obviously, too, such judgments have far-reaching practical implications, ranging from report cards to college admissions. On the other hand, the judging role isn't the only one teachers play—or even the most important one. Good teachers, from Socrates forward, have helped their students meet expectations. They nudge, tease, cajole, and challenge students to accomplish important goals.

The roles of judge and coach are visibly separated in Olympic athletic events. While judges carefully assess performance skills in high-stakes competitions, nervous coaches retreat to the sidelines to chew their nails.

In secondary schools, however, the roles become fluid and slippery. On one day, the teacher is a judge, assessing student work against the criteria of district, state, or national standards. On the very next day, the same teacher is working side by side with students, helping them decide how to weave vivid examples into a text, find a better lead, or reorganize its paragraphs. Such shifting roles can present problems.

For example, you might meet with a student to review her research report. Like any good coach, you're positive and encouraging—pointing to strengths she can build on, and inviting her self-assessment. There's a pause between the two of you.

"So it is good enough?" she asks. "What's it worth?"

And your heart sinks because you've been suckered again. You've had a coaching aim—to help her do good work and feel the pride of achievement—but her aim has been to get a judgment from you (a "grade") and do as little work as possible. You've been on very different wavelengths.

How can this problem be addressed? Talk it through with your classes. Explain that you're interested in education, not game-playing. Remind them that they're not well served by sloppy judging—that is, by low standards and the judge playing favorites—or by lazy coaching. That's why you'll wear a judge's hat when final papers are due and the coach's cap when you're setting up assignments and commenting on drafts-in-progress. You can dramatize these roles by using *real* props—a literal "judge's hat" and "coaching cap."

Emphasize that the judge expects their best work, on time, with no excuses; but that the coach can always be consulted on follow-up tasks to help them *learn* from mistakes. Thus, the judge strives to be honest and fair, and the coach strives to be helpful and encouraging. Finally, help students understand that coaching occurs "up front"—in advance of writing—as well as during their good-faith efforts to draft a paper.

We'll deal with both coaching contexts in this chapter. And later we'll turn to judging and grading, which will hold some unexpectedly pleasant surprises for you.

Getting Ready to Coach

To set up the advice that follows, let's review three common-sense principles of good assessment. Then we'll look at coaching strategies *before* academic writing and *during* it. This information will help you feel prepared to handle the academic writing that comes your way—but also to feel less guilty about *not* correcting the essays that students toss in the trash can, never to be revised.

Principle 1 (Models)

To create positive contexts, give students a few samples of written work, ones that illustrate concretely and specifically what you want and don't want in their writing. Such samples come from previous classes—or from colleagues down the hall—and they are always shared without identifying names. As you point to specific features of strong and weak writing, your students will better understand your expectations. In sharing lab reports, for example, ask students for their responses to a well-formatted, thoughtfully presented report versus one that seems to have been thrown together at the last minute. Have students contrast the "telling details" of two (or more) reports. Share your responses to samples and the grade each would get.

Principle 2 (Rubrics)

In Chapter 6, "Designing Assignments and Rubrics," you learned about grading rubrics (the listing of text features and qualities). By openly sharing rubrics in advance, you help students anticipate your standards, particularly as sample papers are used to illustrate what you expect. Basically, you're teaching *to* the standards you've created. That is, instead of merely "assigning" writing—something the school janitor can do—you're actually "teaching" it in a scaffolded, step-by-step way. For example, as students revise, they can use the grading rubric to assess papers in small groups—or an anonymous paper can be used in a large-group workshop. The rubric's framework helps students to self-assess, and it helps you remain focused and fair in your feedback.

Principle 3 (Response)

When we respond to drafts in progress, our response should be *timely, focused,* and *balanced.* The aims of education are poorly served when papers stack up, instructional aims get forgotten, or comments become vague, mechanical, or just plain nasty. If students wait more than a week for response, their attention wanes. Feedback should center quickly on each student's demonstrated effort to meet the assignment's goals. Finally, comments should be balanced—offering praise for something done well, a suggestion or two, and closing words of encouragement. This three-part "sandwich" formula—praise, specific advice, and encouragement—helps students learn from your feedback.

These ideas deserve serious reflection. Why? Because it's easier to anticipate and avoid problems than to remediate situations we inadvertently create for ourselves. I say this humbly as one who has made countless mistakes in responding to student writing. I hope these pointers help you to avoid some response pitfalls.

Up-Front Coaching

Many students lack knowledge of basic academic "moves" for typical tasks. For example, novice writers may lack skill in framing a response to an essay question, or providing support for their views—or using language appropriate to the academic occasion. That's where "up-front" coaching, linked to content area expectations, can help.

Let me explain. In Chapter 1, "Writing from the Inside Out," I describe my fourth-grade writing experience at a Catholic elementary school. But there's more to the story. In the intermediate grades, I was also taught a formula for catechism questions—namely, to begin each answer with key words from the question and then to write in complete sentences. So imagine my surprise when I moved to a public junior high school where few of my classmates knew how to do this. To me, writing short essays based on content knowledge in geography, English, or science was utterly natural because I had practiced it hundreds of times. To my friends, it was a new experience.

So imagine that your students don't have a clue about **thesis statements**. No, you're not an English teacher; but, yes, you do think it's useful for secondary learners to have some skill in presenting a problem, stating a thesis, and outlining their approach to an issue in an opening paragraph. How can you coach this skill?

You might begin by contrasting "knowledge dump" essays in your content area with ones that begin by identifying a problem, articulating a thesis, and framing a response. And then you might give students sentence-level practice in crafting (and responding to) thesis statements based on the models you provide. Here are a few in the area of science:

Global warming does/does not present a serious threat at this time.
Manned space flight to other planets is/is not worth the cost.
Evolutionary theory should/should not be the basis for modern science.

Afterwards, you could convert expressive writing into thesis-training activities. We saw the "Take a Stand" activity in Chapter 3, "Exploring Expressive Writing," but students might also write up "award nominations" related to a content area. Here are some ideas:

In English, awards could be based on character behavior in a novel, such as the most supportive person, greediest person, and so on.

In physical education, students could nominate the most accessible sport, the sport that works muscle groups, and so on.

In social studies, students could nominate and give awards to people, eras, actions, and events.

(Mitchell, 1996, p. 95)

Of course, for each award nomination, students are actually framing thesis statements that invite supporting details like specific facts and content information.

It will come as no surprise that up-front coaching also works with **supporting information**. You contrast bare-bones essays with well-developed ones, offer content-related practice to develop the skill, and then ask students to apply what they have learned in essay exams and short papers.

And finally, such coaching helps address **proofreading and editing** issues. We can collect garbled or confused sentences from exams and papers so that students have raw material for proofreading practice. By putting anonymous sentences on handout sheets, transparencies, or computer screens, students quickly *see* the importance of editing and learn how to do it by using a "common code" for proofreading. This simple code, set above errors or in the text's margins, is one you'll also use:

✓ C	=	Check capitalization
✓ P	=	Check punctuation
✓ R	=	Check reference (pronouns)
✓ W	=	Check wording
✓ Sp	=	Check spelling

Here are just a few of the many careless sentences I've collected from short in-class essays in content area literacy classes. Remember, these sentences are written by junior and senior college students, not by middle school and high school students.

Proofreading and Editing Practice

- I possible have somebody eltse read your Paper for clairity, Grammar and spelling. Then make revisions as needed.

- May I suggested though no writing is ever finished or prefect. We are always changing are minds so lets not bc afraid to change and recreate out writing.

- Read your paper to you mom or friend get their oppioion on it. We will also be reading papers in small groups so we can get peers oppinion. Then you make changes don't worry about spelling just change the organization and content of your paper.

After students are reminded of the need to proofread and edit careless errors, they are more inclined to look over their own papers more carefully.

Coaching as Response

As I pointed out earlier, even the best assessments don't address the critical question of effective instruction, or what I've characterized as coaching. Wandering up a row of desks, sometimes dropping in for a brief conference, the coach works in a more personal way than the judge. Good coaches circle errors on drafts and raise questions about organization, but no grades are attached to this advice.

Understanding that learning is an individual matter, the coach uses "different strokes for different folks." A supportive coaching style works well with most students, but others need directive "no-nonsense" feedback, a little like my microtheme response in this chapter's opening vignette.

Before responding to the written text of any student, ask yourself some basic questions. By having clear answers to these questions, you increase the likelihood of working smarter, not harder.

- *Is this an early or middle stage text?* Early on, ask questions about ideas and make suggestions on development. Later—assuming the ideas are clear—comment on form and organization, then urge some attention to conventions such as spelling, usage, or punctuation. Skill-deficient students may be coached by peers with better skills or referred to a number of Internet sites that help with writing.

- *What kind of reading is required?* Skimming a learning log may require only a check mark. Scanning an essay exam for specific content may lead to grading points. Quickly reading a draft essay may prompt coaching comments in a "sandwich" formula—praise, specific advice, and final encouragement. And then there's the quick joyful read of home-run texts when you simply shout "Hallelujah!"

- *What form should our coaching take?* We can talk with students in class, or we can audiotape or podcast our suggestions. We can make notes directly in the margins of student papers, or we can use sticky notes, leaving the student's text unmarked. We can respond electronically, layering in suggestions as the student's text scrolls down the computer screen. In what follows, I offer suggestions for traditional marking, but I encourage you to experiment with other coaching approaches.

- *How can we signal what's working and not working?* In a quick first read, lightly underline parts of the text that read well; use a wavy underline for confusing or awkward parts. For a paragraph or two, circle spelling and punctuation errors or use check marks to identify problems—but signal where your "close reading" stops. Students must confer with peers or their teacher to find out what's wrong and apply this learning to the rest of the paper. As students do so, they often see repeated errors (such as using commas between complete sentences). "Oh, I get it," they say.

- *How should we praise writing?* As a rule of thumb, praise should be sparing and specific, not gushing and global. Students will remember "Stunning image!" but dismiss global comments such as "Effective use of language." Try using plus (+) signs or smiley faces (☺) to mark an exact word choice or a finely crafted sentence. Use simple exclamations like "Wow!" or "Tell me more!" or "I'm hooked!" to let students know that their good writing gets results.

- *How should we criticize writing?* We should criticize writing in the same way that porcupines make love—*very* carefully. Helpful criticism centers on one or two key points. Be clear and personal. Say "I'm lost here" or "Give an example" or "I don't follow this." Report your experience rather than speaking for readers in general. Comments like "Confusing" or "Unclear reasoning" sound like Olympian pronouncements. Show respect with open-ended questions ("How could you introduce this idea earlier?") and other requests ("For your final paper, please edit with care").

Here are some specific coaching tips, assuming that comments (or corrections) are made directly on the student's paper during drafting and revision stages of text development and that students resubmit final work.

- Remember: the job is to teach the student, not to fix the text.
- Know why you are reading and what your focus will be.
- Be alert to the student's self-assessment questions and requests.
- Use the student's name as you make comments or suggestions.
- Have a grading rubric as a frame of reference for your comments.
- Lightly underline strong parts; use a wavy underline for problems.
- Tell how the text affects you as a reader, not readers in general.
- Don't waste time with a text that falls below your basic standards.
- Try to "sandwich" your criticisms between statements of praise.
- Raise questions to prompt reflection about content or form.
- Couch advice in open-ended language (e.g., "Consider . . .").
- Try to use full, elaborated sentences in brief summary comments.
- Use the Common Code (see Chapter 7, p. 108) employed by peer groups.
- Circle (or check) misspelled words, punctuation errors, and so on.
- Limit yourself to a paragraph or two of close editing, then move on.
- Use smiley faces or other icons to signal your responses to text.
- Try using sticky notes so that you don't write on the student's text.
- Work as fast as you comfortably can; take breaks to stay focused.
- Ask students to jot down their candid responses to your comments.

Source: Coaching Writing: The Power of Guided Practice (Heinemann, 2001).

And finally, I offer the expert strategies of Donald Daiker (1989), an award-winning teacher of writing, and the late Donald Murray (1990), godfather of the process writing movement in North America. Daiker allowed himself *only* positive comments in a first reading, and Murray's favorite response to a student writing began with, "I like the way you _____" (p. 111). Such practices deserve emulation.

Audiotape Coaching

Let me also make a brief pitch for the use of audiotape, recounting what biology teacher Bob Tierney did with his **Neuron Notes** homework assignment. You'll recall from Chapter 2 that students wrote down their actual understanding of a concept or process, but without the support of books or notes. Bob emphasized that it was okay if students didn't understand a concept, but that they needed to acknowledge this fact in their writing. They received full credit if they wrote a Neuron Note, but no credit if they didn't. And here's how Bob Tierney handled the papers:

> My students, at the beginning of the year, provide me with a blank audiotape. I believe that the best response to student writing is the oral response, not the written reply. I put the tapes in a bag, by period, and when they turn in a Neuron Note, I reach into the bag, find the tape, and then find the student's paper. As I read the paper, I talk to the student. I am able to coach each student, one on one for the upcoming test. I do not provide answers. Like [the legendary Harvard naturalist] Louis Agassiz, I ask questions that allow the student the exhilaration of their own discovery.

(2002, p. 16)

Using another audiotape approach for essays, you can have students activate the "line numbering" feature on their word processors. Thus, all the papers you receive will have their lines numbered in the margin. As a reader, you first skim the text, underlining strong sections with straight lines and weak sections with wavy underlines. Then you drop a labeled audio cassette into the tape recorder and begin your comments in a friendly, upbeat way. In a personal, conversational tone, you point out strengths of the text, note errors, and give advice. Of course, you use the line numbers as points of reference for your comments.

The audiotape approach is interesting because it's very personal and because papers have *no* correcting marks on them when they are returned! The student's task is to listen to comments, make revisions and corrections on the working copy, and then resubmit the paper for a final (graded) reading. Of course, students should also submit a self-assessment sheet with their final paper, describing changes and improvements.

What I like about audiotape is that it forces active response to teacher advice. In other words, the *student* jots notes in the margin, or checks the punctuation mistakes, or draws reorganizing arrows. If your school has a set-up for audio playback in its media center (playback units plus headphones), audiotape response is certainly worth a try—if nothing else, as a change of pace in your feedback strategy.

Getting Ready to Judge

To clarify your role as judge and grader, it helps to have explicit criteria for writing tasks. One such set of criteria—widely used standards with validity—is the Six Trait Analytical Model developed by the Northwest Regional Educational Laboratory (1997). By using a framework like the one in Figure 8.1, also available in a set of teacher-friendly rubber stamps (http://www.nwrel.org/comm/catalog/), you can help students better understand the standards used to assess their essays.

Standards like these, scored on a five-point scale, can influence students' thinking when used in workshops, response groups, and self-assessment activities. Equally important, scores on a rubric can help students understand where they need to invest time and effort. Note that

Figure 8.1

Six Trait Analytical Model

Ideas	Organization	Voice
5 The paper is clear and focused. It holds the reader's attention. Relevant anecdotes and details enrich the central theme or storyline.	The organization enhances the central idea or storyline. The order, structure, or presentation of information is compelling and moves the reader through the text.	The writer speaks directly to the reader in a way that is individualistic, expressive, and engaging. Clearly, the writer is involved in the text, is sensitive to the needs of an audience, and is writing to be read.
3 The writer is beginning to define the topic, even though development is still basic or general.	The organizational structure is strong enough to move the reader through the text without undue confusion.	The writer seems sincere, but not fully engaged or involved. The result is pleasant, or even personable, but not compelling.
1 As yet, the paper has no sense of purpose or central theme. To extract meaning from the text, the reader must make inferences based on sketchy details. The writing reflects more than one of these problems.	The writing lacks a clear sense of direction. Ideas, details, or events seem strung together in a loose or random fashion—or there is no identifiable internal structure. The writing reflects more than one of these problems.	The writer seems indifferent, uninvolved, or distanced from the topic and/or the audience. As a result, the writing is lifeless or mechanical; depending on the topic, it may be overly technical or jargonistic. The paper reflects more than one of these problems.

Word Choice	Sentence Fluency	Conventions
5 Words convey the intended message in a precise, interesting, and natural way	The writing has an easy flow and rhythm when read aloud. Sentences are well built, with strong and varied structure that invites expressive oral reading.	The writer demonstrates a good grasp of standard writing conventions and uses conventions effectively to enhance readability. Errors tend to be so few and so minor that the reader can easily overlook them unless hunting for them specifically.
3 The language is functional, even if it lacks punch; it is easy to figure out the writer's meaning on a general level.	The text hums along with a steady beat, but tends to be more pleasant than musical, more mechanical than fluid.	The writer shows reasonable control over a limited range of standard writing conventions. Conventions are sometimes handled well and enhance readability; at other times, errors are distracting and impair readability.
1 The writer struggles with a limited vocabulary, searching for words to convey meaning. The writing reflects more than one of these problems.	The reader has to practice quite a bit to give this paper a fair interpretive reading. The writing reflects more than one of the following problems.	Errors in spelling, punctuation, usage and grammar, capitalization, and/or paragraphing repeatedly distract the reader and make the text difficult to read. The writing reflects more than one of these problems.

this condensed version of the six-trait rubric yields descriptors for Ideas, Organization, Voice, Word Choice, Sentence Fluency, and Conventions.

My next piece of advice may cause you to raise your eyebrows.

Whenever you wear the judge's hat, I urge you to work swiftly—*not* marking up papers or correcting usage errors or offering advice on organization. Why? Because that's the job of the coach—and because the timing of your feedback, after the paper is completed, will be absolutely wrong. *Remember: The optimum time for coaching is when students are working toward a final product, not when the product is completed.*

Think about it: After the train has left the station, are you really all that interested in knowing what you could have (or should have) done to be on board? Pay attention to your students. Once they get their grades, many will ignore your advice and careful corrections. In other words, when the students' minds are elsewhere, your marking efforts are pretty much wasted.

"Wait a minute," you might be thinking. "If I *don't* correct my students' writing on that final product, they'll assume everything is okay. And they'll question their grades." And now we get to the root of the problem.

Instead of giving students the coaching they need at the right time—when the paper is being developed—most of us try to use after-the-fact feedback and corrections to justify some grade or another. Thus, we're confused about what we're doing and why.

I'm saying that *grading* (a judging activity) has little to do with *advising and correcting* (a coaching activity). Students should receive grades based on the quality of their Ideas, Organization, Voice, Word Choice, Sentence Fluency, and Conventions. The scale-point descriptors give students feedback on their writing performance, but it's usually not helpful to use that performance as a teaching moment. Think about it. Do we see Olympic judges (or coaches, for that matter) rushing to the side of competing athletes to point out their mistakes? Of course not. The hard work of coaching comes *in between* the assessments, not during them.

For some teachers, the advice to not correct final papers is utter heresy. "I have to mark *something* and give *some* comment," they tell me. As an unreformed English teacher, I understand completely. So my admonition is to limit your comments and to tie them closely to the criteria for the assignment. Here's an example of what I'm advocating by way of grading feedback:

> Jody, you've done a nice job on your "Real World Math" paper. Check out those good scores on Ideas, Organization, and Voice. Other areas need work. I marked a paragraph with three run-on sentences, so pay attention to this. I enjoyed your paper's creativity. Score: 23/30.

Judging Portfolios

Portfolios are collections of your students' best work. Today, increasing numbers of secondary school and college programs encourage the keeping of portfolios, because they showcase learning over a semester or year. Moreover, portfolios clearly reduce the corrosive effects of high-stakes grading as described in Chapter 2. But, perhaps most importantly, portfolios extend the amount of time that teachers can coach, rather than judge student work. Final grading gets delayed.

The mechanics of portfolios are straightforward. Typically, students keep a **working portfolio**, a folder or notebook that warehouses all of their academic work over a semester—the good, the bad, and the ugly. From the working portfolio, they select several examples of their best work, called *artifacts,* which go into a **learning (or "presentation") portfolio**. Before submitting this portfolio for assessment, students must prepare a *cover letter* that discusses the artifacts and the growth (or learning) they represent.

The learning ("presentation") portfolio—coupled with a **cover letter**—constitute each student's case for a passing grade in the course. Of course, the teacher has shared explicit (minimum) standards for the portfolio—the number of artifacts, the types of artifacts—that relate to course goals. For example, a health education teacher might have students include their three most insightful learning logs, their most thoughtful in-class essay, the two (out of five) exams that represent their best work, and their most engaging piece of collaborative research. To create a cover letter, students examine all their work over a semester, select artifacts, and lay out their case. In this way students get deeply involved in ongoing self-assessment, an essential frame of mind for lifelong learning.

Of course, rubrics can be developed for portfolios, just as they are developed for individual assignments. Such rubrics provide a kind of checklist of expectations. But to scaffold the portfolio task for students, it helps to have exemplars of good portfolios from previous classes. For all their differences in style, such portfolios always share certain common features, such as an array of top quality artifacts and detailed cover letters. It's also useful to set up a series of portfolio checkpoints, so that procrastinating students aren't scrambling at the last minute to pull it together.

Portfolios represent a real leap of faith, a partnership approach to assessment. As teachers, some of us take security in traditional teacher/student roles—the fact that we're in charge and students must please us to get the grades we dispense. However, portfolio assessment changes this dynamic. It forces us to see students as individual learners again, not as grade points on a distribution curve.

Students find it difficult to fake their portfolios. Inevitably, their focus shifts from whining and making excuses to laying out their best work and making their best case. And grading gets easier because the standards are explicit and public.

Coaching as a Lifetime Sport

Let's recall the student whose story opened this chapter. Our aim is to help such students internalize self-assessment strategies—or what some teachers call "think-for-yourself" skills. Helping students self-assess is a lifetime sport. But as I pointed out in Chapter 2, the school's hidden curriculum can often work against our coaching.

Consider having an explicit policy on feedback: *I read only papers that have been proofread by the student author and one or more peers.* As students sign this contract, you gain some protection from being "used" by lazy ones. Explaining (and, if necessary, re-explaining) your roles of coach and judge will be a first step in creating a positive work environment. As learners see you move back and forth between these roles, they begin internalizing such roles for themselves.

The best time for coaching, I've emphasized, is *before* the final paper comes in. Of course, big classes mean that you must budget the amount of time for feedback. Earlier I also mentioned the rubber stamp kit from the Northwest Regional Educational Laboratory. Using this kit, you can mark the point where you have to stop. Obviously, some coaching is better than none, and students get the message that their revision matters.

When it comes to feedback, problems arise from trying to do too many things at once. For example, we might want to give advice about using vivid examples (probably a prewriting lesson), finding a clearer voice (a drafting lesson), organizing better (a revision lesson), and checking sentence mechanics (an editing lesson). Overloaded circuits result if we succumb to this temptation.

My advice is to work smarter, not harder.

Repeating earlier advice, praise what the student is doing well and "sandwich" a suggestion or two within your note. And then move on!

Given these points, it will come as no surprise that I urge *balance* when commenting on student papers. Traditional approaches emphasize criticism over praise and form over content. Unfortunately, such feedback typically has an unhappy legacy—discouragement. The approach offering the best hope for growth in writing balances praise *and* criticism, content *and* form, questions *and* directions.

Finally, after good-faith coaching efforts, no one should feel guilty about asking students to rely on themselves for exams and in-class papers. There comes a time to assume the role of judge, without guilt or apology. The point of this switch is to assess what students can do *on their own,* without peer or teacher support. And if you're lucky, you'll someday get a surprise note or phone call from a grownup who wants to communicate, belatedly, the positive effects of your coaching.

For me, the phone call from South Dakota came 15 years after my high school teaching career—a summer evening as I stood at a kitchen window, listening to a voice that had tracked me down across three states. In that conversation, I learned how my former student had come home from the trauma of Vietnam and reread my words in his saved journals and class papers. It was thanks to those words, he said, that he now worked in special education and school counseling, helping kids just like the one he had been, seriously at risk of dropping out. His voice was strong and clear, the voice of a coach.

So, believe me: good coaching matters.

Write-for-Insight Activity

This chapter deals with the ideas of "coaching" and "judging" as applied to your work with student writing. It makes the point that students can easily get confused when we send mixed signals about these roles.

Let's assume that you want to head off such confusion—and let's also assume that you want to use writing as your mode of explanation. Having a thoughtful, rational policy about such issues—one that both students and parents can understand and support—will help to make your life as a teacher more positive and effective.

Develop a one-page classroom handout that communicates your expectations for the written work in your content area. Remember, the audience for this text is both students and their parents. Describe how you plan to approach drafts-in-progress and final papers. Use language that students and parents are likely to understand. Express your desire to help students develop quality writing, but also speak about *their* responsibilities to work with each other and you.

For obvious reasons, make sure to use your spell checker and grammar checker as you shape this text into its final form. After developing this one-page classroom handout, share it with your classroom colleagues and your instructor or workshop leader.

Researching Outside the Box

We do not write what we know; we write what we want to find out.

—Wallace Stegner

A Research Story

Sometimes questions hook us.

For me, the quest began shortly after the horror of 9/11, when I worked on a keynote talk for Colorado teachers on the theme of "Taking Stories to Heart." I wanted to think hard about the personal side of research—how narrative can help students negotiate the thinking challenges posed by informational tasks as well as ones requiring argument or persuasion. Here's what happened.

On the library's shadowy fourth floor, I find a hopeful title—*Tell Me a Story*—but then I read the subtitle, *A New Look at Real and Artificial Memory*, and my heart sinks. The author may have programmed computers at major universities, but it's not likely he'll help frame a rationale for taking stories to heart. Still, I crack open the Preface.

> We assess the intelligence of others on the basis of the stories that they tell and on
> the basis of their receptivity to our stories. . . . We have a memory full of experiences
> we can tell to others. Finding the right ones, having the right ones come to mind
> at the right times, having created accounts of the right ones in anticipation of their
> eventual use in this way, are all significant aspects of intelligent behavior.

> (Schank, 1990, pp. xi–xii)

The book feels weightless in my hands, its cover the color of wheat straw in winter. I learn that two aspects of intelligence are critical for both humans and computers: "One is having something to say, to know something worth telling, and the other is to be able to determine others' needs and abilities to know what is worth telling them" (p. xii).

Schank has a little taxonomy of stories—personal experience, secondhand accounts, official stories, and so on. It's like I'm sleepwalking now, still reading, pausing on the landings between each floor, then out the library door into the sunny Utah cold. Over the next week, I reread Schank's argument about the role of stories in shaping memory and intelligent behavior. He explains how stories compress experience into chunks of memory and how, over time, these chunks tend to get smaller with each retelling. To tell a story is to create the gist of an experience that we can recall and use whenever the need arises. Intelligence amounts to accessing the right story at the right time.

That's the point, I find myself thinking. Stories scaffold our lives. They make it memorable and help us live it over and over. And especially after 9/11, they connect us—to ourselves and others. So the rationale for taking stories to heart is all about memory.

We need to tell someone else a story that describes our experience because the process of creating the story also creates a memory structure that will contain the gist of the story for the rest of our lives. Talking is remembering. It seems odd, at first, that this should be true. Certainly, psychologists have known for years that rehearsal helps memory. But telling a story isn't rehearsal, it's creation. The act of creating is a memorable experience in itself.

(Schank, 1990, p. 115; italics in original)

I pause to picture classrooms of secondary students with slack, bored faces—because their experiences so often go untold, unwritten, unremembered.

There are two kinds of memory, I learn—the *semantic* kind that's organized hierarchically, and that amounts to shared world knowledge about biology and literature and really cool rock groups—and *story-based* memory, the kind activated as we process our experience. Semantic memory is like Chinese boxes—concepts nested within concepts. But story-based memory involves the creation of gists, ones that we mull over so we can be reminded of them later. Put another way: stories are the glue for making our semantic memory personal, connected, and accessible to self.

Intelligence, according to this view, is a set of behaviors linked to stories. People labeled "intelligent" get reminded of relevant stories in their repertoire more often. They adapt old stories to new situations. They connect new and confusing experiences to old stories—actively seeking to make sense, to figure things out and make a new story. They generalize or explain from their stories, including stories in which things do not go well. They use stories to plan future action. They tell or write elaborated stories, ones that share insights not obvious in the original. And of course intelligent people also seek to know the story behind the story, betraying a trait called "curiosity."

Eventually I travel to Colorado, where I tell three stories to illustrate these points. What I say finally is that, yes, five-paragraph themes have their place and, yes, it's important for kids to write simple reports, but it's through **research stories** like this one that we express our intelligence insightfully. After all, in sharing our insights we come to know what we really know. Indeed, we *are* the stories we tell.

Personalized Research

My research story dramatizes my interaction with ideas. The narrative creates a current that carries the ideas and information forward. In other words, personalized research is a cognitive tool for developing intelligence and insight.

So I again return to this book's basic theme, that writing can empower personal knowledge construction. But unlike earlier chapters, this one deals with research tasks that students mostly define for themselves, sometimes by teaming up with others. The aim of such writing, as with the traditional research paper, is *higher-order thinking*. To engage in such thinking, students document and analyze others' ideas, then synthesize and evaluate those ideas in meaningful ways.

However, personalized research isn't constrained by rigid expository formats and the dry voice of academic detachment like that of the papers some students cavalierly download from the Internet. Instead, these are papers "outside the box" of typical conventions, ones that invite *genuine* research. Of course, to achieve this aim, students are asked to pursue questions of real interest—and not to waste their time (and ours) by doing fake inquiries that result in fake writing.

Some will say that personalized research won't prepare students for the rigorous demands of college writing—an argument based on the premise that the traditional research paper now accomplishes this goal. Respectfully, I must question such a claim, based on my 40 years in higher education. In my view, far too many college students have perverse and cynical conceptions of research writing, often construing it as a meaningless patchwork of quotations. This is hardly a helpful or positive frame of mind for college work.

Getting students involved in authentic research when some are either sleeping or neurotically seeking approval is no easy task. However, it *does* help to begin with the truth: that life is too short (and education too important) for self-deception and going-through-the-motions fakery. In this dialogue you can challenge students to explore content-related topics of personal interest—their real questions and curiosities. Explain that research writing may be a requirement, but this doesn't mean it has to be boring. In fact, such writing is a chance to have some fun and come alive intellectually.

This chapter examines how to teach research-based writing without distorting its underlying values. Students conduct interviews as well as review print sources in the library or via the Internet. We'll explore three contexts for personalized research—the **Saturation Report** (Bernstein, 1997; Olson, 1997a, 2003), the **I-Search Paper** (Macrorie, 1988, 1997; Olson, 1997b), and the **Multigenre Research** Project (Romano, 1995, 2000). These tasks invite description and narration as well as explanation, analysis, and evaluation. Each is adaptable across content areas, and each has the potential to engage the creative and intellectual abilities of students. You'll find additional ideas to motivate research writing in Chapter 10, "Writing in a Digital World."

Toward the end of this chapter, we'll consider **Guided Research**, an approach to content-based teamwork that can be structured to discourage cut-and-paste behavior.

Of course, by inviting real-world formats—such as a feature article for a science magazine or history journal—even traditional papers get more lively. High-quality multimedia presentations can fuse image, sound, and text to make student research public.
Finally, a key issue for *all* teachers is academic honesty. Therefore, this chapter concludes
with basic strategies and Internet resources for dealing with rampant plagiarism and
research fakery.

The Saturation Report

Let's examine some features of the Saturation Report, as developed by high school teacher
Ruby Bernstein. Such a report involves:

- Writing about some place, some group, or some individual that you know well or
  can get to know firsthand. You "saturate" yourself with your subject.
- Writing a nonfiction article using fictional techniques. There will be scenes, characters and characterizations, dialogue, and a subtle, rather than overt, statement.
- The appeal of information and facts. You are writing nonfiction, and the reader
  will want to "know" about your subject; in short, be sensitive to this thirst for facts
  on the part of your reader.
- Author identification. Your point of view can be quite flexible. You can be an active
  participant in the action; you can remove yourself; or you can come in and out.
- Microcosm. You are focusing on some particular subject, but in so doing you are
  saying something more. As you capture an isolated segment of today's world, you
  say something about the total world.
- Implication. Much of what you attempt to "say" in your article (because of your
  use of fictional techniques) will be said through implication—through dialogue
  and through your manipulation of details.
- Reporting. You will observe your subject with a keen eye. You note interesting
  "overheard" conversations. You might want to interview someone.
- Form. You might write your article in pieces—conversations, descriptions, interviews, facts—and then piece it together, finding the best form for your subject
  (time sequence and so forth). A "patchwork"—working sections together with no
  transition—can be quite acceptable.
- Choice of subject. You can pick some subject from the present or recreate some
  subject from your past.

(1997, p. 137)

In contrast to traditional research, the Saturation Report challenges students to
exercise both narrative and expository techniques. Bernstein asks them to show personal involvement as they report the information gleaned from research. In other words,

the mind-numbing "knowledge dump" paper simply doesn't pass muster in Bernstein's class. She expects more, and she gets it.

Here's how Bernstein frames the Saturation Report assignment.

This paper will bring together some of the techniques you have practiced: use of descriptive detail, dialogue, narrative, close observation. For the saturation report you may do one of the following:

1. Teach or be taught a task.

2. Visit a place.

3. Capture an event.

4. Vividly describe a person.

5. Show your job in action.

No matter what you do, you will need to bring in an abundance of notes in which you have recorded your feelings, your detailed observations, conversations you have heard, people you have spoken to, and descriptions. After all your visiting, looking, and listening, bring your notes in (more than you need, please), focus on your subject, and then write. Remember that your paper should make some kind of statement about a lesson, place, event, person, or job. That statement may be stated or unstated as your material demands.

(1997, p. 137)

Thinking outside the box, let's imagine math students in writing teams. Their challenge is to explore how math is used in the modern workplace. Their parents may be sources of information, but they can also arrange visits to local businesses, construction sites, and professional offices for real-world applications. Imagine seventh-graders sitting down with a factory manager and learning the inside story of math. Imagine tenth-grade girls linking up via email with female engineers in the aerospace industry. The reports of such real-world experiences can resonate with students for the rest of their lives.

Or let's think about health education students doing Saturation Reports on human health stories—families and individuals who struggle with Alzheimer's disease, diabetes, alcohol or drug addiction, obesity, physical disabilities, and other problems. Human dramas surround us. As students respectfully depict the saga of human stories, taking care to protect privacy, they develop compelling reasons for learning more about a specific condition and communicating what they learn. Research has a human face.

Building on Bernstein's ideas, Catherine D'Aoust (1997) adapted the assignment to include historical figures, asking students to do background reading and focus on a key moment in a famous person's life, weaving in elements of setting, action, and interior thoughts. Carol Booth Olson (1997a) further developed the task to allow students the option of witnessing a person, place, or event, with the goal of creating a "you-are-there" effect for the reader. Olson (2003) requires students to document at least three sources, using in-text citations and a reference list in APA style.

A Student Saturation Report

Here's an excerpt from "Just the Facts," an eight-page Saturation Report by Missy Tierney, one of Olson's students. In this paper, we go inside the media frenzy surrounding the indictment, trial, and execution of Julius and Ethel Rosenberg, both convicted of espionage during the ramp-up to the Cold War in the early 1950s. While most Saturation Reports have a single viewpoint, this one has two voices—that of Ethel Rosenberg as she is strapped into the electric chair at Sing Sing Prison on June 19, 1953, and that of a reporter/narrator who has covered the Rosenberg drama and has helped hype the story at his editor's urging. In the following monologue, while the reporter watches final preparations for Ethel Rosenberg's death, we get the behind-the-scenes story.

> Over the past three years I feel like I've traced Ethel's every movement. Every emotionless gaze, straightening of shoulders, pursing of lips and unfeeling blink has been documented into my notebook. It's almost eerie to see that she hasn't changed that demeanor since the first day I saw her at their tiny apartment in the Knickerbocker Village (Neville, 1995, p. 16), through her testimony, to the reading of the verdict, and even now she sits there in the electric chair. But first impressions always stick. That first encounter, observing her coldness and detachment, set the tone for the stance that I and other members of the press took through this ordeal. And even though the charges brought against her should not have been enough to put her in that chair, the impressions she gave to the press and public were sufficient to convict her.
>
> I should have known that when my editor stormed through the office door three years ago, hair on end, tie undone, shirt unbuttoned, cigar in tow, he wasn't going to be the bearer of glad tidings.
>
> "We've got to keep on top of this Rosenberg scandal," he barked at me. "All of our competition's already on the case. The *Times, Herald Tribune, Post, Journal-American,* and *World-Telegram and Sun* are on assignment. Hell, the *Jewish Daily Forward* and the *Daily Worker* are even runnin' the Rosenbergs as headlines (Neville, 1995, p. 35). The *Daily Mirror* has got to keep up. The police only arrested Julius yesterday, but that means the FBI's been on their track (Neville, 1995, p. 17). But this has all the makings of a great story! Espionage, the reds, brothers, sisters, the atomic bomb. Our readers will eat it up. Now, the wife will be granting interviews at her apartment tomorrow. Looks like you've got yourself an assignment."

With her narrative, Missy Tierney had skillfully set up a scene that will show the first press interview with Ethel Rosenberg. But now she can also fold in relevant factual information about the political context—how "all of the major newspapers were featuring stories on McCarthy, Korea, and Russia," and how syndicated columnist Bob Considine "had whetted the public's appetite for 'patriotic' news." Of course, the reporter/narrator is swept along by the political tide. In order to "suggest Ethel Rosenberg's involvement in the trading of secrets about the atomic bomb," he acknowledges writing about "the messy state of her apartment, her pithy answers, her aloof attitude, and her seeming incapacity to show emotion." And here we again pick up the story.

The following day, I picked up a copy of the *Journal American* and *Daily News* to compare my colleagues' accounts with my own. Emblazoned across the top of the *Journal American* was the headline "Doubts FBI Charge: Wife Defends a Spy Suspect" (Philipson, 1998, p. 375). The angles of their articles were almost identical to mine. And mine, I couldn't help notice as I glanced over my name in the by-line of the *Daily Mirror,* had an awful lot of text taken straight from the "commentary" side of my notebook.

The newspaper articles that covered Ethel Rosenberg from that day forward followed the same formula as those my colleagues and I published after that first interview. An eye-catching headline with the word "spy" was inevitably included, along with text that we liberally peppered with words like "cold," "emotionless," "Communist," "guilty," and "unfit mother." Looking back, that first interview must have set the tone for the way the press treated Ethel. I don't think any of us realized how much clout we had in influencing public opinion. No, there wasn't enough evidence to convict Ethel, let alone send her to the chair. But these days, a drop of suspicion is evidence enough.

Clearly, such powerful prose has been informed by lots of background research. This Saturation Report concludes with an unforgettable description of the execution—"I'll never forget my last sight of her, slumped in the oak chair, smoke rising from her pores, and the last morbid stench of burning flesh"—followed by the reporter's thoughts and his decision to publicize a wrongful execution.

The I-Search Paper

It's a warm Saturday in October, and I've just come in from a walk along the river, where the leaves are turning yellow and asters bloom in purple profusion. Earlier today, I purchased *The Best American Essays 2003* (Fadiman & Atwan, 2003), and I've now spent a few autumn hours getting acquainted with several fine writers. Scan these opening lines. Do they share common features?

- The first time I opened Peter Singer's *Animal Liberation,* I was dining alone at the Palm, trying to enjoy a rib-eye steak cooked medium-rare. If this sounds like a good recipe for cognitive dissonance (if not indigestion), that was sort of the idea. Preposterous as it might seem, to supporters of animal rights, what I was doing was tantamount to reading *Uncle Tom's Cabin* on a plantation in the Deep South in 1852.

(Pollan, 2003, p. 190)

- The patient needed a central line. "Here's your chance," S., the chief resident said. I had never done one before. "Get set up and then page me when you're ready to start." It was my fourth week in surgical training. The pockets of my short white coat bulged with patient printouts, laminated cards with instructions for doing CPR and reading EKGs and using the dictation system, two surgical handbooks, a stethoscope, wound-dressing supplies, meal tickets, a penlight, scissors, and about a dollar in loose change. As I headed up the stairs to the patient's floor, I rattled.

(Gawande, 2003, p. 83)

■ My daughter, Olivia, who just turned three, has an imaginary friend whose name is Charlie Ravioli. Olivia is growing up in Manhattan, and so Charlie Ravioli has a lot of local traits: he lives in an apartment "on Madison and Lexington," he dines on grilled chicken, fruit, and water, and, having reached the age of seven and a half, he feels, or is thought, "old." But the most peculiarly local thing about Olivia's imaginary playmate is this: he is always too busy to play with her.

(Gopnik, 2003, p. 107)

■ It was a silver Seiko watch with a clasp that folded like a map and snapped shut. The stainless-steel casing was a three-dimensional octagon with distinct edge, too thick and ponderous, it seems now, for a thirteen-year old. Four hands—hour, minute, second, and alarm—swept around a metallic blue face. I received it for my bar mitzvah. . . .

(Fisher, 2003, p. 61)

What you notice is the vividness of these leads, their "voice." All of these nonfiction essays use fiction techniques—description, dialogue, and characterization—and like most pieces in the volume, they're written from a first person ("I") viewpoint.

Also, each article reveals the author's deep involvement in the topic. For Pollan, the topic is the animal rights movement and the grim industrialization of farming in America. For Gawande, the topic is an inside look at surgical training. For Gopnik, the topic is children's psychological development—and what Charlie Ravioli's behavior may reveal about the disquieting character of urban life. For Fisher, the topic is our relationship to the relentless advance of modern technology.

In the 1970s, legendary teacher Ken Macrorie challenged the status quo. Why is it, he asked, that we insist on voiceless research papers written in a dry, academic style? Why not invite students to think outside the box—and use the techniques of real writers? Macrorie argued that vacuous, pedantic prose should be *devalued* in schools, not rewarded.

Macrorie's antidote to traditional research toxins was the "I-Search" paper (1988), a narrative rendering of research. Following the methods of good nonfiction, Macrorie encouraged students to tell the story of their research simply and clearly, showing their investment in knowledge construction. He also urged young writers to drop the phony pretense of academic detachment. Of course, this frontal assault on traditional research writing was controversial. Some viewed "I-Search" ideas as a breath of fresh air; but to others, they suggested the imminent collapse of western civilization.

Drawing upon Macrorie's work, Carol Olson (2003) developed a clear set of directions for the "Personalized Research Paper":

Personalized Research Paper
Description

The personalized research paper is designed to teach both the writer and reader something valuable about a chosen topic and about the nature of searching and discovery. Unlike the standard research paper, in which the writer usually assumes a detached and objective stance, this paper allows you to take an active role in your search, to experience some of the hunt for facts and truths firsthand, and to create a step-by-step record of the discovery process.

Topic

The cardinal rule in the personalized research paper is to select a topic that genuinely interests you and that you need to know more about. The important point is that you choose the topic rather than having the instructor select a topic or a choice of topics.

Format

The personalized research paper should be written in three sections. These can be organized either explicitly, with subheadings, or implicitly. The sections are:

   I What I Know, Assume, or Imagine

   II The Search

   III What I Discovered

I: What I Know, Assume, or Imagine. Before conducting any formal research, write a section in which you explain to the reader what you think you know, what you assume, or what you imagine about your topic. For example, if you decided to investigate teenage alcoholism, you might want to offer some ideas about the causes of teenage alcoholism, give your estimate of the severity of the problem, create a portrait of a typical teenage drinker, and so on. This section can tell the story of how you came to be interested in your topic.

II: The Search. Test your knowledge, assumptions, or conjectures by researching your topic thoroughly. Conduct firsthand activities like writing letters, making telephone calls, initiating face-to-face interviews, and going on field trips. Also, consult useful second-hand sources such as books, magazines, newspapers, films, tapes, electronic sources, and so forth. Be sure to record all the information you gather. For a search on teenage alcoholism, for example, you might want to do some of the following: make an appointment to visit a rehabilitation center, attend a meeting of Al-Anon or Alcoholics Anonymous, consult an alcoholism counselor, or interview your peers; you would also need to check out a book on the subject, read several pertinent articles, and perhaps see a film.

Write your search up in narrative form, relating the steps of the discovery process. Do not feel obligated to tell everything, but highlight the happenings and facts you uncovered that were crucial to your hunt and contributed to your understanding of the information; use documentation when appropriate.

III: What I Discovered. After concluding your search, compare what you thought you knew, assumed, or imagined with what you actually discovered; assess your overall learning experience; and offer some personal commentary about the value of your discoveries and/or draw some conclusions. For instance, after completing your search on teenage alcoholism, you might learn that the problem is far more severe and often begins at an earlier age than you formerly believed. Perhaps you assumed that parental neglect was a key factor in the incidence of teenage alcoholism but have now learned that peer pressure is the prime contributing factor. Consequently, you might want to propose that an alcoholism awareness and prevention program, including peer counseling sessions, be instituted in the public school system as early as sixth grade.

Documentation. Include in-text citations and a list of works cited to document the research sources you consulted.

Source: Olson, THE READING/WRITING CONNECTION, "Personalized Research Paper" pp. 250–251, © 2003. Reproduced by permission of Pearson Education, Inc.

Olson's prompt can help your students know what's expected in terms of process and product. However, many students will need more guidance. To download the prompt and a model student paper electronically, visit Olson's website for her excellent book *The Reading/Writing Connection: Strategies for Teaching and Learning in the Secondary Classroom* (2003) (http://www.ablongman.com/olson) and find the pull-down menu for Chapter 9, "Alternative Approaches to the Research Paper." Look in the list to the left for the "Student Model of Personalized Research," a well-written paper on canine parvovirus. While there, make sure to check out the other support materials.

Multigenre Research Project

Like other papers we've discussed, the Multigenre Research Project involves deep immersion in a topic. However, multigenre writing asks students to *transform* what they have learned into a collage of different types of text. In other words, besides including straight-ahead informational writing—usually in an introduction or prologue—the multigenre project may include poetry, fiction, letters, advertisements, dialogue in play format, or visuals. The idea is to interweave factual, emotional, and creative material to address a research topic. It's fun for students to write and exciting for teachers to read.

For example, middle school teacher Amy Anson (personal communication, 2003) wanted to teach historical research by having her students investigate a family ancestor. To set up the research, Anson stipulated that the ancestor had to have been dead at least 10 years and that students had to have sufficient information to get deeply involved. A minimum of three research sources—biography, autobiography, journal, family history records, photographs, Internet, magazines, or interviews—were required. Students who couldn't meet these basic requirements for an ancestor were allowed to research a famous historical figure of their choice.

As scaffolding for research, Anson and her colleague Jacoy Blair created a "Fact Sheet" prompt that outlined basic questions and that students used for note-taking. One important feature of the Fact Sheet was the documentation of all facts, including title, author, and page number for books; web address and log-on date for Internet sites; and name of interview subject and date for all interviews.

Here are questions Anson and Blair used to spark student research. Of course, students were encouraged to go beyond these questions in pursuit of historical truth.

Fact Sheet

1. What is his/her full name?
2. When was he/she born?
3. Where did he/she live?
4. Who were the other members of his/her family?
5. What did he/she do (job, chores, responsibilities, etc.)?
6. Whom did he/she marry?
7. How many children did he/she have and what were they like?
8. What was happening in the world during his/her life?
9. What was happening in the country where he/she lived?
10. What kind of person (happy, mean, shy, etc.) was he/she?
11. What is something ordinary this person did?
12. What is something extraordinary (special) this person did?

(Anson & Blair, personal communication, 2003)

After students became deeply immersed in their material, Anson and Blair shared a writing framework. Students were asked to take imaginative risks and to choose a genre that could communicate the rich texture of a person's life. As minimum requirements, young writers had to include four genres from Column 1, two genres from Column 2, and two genres from Column 3. (Note that some contemporary genres are familiar to middle school students but would not have been available to ancestors or to other historical figures.) Of course, there are many format possibilities beyond those listed in the following table (see Figure 3.2, p. 33).

Multigenre Options

Short Written Genre (choose four)	Long Written Genre (choose two)	Visual Arts (choose two)
birth certificate	journal entry (one page)	game
wedding invitation	personal letter (one page)	fashion doll (clothes)
passport	childhood memory (one page)	wanted poster
obituary	conversation or dialogue (two pages)	clay sculpture
grocery list	song (two pages)	movie poster
recipe	interview (20 questions and answers)	map
post card	play (two pages)	scrapbook page

(continued)

Multigenre Options *(continued)*

Short Written Genre (choose four)	Long Written Genre (choose two)	Visual Arts (choose two)
receipt	compare/contrast essay (two pages)	CD jacket
memo	magazine article (one page)	portrait
poem	movie preview (one page)	cartoon character
advertisement		book cover
tabloid cover		video game cover
radio announcement		
email		
home page		
photo caption (with photo or drawing)		
suitcase packing list (15 items)		

Source: Anson & Blair, personal communication, 2003.

To begin writing, each student used his or her Fact Sheet as a prewriting tool. The choice of genres coupled with an emphasis on creativity led to high writing motivation. Later, as students engaged in revision, Anson and Blair created a "Multigenre Reality Check," so they could discern each paper's fictional material from its factually based content. This basic disclosure statement, filled out by each writer, anchored the students' texts in research-based fact rather than allowing for untethered flights of fancy.

Multigenre Reality Check

Made-Up Information (things you imagined or invented)	Filler Information (your inferences that don't change history)	Research Information (facts from your research or notes)
1.	1.	1.
2.	2.	2.
3.	3.	3.
Etc.	Etc.	Etc.

Source: Anson & Blair, personal communication, 2003.

Having done their research and having imagined their way into a life history, students were eager to share what they had learned with classmates. They learned the *skills* of research—a goal of the state's core curriculum—but they also learned the *pleasures* of sharing knowledge, an equally important goal.

Challenging Advanced Students

Of course, multigenre research becomes more challenging in the upper grades. For example, high school teacher Warren Bowe asks students to choose topics in one of four areas: biographical (a deceased famous person); historical (a specific event in history); scientific (a specific discovery, invention, disease cure, etc.); or social (e.g., a specific organization founded to help people). Bowe's overview is a model of clarity:

> In this paper, you will choose different forms of writing and create a paper that clearly informs the reader about the topic you have selected. You will still use sources to investigate your topic, and you will use these sources to inform your readers. But you will expand on the ways you use this information. Within this one paper, you might write an editorial, a poem, and a letter, in addition to a "traditional" essay. But you won't just "make up" or create these pieces of writing out of thin air; instead, these creative efforts will be informed by, based on, and shaped by your solid research, just as any traditional research paper would be.

> (Bowe, personal communication, 2004)

Bowe's multigenre assignment stipulates several basic expectations (a typed document of at least 2,000 words, parenthetical documentation, annotated bibliography and Works Cited page, plus the inclusion of graphics and/or photos). He also asks for no repetition of information in the genres and for transitions among them; for five different writing formats and a minimum of six research sources; and for a half-page (minimum) reflection on each genre included. Clearly, such expectations cannot be met in a marathon writing event the night before the paper is due. Of course, Bowe's grading rubric is linked to these expectations. It's based on a one-hundred-point framework in six sections, each of which has elaborating detail (not shown here).

1. Purpose	/20 possible
2. Word Choice	/10 possible
3. Organization	/20 possible
4. Documentation	/20 possible
5. Conventions	/20 possible
6. Layout/Presentation	/10 possible
Total Points	/100 possible = _____ Grade

Finally, there's the dynamic teaching of Tom Romano (1995, 2000), who promotes multigenre research in secondary schools. In his teacher education classes, Romano insists on a minimum of 10 sources—other than the Internet—to be cited in the bibliography and used in the paper. He also encourages primary material such as interviews, testimony, and observations. Consider the tone of Romano's admonitions to students, especially his emphasis on quality and his passionate insistence on originality:

> The Internet contains the good, the bad, and the ugly. It is democratic, but there is no screening for quality as there is in journals and books. So gauge the quality of what you find in cyberspace. And I definitely don't want you to simply paste material from the Internet into your paper. I want to see an original piece of work from you, one grounded in a thorough research understanding of your topic. I want to see you expand your learning and content knowledge about some subject; I want to see you stretch and refine your writing skills and powers of communication. I want to read your paper and be informed, but even more, I want to be *moved*.
>
> (Romano, personal communication, 2001)

As a savvy, veteran teacher, Romano knows how important it is for students to begin early and to avoid the pitfalls of procrastination. He therefore insists that they produce a "Multigenre Research Design" paper early in the semester. Because the design paper is worth 25% of the grade for the final project, students are motivated to knuckle down. Of course, Romano uses these papers to guide and assist students' research. Here are the seven points that frame each student's design paper:

1. What is your topic?
2. Describe what you know about your topic.
3. Tell what you want to learn about.
4. Describe the origins of your research. What sparked your interest in the topic? Why do you want to know more about it?
5. List at least a dozen questions you have about your topic.
6. Describe your plan for collecting information about your topic.
7. Provide a preliminary bibliography.

(Romano, personal communication, 2001)

Later, as students begin to convert their research notes into creative texts, Romano helps them frame introductions that will guide the reader into the paper. Students are coached in specific writing strategies that enhance the effectiveness of various genres. To help them better understand the standards for the assignment, they are also given model papers and grading rubrics. Here's a typical research rubric developed by teacher Karen Blanchette and cited by Romano (2000, p. 166):

Multigenre Research Paper Guide

5 genres present (minimum)	50 points	_____
6–8 typed pages	25 points	_____
Content/historical accuracy	100 points	_____
Mechanics/presentation	25 points	_____
Documentation/bibliography	50 points	_____
Total possible	250 points	_____

For tips on teaching—and many models of successful multigenre writing by students—I highly recommend two books: *Blending Genre, Altering Style: Writing Multigenre Papers* by Tom Romano (2000); and *Writing Multigenre Research Papers: Voice, Passion, and Discovery in Grades 4–6* by Camille Allen (2001).

Traditional Guided Research

If the idea of personalized research makes you nervous, consider a more traditional approach to research writing, one that defines the territory to be researched as well as methods of inquiry. Such an approach makes perfect sense if you're doing an inquiry unit—for example, a social studies unit on inventions, a science unit on marine mammals, a history unit on minority leaders, or a vocabulary unit on word histories.

In **guided research**, each student takes an aspect of a topic being studied and becomes a class expert. For example, middle school earth science students might be divided into teams—igneous, sedimentary, and metamorphic—for the three rock classifications. Each team member would choose a specific rock for research. The teacher could lead imaginative in-class activities for "getting to know your rock"—close observation, dialoguing with the rock, and imagining the rock's history. Then the teacher could provide a guide for research, suggesting Internet strategies but also teaching about direct quotation, paraphrasing, and citation conventions. Eventually, each report could become part of the team's oral presentation and be posted on the "Hard Rock" website.

Instead of exploring vast unwieldy topics, students are challenged to focus their research. Thus, a high school art teacher might provide an overview of the impressionist movement—its major figures and features—but students will probably get personally *engaged* when they come to know single paintings in depth. Therefore, a class might be organized into research teams—Monet, Degas, Renoir, Van Gogh, and so on. Each team would explore an artist's work, with each member reporting on a single painting. Of course, the teacher could use questions to guide writing: How does your painting represent the artist's work? In what sense is it different, unique? What are its key technical elements? What story do you see in the painting? What drew you to this painting initially and how do you now view it? What do art critics say about this work's significance?

Although this chapter has argued for "Researching Outside the Box," traditional research still has its place, especially when supported by good teaching. What matters most is the *context* of inquiry. Students notice whether we structure the research process into stages, with explicit expectations. They notice whether we encourage teamwork, provide model papers, and welcome conferences. They notice whether we're open to real-world formats such as magazine articles with graphics, websites, CD-ROMs, and multimedia presentations. In Chapter 10, for example, you'll visit a social studies class taught by Kathy Christiansen, a master teacher in northern Utah, to see her world geography project.

And even with traditional reports, it's vital to let students know that their job is to *teach* us with their writing. We're like them. We hate being bored, and we like being stimulated.

Tell students the truth—that quality research writing can not only earn a high grade but also make your day.

The Problem of Fakery

Here's a sure-fire way to get really depressed as a teacher: Simply type the words "research paper" into your Internet browser. You'll come up with hundreds of commercial websites that provide reports, term papers, and "custom writing" to the student market.

Of course, it's hardly a secret among informed teachers or work-averse students that the Internet can support intellectual dishonesty, as papers are downloaded with impunity, then handed in with a sly smile. This fact simply provides one more reason for guided inquiries and for Saturation Reports, I-Search Papers, and Multigenre Research Projects.

Sadly, the fakery problem is corrosive in two key ways: Not only does it deprive students of the opportunity for real intellectual development, but it also undermines the basic moral contract between teacher and students. And the problem is growing. For example, in a national survey conducted by *Education Week,* 54% of students admitted to Internet plagiarism, and 74% of students admitted to "serious cheating" during the past year (http://www.plagiarism.org).

Should such ethical issues be addressed in class? Absolutely. Students should know where teachers stand. They need to know what plagiarism is and why it's sleazy to use someone else's words and ideas without attribution. A wonderfully helpful (and free) site for teachers is available via the "Research Resources" link at http://www.plagiarism.org. Here you can get student handouts that define plagiarism, give tips on avoiding it, and offer citation guidelines. I highly recommend this site for both teachers and students.

Beyond these basics, discuss plagiarism as the moral equivalent of a performance-enhancing drug, and note that the International Olympic Committee strips athletes of medals when they take such drugs. To situate the Internet downloading issue starkly, you can relate how the careers of reporters and editors at the *New York Times, USA Today,* and other media outlets have been ruined because of plagiarism, fabrication, and intellectual cheating. Look students in the eye and let them know that you expect better of them.

In the August 1, 2010 *New York Times,* writer Trip Gabriel reported that the Internet may be "redefining how students—who came of age with music file-sharing, Wikipedia, and Web-linking—understand the concept of authorship." But although definitions of authorship may be changing, plagiarism remains serious business on college campuses. According to one college student, Sarah Wilensky, "The main reason it occurs is that students leave high school unprepared for the intellectual rigors of college writing. If you're taught how to closely read sources and synthesize them into your own original argument, you're not going to be tempted to plagiarize in college, and you certainly won't do so unknowingly." (http://www.nytimes.com/2010/08/02/education/02cheat.html)

Linked to http://www.plagiarism.org is a commercial website, http://www.turnitin.com. This site makes a "digital fingerprint" of submitted documents and uses the Internet to cross-reference research across multiple databases. The incredible detection abilities of this site are purchased annually by individual schools, districts, or colleges.

An integrated vendor service—**MY Access!**—provides plagiarism checks as well as responses to student writing. This suite of services has been popular with many districts in the intermountain west as well as nationally. Administrators can visit the MY Access! website (http://www.myaccess.com/myaccess/do/log) for overview information.

With Internet tools like these, maybe teachers can get back to doing what we do best: helping students learn. Let's hope so.

Write-for-Insight Activity

Choose one of the following tasks for your learning log. Then share this writing with your colleagues and your instructor or workshop leader.

1. Tell a remembered story of your research writing in middle school, high school, or college. What did you write about and why? What do you now remember about your topic and the research process? How does your experience—positive, negative, or neutral—now inform your thinking about involving students in research writing?

2. Develop a statement on how research writing should be approached in your content area. What topics hold interest for your students? What kinds of research formats or methods do you see as practical and educational? How might your imagined approach teach the "habits of mind" valued in your field?

3. Do Internet research on the topic of "research papers." As you visit several websites, take notes on the offered services. How do you feel about these websites? Also, visit the website http://www.plagiarism.org to explore the resources available for teachers and take notes on these. Use your notes to write up a summary for your colleagues.

10

Writing in a Digital World

I'm rewriting it while I'm writing it. It's changing itself.
—Max Apple

Cultural Divide

At eight and twelve, Laura and Dana Strong are true "digital natives"—totally comfortable with many forms of information technology—unlike their Grandpa Bill, a self-confessed "digital immigrant" who still gets queasy navigating functions of his new cell phone, not to mention the shift from Web 1.0 to Web 2.0 (Prensky, 2001).

At their age, I thumbed musty references for information, enjoyed comic books and after-school radio dramas, and chatted on a "party-line" telephone. My early teachers eschewed the newfangled technology of ballpoint pens, so I used a metal-tipped quill, dipped carefully into an inkwell, for handwritten essays. Pretty good penmanship—with dangerously leaking tools of advanced technology called fountain pens—carried me all through high school and well into college, where I finally bought a portable typewriter, "erasable bond" paper, and small bottles of Wite-Out Correction Fluid. Ten years later, writing a doctoral dissertation, I owned an electric typewriter with built-in correction tape. I was a full professor when my first desktop computer arrived.

For Laura and Dana, the world is a very different place. They access the Internet for information and many forms of visual, auditory, or game-based entertainment—and they use electronic text and digital images to communicate with friends, family, and teachers. They are totally comfortable with keyboards, touch-screen technology, and joysticks. As early subscribers to Club Penguin and Wee World websites, they know all about cute avatars, advanced membership levels, and the dangers of online predators. They explore the digital landscape with ease because they were born into a Google-informed reality and have grown up with it. And they—or their tech-savvy friends—are likely to soon cross your classroom threshold. They look forward to tools like digital notepads, video conferencing, and graphing calculators. Will such high-tech expectations be welcomed?

Many observers agree that "there is a vast difference between the ways in which teens read, write, create, and think online and the ways in which they are required to do so in schools" (Wilber, 2008). Of course, this fact creates a profound disconnect, or cultural divide, for today's learners, one that undermines their motivation. Meaningful learning, as all teachers know, requires engagement—but it is hard to imagine how adolescents can be fully engaged when their interests and online expertise are devalued in classroom settings. Therefore, this chapter explores a few ideas for using technology-based writing activities to help students learn new content. Let's begin with easy-to-use applications—or "apps" in the jargon of today.

iPod Inspiration

When future historians document today's education trends, they will surely include the iconic image of iPod-connected kids on yellow school buses. For most teens, devices like the iPod represent the very cool fusion of must-have connectivity and music access—a hand-held delivery system for keeping in touch with friends and for music downloads.

Of course, classroom lessons using music-inspired springboards are nothing new. In ancient times, like the mid-twentieth century, teachers dug past filmstrip projectors and carousel trays in storerooms to unearth dusty record players and reel-to-reel tape machines—followed, only a few decades later, by cassette recorders and CD players.

But times have changed. The Northern Nevada Writing Project (NNWP) now sponsors WritingFix, a superb writing-across-the-curriculum website for content area teachers. This site had nearly four million hits in 2009 alone. Here's how NNWP teacher/consultant Rob Stone, a website host, describes the appeal of today's iPod technology:

> Pull out an iPod in class and watch the interest immediately appear on your students' faces. Put lyrics on the overhead and watch the focus in their eyes. Hit play and they are yours. Implement a well-designed lesson attached to that song and you can do magic....
>
> (Stone, WritingFix website, 2010)

It's an effective pitch, don't you agree?

There's no way to catalogue the many free-to-use resources at the WritingFix website (http://www.writingfix.com/WAC.htm)—but here's a brief sampler to whet your appetite for further inquiry.

- *Art: Tribute to an Artist and a Painting.* Inspired by a Don McLean song ("Vincent") and a Tupac Shakur poem ("Starry Night") that both pay tribute to Van Gogh, student writers research an artist in order to pay a similar tribute.

- *Music: Singing the Blues.* Inspired by some of the blues songs featured on Ken Burns' *Jazz*, student writers draft and publish original blues lyrics. Students may also perform their lyrics by using one of the tracks from Jamey Aebersold's Jazz CDs.

- *History: What's Important in Your World?* Inspired by Billy Joel's song "We Didn't Start the Fire," students catalogue important historical events in their own lifetimes in the form of a free-verse poem.

- *English: CSI: the Cory Crime Scene.* After comparing a famous poem—"Richard Cory"—and a song by Simon and Garfunkel about the poem, students create an interpretation that explains why they think Cory killed himself. Students then create three pieces of evidence that—if found by a CSI team—would lead those investigators to interpret the poem the same way.

- *Science: This I Believe Essays . . . Science.* Inspired by episodes of "This I Believe" and "Science Friday" podcasts, students will write a "This I Believe" essay about a current scientific issue, which can be published on a classroom iPod or web page.

- *Math: Linear & Exponential Growth Poetry.* Students choose numbers and units of measurement, and then create short poems that compare and contrast exponential (or multiplied) and linear growth. This lesson is inspired by several Schoolhouse Rock songs as well as other videos that help students explore numerical growth.

(WritingFix, 2010, http://www.writingfix.com/WAC.htm)

If nothing else, writing activities like the ones in the previous list provide welcome respite from business-as-usual routines in content area classrooms. But if you're interested in *other* kinds of teacher-developed lessons, read on. We've just begun to explore digital teaching.

WebQuest Nation

Since the mid-1990s, tsunami waves of teachers have reached the official home base for WebQuests—http://webquest.sdsu.edu—and found exportable units with clear, easily accessible structure. WebQuests bring fresh approaches to standard curriculum topics and invite students to *use* their technology expertise.

Basically, WebQuests present a question or problem, outline an inquiry task as well as links to preselected Internet sites, and conclude with an evaluation framework. Thus, WebQuests are technology-based "pathways" for students—activities that help learners visit specific resources, collaborate in the process of finding and processing information, and draw conclusions. The product of inquiry—whether multimedia writing posted on the classroom website, in-class presentation, or other artifact—documents student learning.

Typically, learners are given a role as they access websites. Also, WebQuests often stipulate roles for individuals in small groups. For example, in a challenging WebQuest titled *Sights & Sounds of the Harlem Renaissance* by Diane Malzone (n.d.), high school students become video producers. Organized into groups of three, they develop a four-minute video podcast—a video montage with music—focused on a writer, artist, and musician of the era. Students research a single aspect of the overall project from an array of content links, and this expertise enables them to contribute to a final script, which requires both background information and analysis in its voiceover narration.

Obviously, such a WebQuest requires learners to take notes, to integrate and organize information, and to use advanced writing skills of analysis, evaluation, and negotiation. In addition, as they access technical links for producing their video podcast, students must make dozens of decisions about color, font, graphics, music selection, and so on. In short, such a project develops the research and writing skills of tomorrow—skills far more complex than the five-paragraph themes of yesteryear. Moreover, such a project establishes an immediate audience of peers—other students in the classroom community—as well as a potentially vast audience of Internet users.

Of course, not all WebQuests are as technically challenging as the one just noted. Indeed, some WebQuests require only simple reports, narrations, or expository papers—basic assignments familiar to all secondary teachers. However, regardless of their high-tech sizzle, all WebQuests alter the underlying dynamics of instruction, the relationship of "teacher" to "student." No longer is content delivery the teacher's main job. As students click their way through Internet links—some with graphics, streaming video, and music in addition to informational text—the learning context shifts dramatically. Students are individually "empowered" for learning, according to WebQuest enthusiasts.

As of 2010, the WebQuest.Org site invites teachers to search in the QuestGarden with a free 30-day membership. WebQuests are arrayed in reverse chronological order, with newest documents first. Presently, QuestGarden offers three means of access. You can type in a topic of interest such as *fractals, oil spill,* or *Macbeth*; you can use a drop-down menu to select your curriculum area, plus a grade level designation; or you can conduct a "design pattern" search. Among the design patterns are key terms like *analyzing for bias, historical story, simulated diary,* and *persuasive message*—an indicator of the kind of writing prompt you are likely to find in a content area WebQuest.

In thinking about *persuasive message*, for example, let's imagine that your school's students will soon take a state-administered writing test. Imagine too that scores have slumped in recent years, thanks to bulging class sizes. While there's no easy fix for such a situation, it certainly won't hurt if a few colleagues across your school's curriculum agree to focus on persuasive writing as part of their content instruction. Accessing the "design pattern" search in QuestGarden with a focus on *persuasive message*, your colleagues will find over a thousand available WebQuests. Obviously, students will be better prepared for the state assessment after their across-the-curriculum writing practice.

And now a word of caution: Although QuestGarden provides access to many quality lessons, it also contains WebQuests of dubious utility. To limit your frustration, I suggest visiting "Useful Resources" on the WebQuest.Org page and then clicking on *Search Techniques*. Also, make sure to click on *Adapting Existing WebQuests*, a teacher-friendly resource for enhancing an existing WebQuest to meet your classroom's needs.

If you're new to the WebQuest model, I highly recommend "A WebQuest about WebQuests" authored by Bernie Dodge, the WebQuest founder at San Diego State University. This cleverly designed resource, found on the WebQuest.Org site, has different versions for middle school and high school teachers—a welcome alternative to the typical in-service afternoon featuring Guru du Jour, with handsome briefcase, well-coiffed hair, and easy abstractions. After participating in this WebQuest activity with department colleagues, you'll have a good idea of whether WebQuests will work with your students.

PowerPoint Pedagogy

Visit Kathy Christiansen's social studies classroom at Cedar Ridge Middle School in early spring, and you'll find Utah sixth-graders busily polishing their PowerPoint slides, the first part of a larger geography unit. Later on, students will research a country of their choice for the school's World Fair, but for now the class is focused on Greece. Some of the skills they've learned are reminders about note-taking, paraphrasing, and summarizing—as discussed in Chapter 5—but others are straight-up technology instruction for PowerPoint software.

As a star teacher/leader in the region, Christiansen believes in well-scaffolded writing tasks. Her coaching is explicit, her expectations high. And because she knows the motivational power of small groups, especially in middle school, she posts this permanent reminder on her bulletin board: "No one of us is as smart as all of us."

To see how PowerPoint technology is used to prompt writing, let's look at her assignment framework for a mini-unit on Greece, one that draws from Internet research:

1. Your group will be making a PowerPoint presentation, with four important topics, yours included. Individually, read and take notes on the "Informational Text Worksheet." Write your topic and main ideas, plus a key question and its answer, on the worksheet.

2. Use the "PowerPoint Planning Sheet" to design six slides for your part of the group's presentation. A title slide will include your topic and your name. A second slide will provide your question. Three more slides will be needed to teach the answer to your question. Your last slide will be the answer to your question. Remember, our final test will include your question, so design your slides well!

3. When everyone in your group has completed his or her reading, note-taking, and design work, meet to review progress. Write down each member's topic, question, and answer on the "PowerPoint Planning Sheet." Evaluate the work. Then, in the computer lab, develop a creative, well-organized PowerPoint presentation. Along with your group's members, install the presentation on Ms. C's flash drive.

Afterwards, students "present their portion of the group's 10-to-15 minute PowerPoint to the class" (Christiansen, personal communication, 2010). Assessment is based on a simple rubric, and students receive additional points for their oral work:

PowerPoint Checklist	Points Possible	Points Earned
Four main ideas within the group's topic are presented.	10	
Fifteen to 25 slides are used in the presentation.	10	
Four questions, to be used on the final test, are presented.	10	
Answers to all questions are clear in the presentation.	10	
Three slides teach the correct answer to each question.	10	
All words are spelled correctly.	10	
All sentences are properly capitalized and punctuated.	10	
A title page includes the names of all student presenters.	10	

Clearly, Kathy Christiansen wants learners to go beyond the mindless downloading of information, followed by cut-and-paste activity. She knows from experience that middle schoolers *can* engage when they're challenged to read and write thoughtfully, to work with others on presentation content, and to share well-organized information with others.

So PowerPoint provides a medium for collaboration—one that serves her content goals, linked to the state's core curriculum—but it also provides rehearsal for research on individual countries. For many students, it's a versatile tool for creative knowledge construction—plus a chance to show off their multimedia moxy with fonts and graphics, photos and music, and other special effects. Especially important is the fact that presentation software literally *enables* some kids to "stand and deliver" because peer attention is on the screen, not on the speaker's acne, teeth braces, or dorky shoes.

Finally, tools like PowerPoint demonstrate how careless mistakes can have a "black hole" effect, sucking attention from the message. Students also see that dense, text-heavy presentations numb the brain. Although both are familiar lessons, they now have resonance because of the dramatic public context. Of course, with good coaching and further practice, students can give critical thought to headers, word choice, careful phrasing, and sentence mechanics—in addition to the aesthetics of color, typography, layout, and graphics. All are vital lessons in the brave new world of digital writing.

PowerPoint can also be used for traditional review activities in your content area. Type "powerpoint game show template" into your browser, and you'll come up with familiar TV game show formats like "Jeopardy," "Wheel of Fortune," and "Who Wants to Be a Millionaire?" Insert your own review questions and—voila!—it's show-time!

Could presentation software like PowerPoint serve as a student writing tool in *your* content area? It's a question worth considering.

A Gift of Glogs

Cool teachers often follow parallel paths. Like Kathy Christiansen, eighth-grade teacher Laura Miller is constantly searching for innovative ways to connect with her language arts and French students at Heritage Middle School in Hilliard, Ohio, west of Columbus. For example, in one activity linked to a novel, students downloaded midi music files, wrote song lyrics based on their reading, and incorporated those lyrics into a PowerPoint presentation, which they performed karaoke-style. "It's a tough age," this cross-country coach confides, "but we seem to fit together."

It was in 2009—thanks to help from a district technology teacher—that Laura Miller discovered another creative angle for literature instruction, one linked to an Internet site called Glogster (http://edu.glogster.com). At this site students create interactive virtual webposters called *glogs*. Seeing the potential, Miller decided to introduce glogs while teaching *The Outsiders*, by S.E. Hinton. Here's how she sums up the experience:

> The students loved this project because it is similar to a Facebook setup; students design a *wall* where they can post information, including uploaded music, video clips, voice recordings, and pictures. They decide on colors and backgrounds and "themes" of how they want their page to look. They really enjoyed integrating technology and using it as a way to showcase their writing. Because peers were looking at and commenting on the projects, students took care in designing their *glogs*. The teacher has access to all of the pages, but the pages are private, so not everyone in the virtual world can see them.
>
> (Miller, personal communication, 2010)

Stoked by student enthusiasm and an Ohio Writing Project summer institute, Laura now plans to revisit this activity in both her French and language arts classes. Pre-reading activities for *The Outsiders* will still "explore issues of self-reliance, gang involvement, empathy, and personal beliefs"—and she still wants students to discuss whatever they find "significant, thought-provoking, or interesting" in the book. But now the glogging expectations will come early, and students will have in-class writing time to work on genres of their own choosing.

Possible genres might include "a letter from one character to another, a news account of an important event in the novel, a poem, a diary entry, an interview, or a dialogue between two characters"—or whatever learners wish to tackle to stretch their writing skills. Students can earn up to 100 points for their web posters, as described below:

Grading Rubric for Glogs	Points Possible	Points Earned
A photo of you representing your character through clothes, props, and facial expressions.	10	
An audio introduction of your character (one or two minutes long) including physical traits, personality, feelings, thoughts, and ideas.	10	
A genre of your choice about the insights or life lessons your character has gained or learned.	15	
Three different genres of choice revealing various aspects of your character (personality, attitude, thoughts, interests, feelings, appearance, hobbies, dislikes, or response to events in the story). Your content, spelling, and grammar should reflect the character and be supported by the text.	45	
A selection of 1960s music and pictures to fit your character's tastes.	05	
Visual appeal, good organization, and extras (interesting quotes, pictures, artwork, etc.).	15	
TOTAL POINTS POSSIBLE	100	

(Miller, personal communication, 2010)

The Glogster website is easy to use. In fact, a one-period introduction teaches kids how to log in, choose backgrounds ("page wall"), and insert different *papers* and *buttons* on their web posters. The "papers" feature enables them to copy their genre writing to the poster. The "buttons" feature enables them to activate audio and video clips. After learning how to upload music, sound, and photos on Day 1, students spend the next four days crafting their written genre and conferencing with their teacher. On Day 6, students and teacher get to explore the different glogs and post their online comments.

If you're curious about student-produced and teacher-produced glogs in your content area, click on the "categories" link at the free Glogster website. This link takes you to specific disciplines—arts, chemistry, earth science, ecology, history, languages, life sciences, mathematics, physical sciences, reading, religion, social sciences, writing, and technology. As you click on the discipline, you'll find dozens—often hundreds—of glogs for you to view and listen to.

Guerrilla Journalism

Travel a hundred miles south of Kathy Christiansen's classroom, and you arrive at Judge Memorial High School, with its backdrop of snowcapped mountains and kids in parochial school uniforms. Find a pair of well-used basement rooms, northwest corner, and you'll meet Chris Sloan, a man happily at home amid the clutter of technology tools, jammed book shelves, and the wall-hung detritus of a 25-year career.

He teaches AP English, digital photography, and a New Media course—newspaper, podcasting, blogging, and TV production—plus workshops for the Wasatch Range Writing Project and national venues. In July, 2010, his Bulldog Press journalism students won first place in statewide competition sponsored by the Utah Press Association.

He's also an articulate voice on the national talk-show and blog site called *Teachers Teaching Teachers* when he's not working on a *Youth Voices* blogging platform he helped develop. As an early architect of Youth Voices—"a meeting place where students share, distribute and discuss their digital work online"—he wanted a secure Internet site for his students' compositions and a way of facilitating their "connected conversations" across the digital landscape. He invites you and other content area coaches to join the *Teachers Teaching Teachers* interactive webcast on Wednesdays, 9:00 p.m. EST / 6:00 p.m. PST, or to access archived programs at its website: http://teachersteachingteachers.org. You'll find *Youth Voices* at http://youthvoices.net.

"It's interesting work," Chris Sloan says, "because to be literate today, you need to read images and other multimedia just as well as you read text. And to be a citizen today, you really have to be able to find digital information and write thoughtfully about it."

He's proud of the way his students handle themselves online—specifically, their intelligence and civility. Helping them acknowledge what others are saying while also providing links and language to advance the dialogue are clearly this teacher's high priorities. When it comes to "netiquette," he sees his students as being light years ahead of some adults who use technology megaphones for their tunnel-vision political rants.

He still remembers the mid-1980s—the really old days—when static texts had to be *retyped* at a print shop, creating columns that were waxed, cut apart, and laid out on light boards. Then, of course, came the Web 1.0 era of stand-alone word processors, followed by networked computers, email, and Internet searches. Today, thanks to the ubiquity of social media, it's easy for anyone with computer access and the right tools to publish digital content online, thus participating in a "culture of authorship" (Rushkoff, 2005, p. 59). Students at Judge Memorial are on the cutting edge of this Web 2.0 trend—the New Renaissance, to use Rushkoff's phrase—doing work of astonishing vitality and outreach. Their teacher calls it "guerrilla journalism."

Which raises a question: Has Sloan's teaching changed over time?

"Originally," Chris says, "I was like a monk. I could go off in a corner and learn stuff. And that's the way I taught."

"Were you a Jesuit?"

Chris laughs. "No, but I knew a few."

The big difference between then and now, he adds, is that he's come to understand "the social nature of learning."

"Meaning what, exactly?"

"Both teaching and professional development are much more social now—and new technology has enabled that."

He contrasts the Youth Voices site, where students house their electronic portfolios, with popular sites like Facebook. One focuses on learning—students' intellectual growth—whereas the other documents students' personal and social lives. Both sites "engage" adolescents, but they engage different aspects of development. Those differences are important enough to get plenty of air time in Mr. Sloan's classes. He's interested in facilitating learning, not in providing a venue for self-disclosure or psychotherapy.

In Sloan's opinion, connecting with others across the digital landscape has given rise to exciting new forms of writing and learning. Today, in his inquiry-based curriculum, students read carefully, research questions of individual interest, post digital documentaries on the Youth Voices website, and use that site to respond thoughtfully to the work of others in far-reaching threaded discussions. Work gets documented in the electronic portfolio and in a hard-copy one, which is kept in the classroom. Writers engage in ways that rarely happened when in-class editing groups focused mainly on "fixing" each other's texts.

"Now there's ongoing documentation of conversation *around* the writing," Chris says. "And that's just as strong and sometimes just as powerful as the original post itself. So the conversation takes on a life of its own."

Sloan's assertion reminds me of a description by Will Richardson, who contrasts the teacher-directed writing of yesteryear with the weblog ("blogging") activities of today:

> Writing stops; blogging continues. Writing is inside; blogging is outside. Writing is monologue; blogging is conversation. Writing is thesis; blogging is synthesis . . . none of which minimizes the importance of writing. But [digital] writing becomes an ongoing process, one that is not just done for the contrived purposes of the classroom.
>
> (Richardson, 2006, p. 31)

The idea that weblogs create motivational force-fields—enabling a learning conversation to take on "a life of its own," in Sloan's words—sounds very different from the traditional classroom, where teachers often act as lonely sparkplugs for student motivation.

So has Chris Sloan given up on teacher-directed writing?

No way. In July, 2009, for example, his students published Volume 1 of *The Judge History Project*, a handsome, artfully constructed book of 116 pages that features stories of the school's alumni. Team-written and self-published (http://www.lulu.com), the book features a wealth of scanned photos and interesting, well-written profiles, including one profiling a graduate of the 1927 class with an undiminished sense of humor. To do this project, students had to connect with older people in the community—often in person or through snail-mail— then post their drafts online so they could be shared, discussed, and commented on by all members of the writing team. For Sloan's students, and especially for editor Emily Andrews, the book became a labor of love.

"A lot of tech talk is about bells and whistles," Chris says. "And yet we've been doing *great* things for a long time that shouldn't ever go away. So, to me it's about balance—how can I blend the technology with projects worth doing?"

It's another question worth thinking about.

Classroom Demonstration

It's late April, after lunch, and natives are restless in the hallway outside. Mr. Sloan glances at the wall clock, wrapping up a preview of today's lesson for seniors. Today they'll work on the Tribute Essay, he explains, which is part of a larger, long-standing capstone project called the Graduation Gift. Students have already decided on the specific audience for their multigenre and multimodal Graduation Gift—whether parents, siblings, extended family, close friends, or mentors. The Tribute Essay, addressed to the Graduation Gift recipient, is an end-of-year assignment, but his students are pumped.

"We often start with pen on paper in a writer's notebook," he explains. "There's a linear kind of thinking when you read carefully or write by pen that's very important. But we also compose digitally—because there's a connected kind of thinking that happens online. You can't do one and not the other. You have to learn the rules for both."

And that's what today's demonstration is all about.

Next to a big SmartBoard screen, with its wireless connection to Sloan's laptop, stands a wheeled cart, about the size of a small refrigerator. It's loaded with a classroom set of wireless laptops, each one charged through the cart's wiring. Both cart and teacher are ready to roll.

As students drift in from lunch, notebooks in hand, I look back at prewriting prompts from the previous week. One calls for an inventory of details to begin the profile:

- physical description: what does the person look like, sound like, talk like
- sensory details: use as many senses as appropriate
- personality, gestures, character traits
- dialogue

Another sets up questions for the writer's notebook, each centered on the significance of the individual being described:

- What are the first words that come to mind when you think of your person?
- What qualities stand out?
- What's your attitude toward them?
- How do they make you feel?
- What have they taught you?

- What have you taught them?
- Consider using figurative language in addition to your description.

A third urges students to study the craft of a skilled writer and to borrow strategies as they do some drafting work:

In Chapter 15 of *I Know Why the Caged Bird Sings*, Maya Angelou shows Mrs. Flowers' significance right away:

- "the person who threw me my first life line"
- "when she chose to smile on me, I always wanted to thank her"
- "she remains the measure of what a human being can be"

(Sloan, personal communication, 2010)

Chris Sloan begins class with a workshop focused on autobiographical significance. Students swap notebooks and read each other's drafts to find examples of good description and other techniques to be shared aloud. There's a happy buzz of activity as kids make notes and confer with partners. Things are going well, and everyone seems eager to hear brief illustrations of good writing in the large-group follow-up.

Afterwards, Sloan returns to audience consideration for the Tribute Essay. A tribute is a direct address, he explains, but the drafts are presently "third person" narratives. "Let's think about that," he says. He gives examples of how the shift to "you" pronouns enhances the text from the perspective of a Tribute Essay recipient and then leads a few minutes of back-and-forth discussion.

Finally, he assigns students to enter their notebook drafts onto the laptops, making pronoun shifts and whatever other changes they'd like. These are Google.doc texts that enable their teacher to monitor the revisions being made around the room and to find, in advance, examples for SmartBoard projection to the group. Of course, this teacher knows his class well. There are certain students he can "choose" to volunteer, if necessary.

Twenty minutes later, the seniors have composed large chunks of Tribute Essays, and their teacher is making the transition to a lively SmartBoard discussion. Freshly minted texts, still smoking from the heat of composition, are projected in large, easy-to-read font. Are these learners engaged? Can new technology like wireless laptops and SmartBoard projection enhance the work of good teachers? Does Utah have the greatest snow on earth? Answer *yes* to all of the above, and proceed to the next section.

Blogging Basics

For Chris Sloan, student weblogs (blogs, for short) provide a tool for motivating kids and expanding their content knowledge. And Chris is not alone. Pick up your favorite professional journal these days, and you will likely find an enthusiastic article or two focused on blogs. Typically, such essays outline a discipline-specific application and offer tips to technophobe teachers. But if you need a one-stop introduction to blogging basics—plus the wonderful world of wikis and the potential of podcasting—you won't go wrong with *Blogs, Wikis, Podcasts, and Other Powerful Web Tools for Classrooms* (Corwin Press, 2006) by Will Richardson, or the updated 2010 edition. It's a great read.

So, what exactly *is* a blog? Are they truly the real deal as an education innovation—or just a gimmicky fad like the Lone Ranger's silver bullets of years gone by? Let's briefly consider these questions.

Simply put, student blogs are interactive online journals. As personal websites, blogs enable students to collect archived entries (called posts). These posts may contain text, still images, video, or audio via hypertext links to websites and other blogs. The attraction of blogs for most adolescents is their ease-of-use and interactivity, plus the topic freedom they typically afford. When students click to publish, their words are suddenly and irretrievably "out there." Such digital publication is *exciting* for students, and it's made even more so when they get response from peers, whether across the room or thousands of miles away.

And, yes, blogging can be addictive. Being validated as a human being feels good any time, but especially so when one is an adolescent, hungering to be acknowledged. It's therefore useful to view blogs as technology tools for establishing identity and discovering personal potential, with the added benefit of fluency development. Of course, such needs can also be met in traditional classrooms, where students share writing face-to-face with peers. But blog posting to a potentially vast audience is actually *less* scary for many learners than in-class workshops. Paradoxically, the "digital distance" afforded by technology helps many students feel psychologically safe (Read, 2006).

Generally speaking, then, blogging has these key features:

- Blog topics are self-chosen.
- Blog posts are short and of rough-draft quality.
- Blog posts receive peer response.
- Blog posts are responded to quickly, though not immediately.
- Blogs often involve frequent changes of fonts, backgrounds, and other design features, which add an element of "fun."

(Read, 2006, p. 45)

To consider the educational value of blogs for content area coaching, let's return to Chris Sloan's assertion just a few pages back: "There's a linear kind of thinking when you read carefully or write by pen that's very important. But we also compose digitally—because there's a connected kind of thinking that happens online. You can't do one and not the other. You have to learn the rules for both."

Sloan's rationale for pen on paper—the special thinking it evokes—reminds me of a landmark essay by Sondra Perl, who documented that composing is hardly a straight-ahead process, even for skilled writers. To move a text forward, writers continually go backward—rereading, reorganizing, or rethinking their aims from the perspective of an imagined audience. They pay attention to a kind of inner compass:

> When writers pause, when they go back and repeat key words, what they seem to be doing is waiting, paying attention to what is still vague and unclear. They are looking to their felt experience, and waiting for an image, a word, or phrase to emerge that captures the sense they embody.
>
> Usually, when they make the decision to write, it is after they have a dawning awareness that something has clicked, that they have enough of a sense that if they begin with a few words heading in a certain direction, words will continue to come which will allow them to flesh out the sense they have.
>
> (Perl, 1985, p. 31)

So far, so good. This is familiar territory to me.

But what about Sloan's additional assertion—that "there's a connected kind of thinking that happens online." It's through blogging, he says, that "the conversation takes on a life of its own." What does this mean?

And now I'm reminded of "Learning with Blogs and Wikis," an *Educational Leadership* essay by Bill Ferriter, who teaches sixth-grade science and social studies in North Carolina when he's not hosting his blogsite, *The Tempered Radical*, at the Teacher Leaders Network (http://www.teacherleaders.org). Ferriter does a fine job of describing how blog activity has enriched his professional life. And here's what he has to say about his blogging work with young learners—a statement that further explains Sloan's idea of "connected conversations" via technology:

> I teach my students to challenge the thinking of digital peers with their comments— and to enjoy the challenges that others make to their own electronic thinking. At the same time, my students are learning to create, communicate, and collaborate—and to manage and evaluate information online. . . .
>
> Blogs and wikis are changing who we are as learners, preparing us for a future driven by peer production and networked learning. All you need to get started is a willingness to explore and a sense of the kinds of tools that make this work easy.
>
> (Ferriter, 2009, p. 38)

So, what are we waiting for? Let's get started.

Exploratory First Steps

High school teacher Staycie Duplichan uses blogs to help students reflect on Louisiana's real-world environmental issues and form educated opinions about science. Students post entries to writing prompts, read each other's posts, and respond to one another. Entries are stored in a blog folder, which becomes part of an electronic portfolio.

Getting permission from school administrators and from parents is the first step in creating a classroom blog. Of course, students and parents must both be informed about the blogging project, and both must agree to certain conditions with their signatures.

Duplichan uses a permission slip letter that spells out classroom rules and provides signature lines. A paper-and-pencil option is available for students or parents who do not grant permission. The rules are straightforward:

- Think of all consequences before making a post to the blog.
- Keep all personal identification secure. Do not use your last name on any post.
- Do not post any inappropriate images or language to the blog.
- Follow all school and Internet-use policies.
- Remember all copyright rules discussed in class!
- I understand that it is my choice to blog. I can answer my assignments using paper and pencil.

(Duplichan, 2009, p. 35)

A second step is to cruise blogs and websites linked to your content area. Your colleagues can probably provide specific leads, but you can also access discipline-specific blogs at Google by using a "wide net" approach and seeing what you catch. Here, for example, are a few results using very broad descriptors:

- math blogs middle school—over 3 million results
- biology blogs high school—over 3 million results
- music blogs middle school—over 7 million results
- physical education blogs high school—over 7 million results

A third step is to cruise the weblog service providers that you and your students might use. Three popular (and free) weblog sites for teachers appear in the following list:

- *Blogger* (http://www.blogger.com)
- *Edublogs* (http://www.edublogs.com)
- *Youth Voices* (http://youthvoices.net)

A fourth step is to look into the writing potential of wikis. Like blogs, wikis are easy to use, with familiar toolbars. Unlike blogs, however, wikis can be edited by anyone with a shared password, after which the results are posted online. So, if you're interested in having your students work on projects together—following the Wikipedia model—you will definitely want to check out the following websites:

- *Wikispaces* (http://www.wikispaces.com)
- *PB Wiki* (http://pbwiki.com)
- *Wet Paint* (http://www.wetpaint.com)

The fifth and final step, if you're interested, is to drop me a note about how things are going in your classroom coaching work and technology exploration. You can reach me by email at wcstrong@msn.com.

Write-for-Insight Activity

This chapter opened with a discussion of "digital natives" versus "digital immigrants." Consider for a moment your personal comfort level when it comes to accessing and embracing new digital technology. Put this reflection on a 1 to 10 scale—1 being "totally relaxed" and 10 being "totally stressed." Think about past experiences with technology that may help to account for your mindset. Jot them down. Now, ask yourself: What are the key personality traits of those teachers on the cusp of technology innovation—and what are the basic traits of those reluctant to use new tools? Talk over this question with colleagues and then jot down at least three descriptors for each category. You're now ready to write honestly about your own situation. Afterwards, share this writing with your instructor or workshop leader.

Epilogue

Revisiting Insight

Don't get it right, get it written.
— James Thurber

Listening to Students

About 45 years ago, I received an unsolicited and neatly typed two-page letter from Linda, one of my high school students, urging me not to quit teaching. Linda witnessed my daily stumbles, but she also recognized the *value* of write-to-learn activities—this despite the groans of protest from some of her classmates. Here was a quiet, almost invisible learner who saw what a greenhorn teacher was trying to accomplish:

> I must commend you for making your classroom seem like a meeting of the minds more than a class. This is important. I never felt there was a prescribed course of study which had to be finished by the end of the year. Instead, I felt each day was made for discovery.

For me, Linda's idea that each day is "made for discovery" remains exhilarating. As you've engaged in this book's activities, I hope you've realized that writing for insight can enable many of your students to feel just as she did. And, yes, it was thanks in part to Linda's heart-felt advice that I didn't quit teaching.

Today, her words remind me that content area coaching is both personal and strategic. That's why I've used small personal stories in this book and emphasized teacher-tested instruction. You now know that such practice centers mainly on regular write-to-learn activities as preparation for crafted, rubric-assessed writing tasks with explicit grading standards. However, we both *also* know that these ideas must be enacted on *your* terms, on *your* turf. As you listen to students and pay attention to their content learning, you'll discover what works.

I have two aims for this Epilogue. The first is to revisit briefly some of this book's main themes and to share final thoughts on "Leveling with Students." The second is to outline, in broad strokes, a set of research-proven recommendations for adolescent writing instruction. These "best practice" ideas come from an important meta-analysis for the Carnegie Corporation of New York titled *Writing Next: Effective Strategies to Improve Writing of Adolescents in Middle and High Schools* (Graham & Perin, 2007). It's available at the Alliance for Excellent Education (http://all4ed.org/files/WritingNext.pdf).

My expression of faith is this: Life-altering rewards can follow—just as they did for Linda and for me—when good teachers prompt content area insights through writing-to-learn activities. Above all, it's vital to motivate students, scaffold the teaching thoughtfully, and try to manage paperwork with a smile. The next step in that learning is found in the "Write for Insight" activity at the end of this Epilogue.

Coaching with Insight

So let's revisit a few of this book's key ideas to focus on the overarching theme of helping students learn content. Perhaps this summary list will offer some points of departure for faculty workshops, dialogue with your colleagues, or future reading and writing.

- The National Commission on Writing has called for a *doubling* of writing in secondary schools, urged attention to writing across the curriculum, and emphasized that "writing is every teacher's responsibility."

- Content area writing is a way for teachers to "work smarter, not harder." As students write, they learn more actively. Much of the expressive work in learning logs doesn't *need* a grade.

- Expressive writing helps learners connect personally to content learning. It also supports graded writing tasks in the three upper domains discussed in this book's Preface (Figure I-1, p. xv).

- Inviting students to write learning histories is useful in all content areas. Such writing tells a personal story that can inform classroom instruction. A room with stories is a room engaged.

- Many students have learned a "hidden curriculum" of writing by the time they reach secondary school. Such lessons often have to be unlearned for students to become insightful learners.

- As playful expressive writing develops fluency, it reduces the resistance many students feel toward content area instruction. Such writing can occur before, during, or after content lessons.

- Metaphorical thinking supports concept development. By having students talk and write metaphorically, we engage imagination and help them visualize key ideas. Image is a powerful teacher.

- Students with special needs and ESL learners improve writing fluency when they receive help with basic skills. Buddy systems and small groups are great tools to assist such students.

- Ten principles of assignment design help turn perfunctory writing tasks into interesting ones. Teachers can prepare their own rubrics or rely on generic ones such as Six Traits assessment.

- Assigning is not teaching. Challenging academic assignments require prewriting support and response group training. Process writing works when teachers scaffold its instruction.

- Coaching and judging require different skills. The ideal time for coaching is during practice time, *not* when the final papers come in. Most of us need to coach more and judge less.

- Judging (grading) of final papers should be done swiftly, using a rubric. Standards in a grading rubric should be explicitly discussed with students, never hidden. Rubrics save the teacher time.

- Working portfolios archive content area insights and document the development of writing fluency. Learning portfolios showcase the best efforts of each student, thereby building self-assessment skills.

- By inviting students to research "outside the box" of traditional reports, we discourage the recycling of fake research from the Internet and encourage genuinely insightful learning.

- Electronic technology has opened a brave new world of enhanced writing motivation for students as well as exciting new venues for content learning. We prepare students for the future by helping them use new tools.

There's one additional point that needs fuller discussion—the important issue of student resistance to writing, which is faced by many teachers.

Leveling with Students

Ideally, in content area classrooms, students set writing goals, plan strategy, transcribe thoughts into words, revise, and edit. As they engage with text—either with pen on paper or digitally—they monitor its meaning, readability, tone, mechanics, and other features.

Ideally, too, today's learners have multiple opportunities to get helpful responses from peers in workshops and via Internet weblogs. We've learned that digital conversations can not only motivate students to write in new ways—integrating visual and auditory material with text—but also challenge and deepen their thinking about content area topics.

But what if young writers aren't really clear about their writing goals, or have no investment in them? What if they permit negative past experiences to undermine their perseverance? What if they play victim, voicing the wrong-headed idea that "writing is easy for everybody but me"? What if they submit papers or make posts to classroom websites without proofreading or self-assessment? Or what if they substitute the goal of "pleasing the teacher to get a grade" for the goal of a good-faith effort?

The answers are obvious: Writing won't be experienced as "discovery," but rather as a boring, meaningless, even tortuous activity. So what are the conditions that warp the spirits of teachers and students alike? Here are several areas of classroom danger:

- Allowing self-defeating student myths to go unchallenged—that good writing comes from "inborn talent" and that "writers are born, not made."

- Ignoring the power of writing-to-learn activities and then assigning vacuous academic topics with little motivation or direction for students.

- Putting basic writers at the classroom margins, instead of assisting them with peer tutors and instructional scaffolds to develop writing skills.

- Eschewing opportunities for explicit up-front coaching—and then focusing only on deficits in usage and mechanics, without reference to grading rubrics.

- Limiting opportunities for personalized research, restricting publication venues to traditional genre, and ignoring the potential of group research.

The truth is simple: *Quality writing in an academic arena takes hard work—and it's* through *the challenge of writing well that learners experience the deep satisfaction of constructing personal knowledge.*

When we don't level with our students about this basic fact, we help them remain emotionally and intellectually detached—in effect, giving them tools for do-it-yourself frontal lobotomies. Yes, it's inevitable that some students will still "play the game" and engage in academic fakery to avoid the hard work of writing well. However, the personal costs of such cynicism are high. Over time, as these students throttle back their curiosity, devalue their own meaning-making ability, and neglect to develop the skills of thinking and communicating with others, they twist the knife in their own gray matter.

The national interest deserves better from such students, and so do we.

The "Writing Next" Report

Steve Graham and Dolores Perin are distinguished professors at Vanderbilt University and Columbia University, respectively—and eminently qualified to conduct a meta-analysis of effective strategies in adolescent writing instruction. Both understand the realities faced by middle school and high school teachers, so it's no surprise that their work for the Carnegie Corporation of New York carries both academic credibility and classroom utility. For me, the "Writing Next" Report (Graham & Perin, 2007) is landmark research.

Meta-analysis is a powerful technique for aggregating the results of research studies that meet specific criteria—in this case, experimental or quasi-experimental designs with treatment and control groups, plus several other conditions. As described in the following text, the goal of meta-analysis is to compute a useful statistic called an "effect size":

> The effect size is a statistic that represents the difference between the test scores of a group that participated in a given instructional technique and another group that does not. If the group differences are sufficiently large, as expressed by the effect size, the technique is considered effective and teachers are justified in considering it for use. Generally, an effect size of 0.20 is considered to indicate only limited effectiveness, an effect size of 0.50 suggests a medium level of effectiveness, and 0.80 indicates that a technique is highly effective (Lipsey & Wilson, 2001).

(Perin, 2007, p. 247)

A total of 142 studies comprise the Writing Next report, and these are drawn from well-designed research in grades 4 through 12. Based on the calculation of effect sizes from the pooled studies, 11 elements of effective writing instruction were identified. Some elements focus on learning-to-write interventions, others on writing-to-learn activities. The following list features Perin's recommendations for instruction, arranged in order of average weighted effect sizes, large to small. As you take time to read this list, think back to the professional ground you've covered in this book's 10 chapters.

- **Strategy Instruction** (effect size = 0.82). *Teach adolescents strategies for planning, revising, and editing their compositions.*

- **Summarization** (effect size = 0.82). *Teach adolescents strategies and procedures for summarizing reading material, as this improves their ability to concisely and accurately present this information in writing.*

- **Peer Assistance** (effect size = 0.75). *Develop instructional arrangements where adolescents work together to plan, draft, revise, and edit their compositions. Such collaborative activities have a strong impact on the quality of what students write.*

- **Setting Product Goals** (effect size = 0.70). *Set clear and specific goals for what adolescents are to accomplish with their written product. This includes identifying the purpose of the assignment, e.g., to persuade, as well as characteristics of the final product, e.g., addresses both sides of an argument.*

- **Word Processing** (effect size = 0.55). *Make it possible for adolescents to use word processing as a primary tool for writing, as it has a positive impact on the quality of their writing.*

- **Sentence Combining** (effect size = 0.50). *Teach adolescents how to write increasingly complex sentences. Instruction in combining simpler sentences into more sophisticated ones enhances the quality of students' writing.*

- **Process Writing with Training** (effect size = 0.46). *Provide teachers with training in how to implement the process writing approach when this instructional model is used with adolescents.*

- **Inquiry** (effect size = 0.32). *Involve adolescents in writing activities designed to sharpen their skills of inquiry. Provide a clear goal, have the students analyze immediately available, concrete information using specific strategies, and have them apply what was learned from this analysis.*

- **Prewriting** (effect size = 0.32). *Engage adolescents in activities that help them gather and organize ideas for their compositions before they write a first draft. This includes activities such as gathering possible information for a paper through reading or developing a visual representation of their ideas before writing.*

- **Use of Models** (effect size = 0.25). *Provide adolescents with good models for each type of writing that is the focus of instruction. These examples should be analyzed and students encouraged to imitate the critical elements embodied in the models.*

■ ***Writing to Learn*** (effect size = 0.23). *Use writing as a tool to facilitate adolescents' learning of content material. Although the impact of writing activity on content learning is small, it is consistent enough to expect some enhancement as a result of writing-to-learn activities.*

(Perin, 2007, italics in original, pp. 248–257)

Listening to Research

As the meta-analysis recommendations make clear, there is strong empirical support for activities recommended in *Coaching Writing in Content Areas*. For example, "Strategy Instruction" is covered in Chapters 7, 8, and 9; "Summarization" and "Sentence Combining" in Chapter 5; "Peer Assistance" in Chapters 5, 7 and 10; and "Setting Product Goals" in Chapters 5, 6, 8, 9, and 10. Thumb back through this book's pages, and you'll see that good teachers are already implementing many key ideas in the Writing Next report.

But what about the relatively small effect size—0.23—for "Writing to Learn," the content learning recommendation? Should we conclude that various types of expressive writing and journaling in content area classrooms—math, social studies, science, and other subject areas—have only limited utility?

Looking at details of the Writing Next meta-analysis, one finds great variability in the studies examining writing for content learning. Some studies report very positive outcomes, but others report negative effect sizes. Of course, all effect sizes are averaged. Graham and Perin (2007) discuss these results with the characteristic restraint of professional researchers; I have added italics to emphasize a take-away message:

> *Writing has been shown to be an effective tool for enhancing students' learning of content material.* Although the impact of writing activity on content learning is small, it is consistent enough to predict some enhancement in learning as a result of writing-to-learn activities.
>
> *About 75% of the writing-to-learn studies analyzed had positive effects.* The average effect was small but significant. Unfortunately, it was not possible to draw separate conclusions for low-achieving writers, as none of these studies examined the impact of writing-to-learn activities specifically with these students.
>
> *Writing to learn was equally effective for all content areas* (social studies, math, and science) *and grades* (4–6 versus 7–12) studied.

(Graham & Perin, 2007, pp. 20–21, italics added)

An earlier meta-analysis by Bangert-Drowns, Hurley, and Wilkinson (2004) reached basically the same conclusions—that writing-to-learn activities "can have a small, positive impact on conventional measures of academic achievement" (p. 29) and that prompts encouraging students to "reflect on their current knowledge, confusions, and learning processes proved particularly effective" (p. 50). It is through "scaffolding metacognitive processes," the authors believe, that writing can enhance academic learning (p. 51).

Listening to these points, I can't help but revisit the terrain of this book—then write for insight. For me, the writing-to-learn activities in early chapters constitute *a necessary but not sufficient condition* for content learning. Expressive activities serve as "foundation" for the public ("process writing") tasks found in later chapters. In other words, engaging activities like admit slips, Quick-Writes, learning logs, Wall Text, dialogue writing, and metaphor-building are really means to an end—but *not* ends in themselves. They prepare students for various types of assessed academic writing, in which powerful learning effects are likely, according to the Writing Next report. It's there, closing the instructional circle with strategy instruction, that we achieve our true goal.

Our end, in my opinion, centers on meaningful learning—learning through personal insight—because such work is the core of any educational relationship, including the one in this book. As used throughout, "insight" refers to flashes of enlightenment or surprise, a "seeing from within." And to achieve insight, one must be involved, attentive, and relaxed.

Like now: Just ☺ if you're with me.

Write-for-Insight Activity

Unlike other chapters in this book, this one is reflective—and without apology. Its research-based recommendations, drawn from a major meta-analysis on adolescent writing instruction, provide a kind of capstone for the practical strategies discussed elsewhere. Select one of this chapter's ideas for a final writing-to-learn entry that you might share with colleagues. Or, as a learning log alternative, ask yourself, "What can I do to help ensure that 'each day is made for discovery' in my teaching?" Then write for insight.

Appendix A

Literacy Autobiography Case Study

According to teacher education research, "reflective practitioners" make the best teachers. So the idea is to tell a story—*your* story of learning to write—and reflect on it. This writing will be a case study in which you are both the researcher and the subject of research.

One audience is yourself—a writer looking in the mirror of experience to see what it means. Another audience is colleagues. A third is your instructor or workshop leader. All share an interest in what your story can teach, so it's your task to recreate experiences—to "show it like it was"—and then to consider the significance of chosen events. Your paper will probably be about four or five double-spaced pages (1,000–1,200 words).

You may have difficulty remembering past writing experiences. Use the following guide to access your memories. Another kind of writing problem is the selection and organization of memories. You'll need to sort and select what you see as the *most important* experiences to write about; the ones with emotional resonance, either positive or negative.

In preparing a first draft of your paper, you may refer to events involving specific teachers. Refer to these individuals by initials (for example, Mr. S. or Ms. L.), not by their real names. This technique protects privacy. Also, your instructor may organize you into small response groups so that you can try out your text on colleagues and gain insights for revision. This process will be explained by your instructor. You should have three copies of your paper, plus the original, for work in response groups.

Questions to Consider

Here are a few questions to prompt initial thinking about your personal case study:

1. Who were your earliest influences as a writer? Were the influences positive or negative? What role did parents, peers, and other adults play in your development? Have the influences since the early ones helped or hindered your writing? Who in middle school or high school was an especially positive or negative influence on writing? What specific incidents are vivid for you?

2. How have you felt about writing? Do your feelings vary, depending on the type of writing? Have your feelings changed as you've grown older? How would you *like* to feel about writing? What stops you or holds you back? To what extent is writing an activity you do for pleasure and stimulation? To what extent is it work or drudgery? What kind of writing do you find boring or difficult? Why do you think this is so?

3. What kind of kid were you in middle school and high school? Whom did you "hang out" with? Go back to a photo album and see yourself as you were then; then try to develop a "profile" (character sketch) of yourself in relation to the group you identified with. How did the norms of the group relate to literacy activities and/or school? Do you still identify with this social group or have you "moved on"?

4. To what extent does writing help you learn? What do you know about using writing for personal learning? When and where did you learn these lessons? How do you get started when you have a writing project like this one? How do you sustain interest and concentration? How do you organize your time when it comes to drafting, revising, and editing? How successful (or competent) do you feel as an adult writer?

Some of those questions will be more interesting than others. Zero in on those you'd like to explore for a few minutes. Work fast and don't worry about order or whether something is "profound" or well worded. First, just get your thoughts down. After doing this, look back over your work and circle words and ideas that seem to hold particular interest (or surprise) for you. You'll want to follow leads that help you answer the central question: *What literacy experiences have made me who I am today?*

Then, on a separate sheet of paper, try drafting with the focus you've chosen. Think back to incidents from your past that are pertinent to your case study, and use this material in developing your rough draft. Be prepared to read your draft aloud in a small response group. Toward the end of your draft, reflect on the meaning of your experience, as you understand it, and the possible implications for teaching.

Revising Your Literacy Autobiography

What features should you work toward to accomplish this assignment? Here are a few key features of a successful literacy autobiography paper:

■ Has an adult voice—clear, honest, reflective—that uses the "I" pronoun in recalling important literacy experiences and sharing them

■ Narrates selected literacy experiences (writing memories) in an engaging way and discusses connections among those experiences

■ Describes thoughts and feelings about writing as a *learner* and relates those to present attitudes, interests, and skills

■ Reflects on the teacher's role as a model of literacy (for your own children and for adolescent students)

■ Uses standard English conventions (spelling, punctuation, and usage) associated with the professional status of the educator

These criteria are organized into a simple rubric. Note the list of text features. Use this evaluation rubric as you share your work in small groups and self-assess your paper.

Text Feature	Awesome	Very Good	Satisfactory	Needs Work
A reflective voice				
A focus on key literacy experiences ("themes")				
Linkage between past writing events and present skills, attitudes, and interests				
Teacher as a literacy model (adult reflection)				
Standard English conventions				

Remember: Your work should reflect your good-faith effort—and efforts of your writing partners—with respect to writing conventions (paragraphing, sentence structure, word choice, usage, spelling, punctuation, and so on). Your instructor is not your proofreader.

Appendix B

Bob Tierney's Concept-Trigger Words

As discussed in Chapter 4, individual students and small groups can use concept-trigger words to develop extended metaphors that visually depict and/or explain (in writing) key concepts being studied. Students can choose trigger words or let serendipity be their guide. Many teachers use Wall Text with this activity (see Chapters 4 and 5).

skeleton	room	treadmill	oven	filter
valley	fruit	library	purse	molecule
maze	water	air	earth	money
tunnel	altar	diamond	army	computer
amoeba	anvil	bait	balloon	Bible
root	temple	window	star	typewriter
battery	armor	fountain	bed	seed
spice	bell	rock	album	robot
bag	tide	bank	weapon	farm
hinge	horse	image	junk	knot
algebra	alphabet	child	lamp	leg
menu	prison	monster	muscle	nest
pepper	pill	satellite	pod	ring
rainbow	rudder	safe	sauce	saloon
ice	index	key	ladder	landslide
liquid	manual	match	sex	data base
nut	frame	page	parasite	pendulum
port	prism	puzzle	radio	microscope
shadow	shovel	smoke	rash	horizon
lever	lock	machine	map	mattress

meteor	mist	moon	music	net
perfume	pipe	plant	pond	pore
rope	rug	sand	saw	screw
insect	kitchen	ladle	leaf	library
nail	meter	missile	motor	organ
ocean	sphere	paint	passport	glass
prison	pyramid	raft	record	river
shell	signature	herb	hose	icon
lode	magnet	marsh	meat	horoscope
nose	onion	palette	pebble	star
vise	pillow	plate	pool	stamp
robot	rose	sandwich	ruler	scale
vulture	joint	kite	lake	lens
mountain	needle	vertebra	violin	pacemaker
pocket	dung	powder	pump	radar
pulley	quilt	rag	ramp	rifle
script	shoe	siren	house	hieroglyph
milk	loom	mask	medal	lightning
soap	pen	knife	piano	planet
rain	halo	rubber	saddle	parachute
cup	school	program	ship	skin
umbrella	channel	crystal	woman	man
cope	cycle	plow	egg	hook
well	water	treasure	flag	guitar
girdle	glue	hair	template	harbor
zone	road	ball	zoo	trigger
caldron	cannon	chain	chord	cloud
drain	drum	tree	bomb	wing
flood	fog	fork	fungus	furniture
mirror	camera	wedge	wave	sandpaper

bridge	network	staircase	cave	box
folder	dust	eraser	statue	net
antenna	floor	flower	food	block
God	guillotine	bee	plug	blanket
trap	tube	spring	television	toilet
lamp	clock	crown	desert	chessboard
wallpaper	gate	diskette	broom	bottleneck
fossil	funhouse	window	glacier	ratchet wheel
funnel	book	brain	brakes	booby trap
buffer	weed	cancer	cell	cesspool
compass	circle	code	web	dress
factory	fairy	fan	farm	feather
foam	fly	fist	bird	bottle
game	garden	gear	ghost	plastic
circus	hammer	head	heart	family
current	detour	ear	button	face
fertilizer	field	finger	engine	floodlight
hole	color	dope	adult	forge
graph	gun	gutter	bruise	bug
blister	acid	candy	chorus	springboard
meatball	body	drill	eye	song
spotlight	pitcher	glove	hand	vegetable
table	tool	trail	vent	torch
target	telescope	fabric	sword	spectrum
spear	sponge	stomach	memory	dam
fish	fence	festival	film	fire
grave	lever	basement	square	sun
soup	spiral	shaft	market	torpedo
train	triangle	vacuum	ticket	thermometer
telephone	stove	tapestry	car	kaleidoscope

Appendix C

Macie Wolfe's Cubing Activity

This prewriting activity, adapted from the work of Kelly Gallagher (*Teaching Adolescent Writers*, 2006) and others, requires a large (5-inch) die or cube for teacher modeling, plus several small (1-inch) dice—one die for each team of students. Cubing is a literacy strategy that enables students to actively explore a topic from different angles or perspectives with each roll of the die. The idea is to examine the topic with prompts from the six sides of the cube. To introduce cubing, start with a familiar topic and model the process with the class. Then have students practice cubing in small groups with another familiar topic. Students will see that their responses "build" on one another. Assign more complex topics once students have a grasp of how the process works. Prompts can differ in their wording, but basically students are asked to "think aloud" using the following six cues:

1. **Describe it**
   - How would you describe this item, topic, event, issue, person, or living thing?
   - What does it look or feel like? Include color, shape, size, and so on, in your description.
   - What key characteristics, attributes, or properties does it have?

2. **Compare it**
   - What is it similar to or different from?
   - What inferences can you make about it?

3. **Associate it**
   - What does it remind you of?
   - How does it connect to other things, topics, issues, events, and so on?
   - How does this person relate to other persons or characters?

4. **Analyze it**
   - How and why did it happen?
   - What are its contributing factors—or its smaller parts?
   - How is it made? What is it composed of?
   - How is it adapted to live where it lives or to do what it does?

5. **Apply it**
   - What can it do? What can you do with it? How can it help?
   - What lessons or understanding does it generate?

6. **Argue for or against it**
   - I support/oppose this because . . .
   - This works because . . .
   - I think this is good/bad because . . .
   - I would like to be like this because . . .
   - I agree/disagree because . . .

The following chart shows the cubing technique applied to the topic of sea urchins.

ARGUE: Erik would NOT like to be a sea urchin because it has no brain and he likes to think deeply. Hannah thinks it would be cool to live in the sea but not as a sea urchin. She likes being human.

DESCRIBE: Circular body with spines coming out; has five tooth plates in its mouth; radial symmetry; five suction cups along spine; black/brown; varies in size (largest in Red Sea has 7-inch test); 700 different species.

APPLY: It uses spines to protect itself and move; its tubelike feet with suction cups hold onto the sea floor. Has no brain but has clawlike mouth on its underside.

COMPARE: Similar to starfish, spider, and dandelion. Different from dog, shark, and human. Inferences: Not a fast mover and lives in water. Hard, chalky skin is called the "test."

ANALYZE: Small pedicellarines on spines have toxins that can sting their food to help them capture it. Spiny, sharp body shows adaptation to ocean environment.

ASSOCIATE: Reminds us of a porcupine (has sharp spines for protection). Sea otters are the main predators. Collected for home decoration by some people.

Appendix D

Graphic Organizers

A *graphic organizer* is an instructional tool used to illustrate a student's or class's prior knowledge about a topic or section of text; specific examples include the K-W-L-H Technique and the Anticipation/Reaction Guide.

The graphic organizer in Figure D.1 is used to describe a central idea: a thing (a geographic region), process (meiosis), concept (altruism), or proposition with support (experimental

Figure D.1

Spider Map

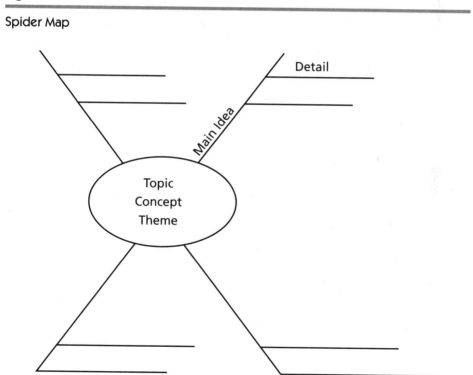

drugs should be available to AIDS victims). Key frame questions include: What is the central idea? What are its attributes? What are its functions?

The graphic organizer in Figure D.2 is used to describe the stages of something (the life cycle of a primate); the steps in a linear procedure (how to neutralize an acid); a sequence of events (how feudalism led to the formation of nation states); or the goals, actions, and outcomes of a historical figure or character in a novel (the rise and fall of Napoleon). Key frame questions include: What is the object, procedure, or initiating event? What are the stages or steps? How do they lead to one another? What is the final outcome?

The graphic organizer in Figure D.3 is used for timelines showing historical events or ages (grade levels in school), degrees of something (weight), shades of meaning (Likert scales), or rating scales (achievement in school). Key frame questions include: What is being scaled? What are the end points?

Figure D.4 is used to show similarities and differences between two things (people, places, events, ideas, etc.). Key frame questions include: What things are being compared? How are they similar? How are they different?

Figure D.5 is used to represent a problem, attempted solutions, and results (the national debt). Key frame questions include: What was the problem? Who had the problem? Why was it a problem? What attempts were made to solve the problem? Did those attempts succeed?

Figure D.6 is used to show causal information (causes of poverty), a hierarchy (types of insects), or branching procedures (the circulatory system). Key frame questions include: What is the superordinate category? What are the subordinate categories? How are they related? How many levels are there?

Figure D.7 is used to show the nature of an interaction between persons or groups (Europeans settlers and American Indians). Key frame questions include: Who are the persons or groups? What were their goals? Did they conflict or cooperate? What was the outcome for each person or group?

Figure D.2

Series of Events Chain

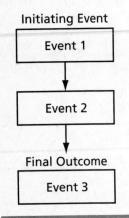

Figure D.3

Continuum Scale

Low   High

Figure D.4

Compare/Contrast Matrix

	Name 1	Name 2
Attribute 1		
Attribute 2		
Attribute 3		

Figure D.5

Problem/Solution Outline

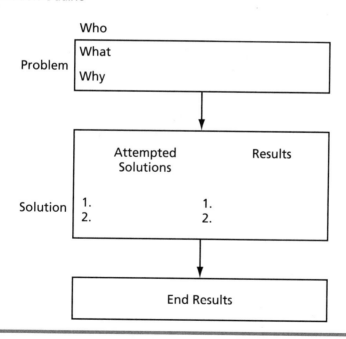

Figure D.6

Network Tree

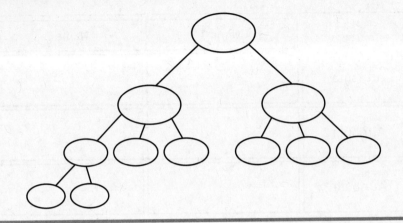

Figure D.7

Human Interaction Outline

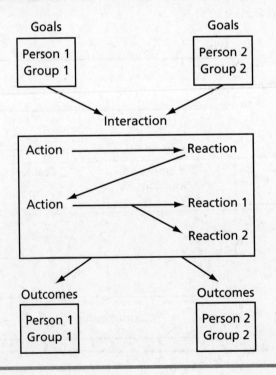

Figure D.8 is used to show the causal interaction of a complex event (an election, a nuclear explosion) or complex phenomenon (juvenile delinquency, learning disabilities). Key frame questions include: What are the factors that cause X? How do they interrelate? Are the factors that cause X the same as those that cause X to persist?

Figure D.9 is used to show how a series of events interact to produce a set of results again and again (weather phenomena, cycles of achievement and failure, the life cycle). Key frame questions include: What are the critical events in the cycle? How are they related? In what ways are they self-reinforcing?

Figure D.8

Fishbone Map

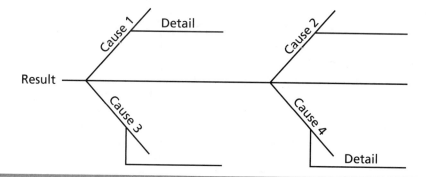

Figure D.9

Cycle

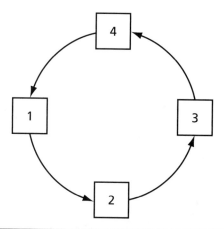

Appendix E

Content Area Writing Assignments

The following writing tasks in health, English, music, mathematics, history, and biology use the CRAFT approach described in Chapter 6, "Designing Assignments and Rubrics." These assignments have been adapted from the work of secondary teacher education students at Utah State University in Logan, Utah.

Health: Ask Dr. Abby Assignment (Tana Johnson)

Today you are Dr. Abby, a medical columnist. People from around town ask for your professional opinion on health issues. Following is a letter from the "Ask Dr. Abby" mailbag. After getting in groups of three, read the letter together and discuss how Dr. Abby should respond. Draw from your reading in health, from class activities, and from Internet research. You should share ideas as a group but write individually. In your Dr. Abby written response discuss possible causes of the problem and offer advice on how the problem might be addressed. Write in a clear, friendly style so that readers of your column can understand and act upon your advice. Your response needs to be about one page in length, double-spaced, and typed in a 12-point font.

Dear Dr. Abby,

My friend eats whatever she wants whenever she wants. I am about 20 pounds heavier than I would like to be so I really watch what I eat. Over the past year I notice she hasn't changed a bit, but I seemed to have gained more weight. It doesn't make sense. I wonder why she can eat whatever she wants and not gain a pound, but I pay attention to my diet and still gain weight. Is there anything I can do to better manage my weight? Thanks for any insight you can provide.

Sincerely,

Frustrated in Florida

After your response is complete, bring it to class and share it with your writing partners. Make sure each person in the group gets to read and respond to your Dr. Abby column. After peer response, make any necessary changes and hand in the final version.

Ask Dr. Abby Scoring Rubric

Discussion of possible causes of the problem (diagnosis)	/20 possible
Answering the question presented in the letter to Dr. Abby	/10 possible
Offering advice on how the problem might be addressed	/10 possible
Format expectations and writing mechanics (conventions)	/10 possible

Total /50 possible

English: *To Kill a Mockingbird* News Story Assignment (Alice Koehne)

You are a journalist for the *Maycomb Times*. The editor has asked you to follow up on an incident that happened during the past three years (the time span covered in *To Kill a Mockingbird*). Pick a major event from the novel and create a newspaper article from it. Make this story real by "interviewing" a character from the novel (what would this person say about the event or situation?) or by reporting what you "saw" first-hand (use your reading to depict how the scene appeared to you). Your article should add some depth or insight to the basic story.

Your story should be one page long and set in a two-column newspaper format. Your page will be published as part of our class newspaper, so make sure it's free of errors in spelling, punctuation, or usage. You will get help with these conventions when we meet in response groups. For now, concentrate on developing a solid, interesting news story, using the journalistic techniques we have studied. When you turn in your story, please include the final copy, rough draft, and any notes you took to brainstorm and set up your story. These provide evidence of your attention to the writing process.

Mockingbird News Story Scoring Rubric

Grading scale: 5 = excellent; 4 = strong; 3 = good; 2 = adequate; 1 = needs work.

Demonstrates knowledge of a specific event in the novel	5	4	3	2	1
Provides clear news article writing and organization	5	4	3	2	1
Uses first-person narration or third-person "interview"	5	4	3	2	1
Shows evidence of engagement in the writing process	5	4	3	2	1
Attends to grammatical correctness (mechanics)	5	4	3	2	1

Music: Bach to Kappelmeister Assignment (Royce Backman)

Imagine that you are Johann Sebastian Bach in the year 1720. You earn a meager living as the organist and choir director for a large church. In addition to these duties, your employer, the Kappelmeister of the church, expects you to compose an entirely new cantata for each week's service. After months of sleepless nights and hundreds of new compositions, the Kappelmeister suddenly demands your resignation, contending that your music is tiresome and too difficult for church patrons to understand.

That night, in a dream, you have a vision of the Modern era. You see concert halls throughout the world, where great musicians perform your work. You see your music widely distributed via modern technology. You see your name used in the same breath as Beethoven and Brahms, who credit your influence. Waking up, you realize that resigning your post may well alter the course of history.

Write a letter to your Kappelmeister to share your dream. Use examples from your dream to persuade the Kappelmeister to change his mind about requesting your resignation. Contrast the Modern era you saw and the Baroque era in which you live, giving examples in areas such as music, industrial progress, and culture. You might even point to dramatic changes in instruments, traditions, and lifestyle. Of course, feel free to do background research to assist with your letter writing.

Letter Writing Scoring Rubric

Grading scale: 4 = outstanding; 3 = very good; 2 = adequate; 1 = needs work.

Uses examples to contrast the Baroque and Modern eras	4	3	2	1
Develops examples through vivid, colorful language	4	3	2	1
Presents clear, compelling reasons for keeping position	4	3	2	1
Has an effective organization of ideas in letter format	4	3	2	1
Shows strong control over writing mechanics	4	3	2	1

Mathematics: Wallpaper Puzzle Assignment (Megan Tanner)

You and your little sister or brother share a bedroom. Your mom agrees to let you wallpaper the room, but you and your sibling can't agree on wallpaper. So she decides to let each of you wallpaper half the wall space in the room. Since you are older and in a great math class, you have the responsibility of deciding how much space each of you gets. Your little sister or brother has no idea how to figure area, so it is your job to first figure this out and then to convince her or him that you are not cheating and using more than half the wall space for your wallpaper.

Your assignment consists of four major parts.

1. For prewriting, measure *all* the walls in your bedroom to figure the total area. You will divide this area in half to determine the wallpaper needed by each of you.

2. Write a paper that describes the process you used. Then describe how you will convince your little sister or brother that the area of a rectangle is length × width, and that you aren't cheating in your calculations.

3. Write a dialogue between you and your little sister or brother in which you describe to her or him how much wallpaper each of you gets to use. The dialogue needs to include an introduction setting up the scene.

4. Make a visual aid to help teach your little sister or brother. Attach this visual aid to the dialogue writing you turn in.

Wallpaper Puzzle Scoring Rubric

Criteria and Points Possible (50)	Comments and Points Earned
Prewriting assignment is completed (+5)	
Math calculations are accurate (+5)	
The process is described in detail (+10)	
Plan for teaching is given in detail (+10)	
Dialogue has setting and clear development (+10)	
Dialogue has visual aid attached (+5)	
Writing shows attention to conventions (+5)	

History: Family History Research Assignment (Katie Carone)

You have just been elected chairperson of the state historical society. As chairperson, one of your duties is to speak at the historical society's annual luncheon. Because this year's theme is "Looking at Legacies," you decide to research your own family legacy and include this information in your luncheon talk. The following writing process will help you accomplish your goal.

Step 1: Gather Histories

Begin by collecting personal histories of three relatives or ancestors in at least two separate generations (parents, grandparents, great-grandparents). If you do not have access to two different generations of your family, you may research personal histories of nonrelatives. Gain access to primary sources (first-hand accounts) as much as possible. Use diaries, journals, personal letters, oral histories, autobiographies, and interviews. Make sure to use personal interviews for at least one of the histories.

Step 2: Organize Information

With your materials collected, begin organizing so that you can compare and contrast the three lives to each other and to yourself. You can use strategies discussed in class (e.g., concept mapping, comparison charts or lists, a table) or create your own method. Part of this comparison will relate to historical events, living conditions, lifestyle, personality, thoughts and feelings, joys and hardships, and so on. This chart should be attached to your final speech.

Step 3: Analyze and Freewrite

What are the major similarities and differences in the three lives? How did historical events affect the lives of these people? What surprises have emerged as a result of your research? What lessons have you learned from researching these stories? Why is it important to keep "Looking at Legacies"? As you think about these questions, begin the process of freewriting. For now, don't worry about spelling or grammar. Just get your answers to the questions down on paper.

Step 4: Write a Speech

Focusing on the theme of "Looking at Legacies" and using your freewriting, develop a three- to five-page speech to present at the historical society luncheon. Use your three histories as examples. Draw upon the comparisons and contrasts in Steps 2 and 3. Describe what you discovered as you delved into family history. Because you are the society's chairperson, members will expect to hear *why* the process of historical research is so rewarding. Of course, make sure your speech has an introduction, body, and conclusion. You will also want to proofread carefully before you turn in a final copy. (The paper itself should be double-spaced, in 12-point font, with one-inch margins.) Finally, don't forget to attach a list of research sources at the end of your paper.

Family History Scoring Rubric

Assignment Criteria	Points Possible	Points Earned	Comments
Research includes three relatives in at least two generations.	10		
Research involves primary sources and one interview (minimum).	10		
Research includes an organizational chart for family history materials.	20		
Speech is organized with an introduction, body, and conclusion.	10		

Speech compares and contrasts the three lives in multiple ways.	40		
Speech meets form requirements and includes a list of sources.	5		
Speech shows good control over basic writing mechanics.	5		
Total points	100		

Biology: Science Fiction Assignment (Jeramy Cook)

As we have learned in class, plants and animals are both classified as *eukaryotes,* meaning they have much in common. However, there are differences between plants and us that are important to understand and remember. A good way to learn biology information is to have fun applying it. This assignment invites you to understand plant and animal differences through creativity.

For this assignment, imagine you are a science fiction writer who has come up with a wonderful idea for your next book. The character you envision has been born here on Earth with many of the structures and functions of a plant, and you want to tell the story of how this person lives. Your story will describe the challenges this person faces as well as the benefits of possessing certain plant-like structures and functions.

You can have your character look like a human but with the cells of a plant, or the character can possess both plant and human traits. It's up to you. With this writing, use your imagination and be creative. However, you should show your understanding of the important structures and functions that make plants different from people. Remember, real learning involves more than just memorizing the parts of a plant or animal.

The following rubric will help you understand my expectations. Meanwhile, have fun, explore, and be nice to plants!

Science Fiction Criteria	Possible Points (100)	Your Points
Appropriate length (3–5 pages, typed, double-spaced)	10	
Character shows challenges of having plant traits.	20	
Character shows benefits of having plant traits.	20	
Paper shows and discusses some specific parts of a plant (e.g., cell wall, plastids, etc.).	20	
Paper shows understanding of the main differences between plant and animal cells.	20	
Paper shows control over writing mechanics.	10	

References

ACT. (2004). *Crisis at the core: Preparing all students for college and work.* Retrieved November 1, 2004, from http://www.act.org/path/policy/pdf/crisis_report.pdf

Allen, C. (2001). *Writing multigenre research papers: Voice, passion, and discovery in grades 4–6.* Portsmouth, NH: Heinemann.

Applebee, A. N. (1981). *Writing in the secondary school: English and the content areas.* Urbana, IL: National Council of Teachers of English.

Applebee, A. N., & Langer, J. A. (2006). *The state of writing instruction in America's schools: What existing data tell us.* Albany, NY: Center on English Learning & Achievement, State University of New York—Albany. Retrieved May 1, 2010, from http://cela.albany.edu

Bangert-Drowns, R. L., Hurley, M. M., & Wilkinson, B. (2004). The effects of school-based writing-to-learn interventions on academic achievement: A meta-analysis. *Review of Educational Research, 74*(1), pp. 29–58.

Bean, J. C. (1996). *Engaging ideas: The professor's guide to integrating writing, critical thinking, and active learning in the classroom.* San Francisco: Josscy-Bass.

Bean, J. C., Drenk, D., & Lee, F. D. (1982). Microtheme strategies for developing cognitive skills. In C. W. Griffin (Ed.), *Teaching writing in all disciplines* (pp. 27–38). San Francisco: Jossey-Bass.

Bernstein, R. (1997). Using fictional techniques for nonfiction writing. In C. B. Olson (Ed.), *Practical ideas for teaching writing as a process at the high school and college levels* (pp. 135–138). Sacramento, CA: California Department of Education.

Boyer, E. L. (1983). *High school: A report on secondary education in America.* New York: Harper & Row.

Bruner, J. S. (1978). The role of dialogue in language acquisition. In A. Sinclair et al. (Eds.), *The child's conception of language* (pp. 241–256). New York: Springer-Verlag.

Casner-Lotto, J., & Barrington, L. (2006). *Are they really ready to work?* New York: The Conference Board.

Catton, B. (1996). *The American heritage new history of the civil war.* New York: Viking.

Chopra, D. (2003). *The spontaneous fulfillment of desire: Harnessing the infinite power of coincidence.* New York: Harmony Books.

College Entrance Examination Board (CEEB), National Commission on Writing in America's Schools and Colleges. (2003). *The neglected "R": The need for a writing revolution.* New York: College Entrance Examination Board.

Collins, J. (1998). *Strategies for struggling writers.* New York: Guilford.

Csikszentmihalyi, M. (1990). *Flow: The psychology of optimal experience.* New York: Harper Perennial.

Daiker, D. A. (1989). Learning to praise. In C. M. Anson (Ed.), *Writing and response: Theory, practice, and research.* Urbana, IL: National Council of Teachers of English.

Dale, H. (1997). *Co-authoring in the classroom: Creating an environment for effective collaboration.* Urbana, IL: National Council of Teachers of English.

Daniels, H., Zemelman, S., & Steineke, N. (2007). *Content-area writing: Every teacher's guide.* Portsmouth, NH: Heinemann.

D'Aoust, C. (1997). The saturation research paper. In C. B. Olson (Ed.), *Practical ideas for teaching writing as a process at the high school and college levels* (pp. 142–144). Sacramento, CA: California Department of Education.

Duplichan, S. (2009). Using web logs in the science classroom. *Science Scope, 33*(1), pp. 33–37.

Fadiman, A., & Atwan, R. (2003). *The best American essays 2003.* Boston: Houghton Mifflin.

Ferriter, B. (2009). Learning with blogs and wikis. *Educational Leadership, 66*(5), pp. 34–38.

Fisher, M. J. (2003). Memoria ex machina. In A. Fadiman (Ed.), *The best American essays 2003* (pp. 61–66). Boston: Houghton Mifflin.

Fry, E., Kress, J., & Fountoukidis, D. L. (1993). *The reading teacher's book of lists* (3rd ed.). Englewood Cliffs, NJ: Prentice Hall.

Gabriel, T. (2010). Plagiarism lines blur for students in digital age. *New York Times.* Retrieved August 2, 2010, from http://www.nytimes.com/2010/08/02/education/02cheat.html

Gallagher, K. (2006). *Teaching adolescent writers.* Portland, ME: Stenhouse.

Gallwey, W. T. (1997). *The inner game of tennis* (rev. ed.). New York: Random House.

Gardner, H. (1982). *Art, mind, and brain: A cognitive approach to creativity.* New York: Basic Books.

Gawande, A. (2003). The learning curve. In A. Fadiman (Ed.), *The best American essays 2003* (pp. 83–102). Boston: Houghton Mifflin.

Gere, A. (1985). *Roots in the sawdust: Writing to learn across the disciplines.* Urbana, IL: National Council of Teachers of English.

Gibran, K. (1923/1975). *The prophet*. New York: Knopf.

Goodlad, J. I. (1984). *A place called school: Prospects for the future*. New York: McGraw-Hill.

Gopnik, A. (2003). Bumping into Mr. Ravioli. In A. Fadiman (Ed.), *The best American essays 2003* (pp. 103–111). Boston: Houghton Mifflin.

Graham, S., & Perin, D. (2007). Writing next: Effective strategies to improve writing of adolescents in middle schools and high schools—A report to the Carnegie Corporation of New York. Washington, DC: Alliance for Excellent Education. Retrieved April 1, 2010, from http://www.all4ed.org/files/WritingNext.pdf

Heilbroner, R., & Thurow, L. (1981). *Five economic challenges*. New York: Prentice Hall.

Hillocks, G. (1986). *Research on written composition: New directions in teaching*. Urbana, IL: ERIC Clearinghouse on Reading and Communication Skills and the National Conference on Research in English.

Johnston, P. (1985). Writing to learn science. In A. Gere (Ed.), *Roots in the sawdust: Writing to learn across the disciplines* (pp. 92–103). Urbana, IL: National Council of Teachers of English.

Langer, J. A., & Applebee, A. A. (1987). *How writing shapes thinking: A study of teaching and learning*. Urbana, IL: National Council of Teachers of English.

Lasky, K. (1994). *The librarian who measured the earth*. New York: Little, Brown.

Lipsey, M., & Wilson, D. (2001). *Practical meta-analysis*. Thousand Oaks, CA: Sage.

Macrorie, K. (1988). *The I-search paper: Revised edition of searching writing*. Portsmouth, NH: Heinemann.

Macrorie, K. (1997). The reawakening of curiosity: The research paper as hunting stories. In C. B. Olson (Ed.), *Practical ideas for teaching writing as a process at the high school and college levels* (pp. 152–155). Sacramento, CA: California Department of Education.

Malzone, D. (n.d.). WebQuest: Sights & sounds of the Harlem renaissance. Retrieved June 1, 2010, from http://questgarden.com/78/41/3/090318104808/index.htm

Martin, J. B. (1998). *Snowflake Bentley*. New York: Houghton Mifflin.

Maxwell, R. (1996). *Writing across the curriculum in middle and high schools*. Needham Heights, MA: Allyn & Bacon.

McKinney, J., & Hademenos, G. (2009). Learning as they write: An assignment to explain physics concepts. *The Physics Teacher, 47*(5), pp. 290–294.

Meeks, L. L., & Austin, C. (2003). *Literacy in the secondary English classroom: Strategies for teaching the way kids learn*. Boston: Allyn & Bacon.

Mitchell, D. (1996). Teaching ideas: Writing across the curriculum and the English teacher. *English Journal, 85,* pp. 93–97.

Murray, D. M. (1990). *Shoptalk: Learning to write with writers*. Portsmouth, NH: Boynton/Cook.

National Center for Educational Statistics (NCES), National Assessment of Educational Progress (NAEP). (2002). *The nation's report card: Writing, 2002*. Retrieved August 1, 2003, from http://nces.ed.gov/nationsreportcard/writing/

National Commission on Excellence in Education. (1983). *A nation at risk: The imperative for educational reform*. Washington, DC: U.S. Government Printing Office.

National Commission on Writing in America's Schools and Colleges. (2003). *The neglected 'R': The need for a writing revolution*. New York: College Entrance Examination Board.

Neville, J. (1995). *The press, the Rosenbergs, and the cold war*. Westport, CT: Praeger.

Northwest Regional Educational Laboratory. (1997). Six-trait analytical model. Retrieved March 1, 2000, from http://www.nwrel.org/comm/catalog/

Olson, C. B. (1997a). Preparing students to write the saturation report. In C. B. Olson (Ed.), *Practical ideas for teaching writing as a process at the high school and college levels* (pp. 138–142). Sacramento, CA: California Department of Education.

Olson, C. B. (1997b). A sample prompt, scoring guide, and model paper for I-search. In C. B. Olson (Ed.), *Practical ideas for teaching writing as a process at the high school and college levels* (pp. 156–161). Sacramento, CA: California Department of Education.

Olson, C. B. (2003). *The reading/writing connection: Strategies for teaching and learning in the secondary classroom*. Boston: Allyn & Bacon.

Perin, D. (2007). Best practices in teaching writing to adolescents. In S. Graham, C. A. MacArthur, & J. Fitzgerald (Eds.), *Best practices in writing instruction* (pp. 242–264). New York: The Guilford Press.

Perl, S. (1985). Understanding composing. In T. Newkirk (Ed.), *To compose: Teaching writing in high school* (pp. 28–36). Chelmsford, MA: Northwest Regional Exchange.

Philipson, I. (1988). *Ethel Rosenberg: Beyond the myths*. New York: Franklin Watts.

Plagiarism FAQ. (2004). Retrieved November 8, 2004, from http://www.plagiarism.org/research_site/e_faqs_text.html

Plessinger, A. (2004). The effects of mental imagery on athletic performance. Retrieved August 1, 2004, from http://www.vanderbilt.edu/AnS/psychology/health_psychology/mentalimagery.html

Pollan, M. (2003). An animal's place. In A. Fadiman (Ed.), *The best American essays 2003* (pp. 190–211). Boston: Houghton Mifflin.

Prensky, M. (2001, October). Digital natives, digital immigrants. *On the Horizon, 9*(5). http://www.marcprensky.com/writing/default.asp

Pugh, S. L., Hicks, J. W., Davis, M., & Venstra, T. (1992). *Bridging: A teacher's guide to metaphorical thinking.* Urbana, IL: National Council of Teachers of English and ERIC Clearinghouse on Reading and Communication Skills.

Read, S. (2006). Tapping into students' motivation: Lessons from young adolescents' blogs. *Voices from the Middle, 47*(2), pp. 38–46.

Research resources (2004). Retrieved November 8, 2004, from http://www.plagiarism.org/research_site/e_home_text.html

Richardson, G. E. (1982). *Educational imagery: Strategies to personalize classroom instruction.* Springfield, IL: Charles C Thomas.

Richardson, W. (2006/2010). *Blogs, wikis, podcasts, and other powerful web tools for classrooms.* Thousand Oaks, CA: Corwin Press.

Rico, G. (1983). *Writing the natural way: Using right-brain techniques to release your expressive powers.* Los Angeles: J. P. Tarcher.

Rico, G. (1997). Clustering: A prewriting process. In C. B. Olson (Ed.), *Practical ideas for teaching writing as a process at the high school and college levels* (pp. 14–17). Sacramento, CA: California Department of Education.

Romano, T. (1995). *Writing with passion: Life stories, multiple genres.* Portsmouth, NH: Heinemann.

Romano, T. (2000). *Blending genres, altering styles: Writing multigenre papers.* Portsmouth, NH: Heinemann.

Rose, M. (1989). *Lives on the boundary.* New York: Penguin.

Rose, M. (1995). *Possible lives: The promise of public education in America.* New York: Penguin.

Rushkoff, D. (2005). *Get back in the box: Innovation from the inside out.* New York: HarperCollins.

Salahu-Din, D., Perky, H., & Miller J. (2008). *The nation's report card: Writing, 2007* (NCES 2008–468). National Center for Education Statistics, Institute of Education Statistics, U.S. Department of Education, Washington, D.C. Retrieved May 1, 2010, from http://nces.ed.gov/nationsreportcard/pubs/main2007/2008468.asp

Schank, R. C. (1990). *Tell me a story: A new look at real and artificial memory.* New York: Scribners.

Schon, D. A. (1983). *The reflective practitioner.* San Francisco: Jossey-Bass.

Shaver, J. P., & Strong, W. (1982). *Facing value decisions: Rationale-building for teachers* (2nd ed.). New York: Teachers College Press.

Sis, P. (1997). *Starry messenger: Galileo Gallilei.* New York: Farrar, Straus, & Giroux.

Sizer, T. R. (1984). *Horace's compromise: The dilemma of the American high school.* Boston: Houghton Mifflin.

Smith, F. (1998). *The book of learning and forgetting.* New York: Teachers College.

Stone, R. (2010). Curriculum: iPod & song-lyric inspired lessons. WritingFix website (Northern Nevada Writing Project. Retrieved April 6, 2010, from http://writingfix.com/ipod_prompts.htm

Strong, W. (1986). *Creative approaches to sentence combining.* Urbana, IL: ERIC Clearinghouse on Reading and Communication Skills and National Council of Teachers of English.

Strong, W. (1994). *Sentence combining: A composing book* (3rd ed.). New York: McGraw-Hill.

Strong, W. (1996). *Writer's toolbox: A sentence-combining workshop.* New York: McGraw-Hill.

Strong, W. (2001). *Coaching writing: The power of guided practice.* Portsmouth, NH: Heinemann.

Tierney, B. (2002). Let's take another look at the fish: The writing process as discovery. In A. Bauman & A. Peterson (Eds.), *Breakthroughs: Classroom discoveries about teaching writing.* Berkeley, CA: National Writing Project.

Tierney, B., & Dorroh, J. (2004). *How to write to learn science* (2nd ed.). Arlington, VA: National Science Teachers Association Press.

Topping, D., & McManus, R. (2002). *Real reading, real writing.* Portsmouth, NH: Heinemann.

U.S. Department of Education, National Center for Education Statistics. (2002). *The nation's report card: Writing.* Retrieved 2004, from http://www.nces.ed.gov/nationsreportcard/naepdata/

Wilber, D. J. (2008). iLife: Understanding and connecting to the digital literacies of adolescents. In K. A. Hinchman & H. K. Sheridan-Thomas (Eds.), *Best practices in adolescent literacy instruction* (pp. 57–78). New York: The Guilford Press.

Wotring, A. M., & Tierney, R. (1981). *Two studies of writing in high school science.* Berkeley: Bay Area Writing Project.

Yoshida, J. (1985). Writing to learn philosophy. In A. Gere (Ed.), *Roots in the sawdust: Writing to learn across the disciplines* (pp. 117–136). Urbana, IL: National Council of Teachers of English.

Zimmerman, P. (1985). Writing for art appreciation. In A. Gere (Ed.), *Roots in the sawdust: Writing to learn across the disciplines* (pp. 31–45). Urbana, IL: National Council of Teachers of English.

Zinsser, W. (1988). *Writing to learn.* New York: Harper & Row.

Index

Academic (public writing) texts, x, xiv–xvi, 100–101
  Literacy Autobiography, 14, 171–173
  Multigenre Research Project, 140–145
  Nature of Science Essay, 62–63, 84
  Personalized (I-Search) Research, 133, 138–140
  Saturation Report, 134–137
  Tribute (Graduation Gift) Essay, 158–159
  See also Process (academc) writing
Activities for writing-to-learn
  admit slip, 23, 35
  biocrostic poem, 55
  biopoem, 56
  cases (dramatic scenarios), 37–38
  cinquain, 53–54
  clustering (mapping), 4–6
  dialogue writing, 41–42
  diamante (poem), 54
  dictation, 67
  double-entry journal, 20–22
  drawing metaphorically, 49
  exit slip, 23
  fact sheet, 69–70, 141
  freewriting, 48, 59, 60, 66
  given language exercise, 68,
  guided imagery, 35–37
  "I Am" poem, 55
  learning logs, 9, 19–20, 32, 62, 66
  letters, 34
  limericks, 53
  metaphor-building, 48–49, 174–176
  microthemes, 38, 116
  neuron note, 22, 124
  note-taking and note-making, 20–22
  oral negotiation, 39
  pattern poems, 53–57
  personal artifacts, 4
  personification, 57
  quick-writes, 24, 32, 61–62
  quotation prompts, 34–35
  role-playing, 39–41
  semantic charts, 52–53
  sentence combining (SC), 73–77
  summarizing and paraphrasing, 68–71
  take a stand, 34
  three words, 33
  transcribing, 66–67
  what if . . . ?, 32
  you are there scenes, 34
  See also Expressive (writing-to-learn) texts;
    Formats (expressive writing); Learning
    logs; Writing-to-learn
Admit slip, 23, 35
Allen, Camille, 145
Anson, Amy, 140–141
Apple, Max, 148
Applebee, Arthur, x–xi, xiii, 9
Arnold, Matthew, 36
Artifacts (personal), 4
Artifacts (in portfolios), 9, 128
Arts education. *See* Fine arts

Assessment, of writing
  ACT and SAT, xi
  coaching versus judging, 118–119
  College Entrance Examination Board
    (CEEB) and, xi
  effects on motivation, 28–29
  National Assessment of Educational
    Progress (NAEP), xi–xiii
  National Commission on Writing in
    America's School and Colleges, xi, xiii
  in national survey research, x–xi, xiii
  nine-step Assessment Support System
    ("ASS-in-Nine"), 80
  with portfolios, 9, 127–128
  rationale for rubrics (grading criteria)
  three levels (Maxwell), 118
  through self-assessment, 109–112
  tool function of, 28–29
  See also Coaching; Grading (judging);
    Rubrics (grading criteria)
Assignments, for writing
  across curriculum (RAFT examples),
    87–88
  case study of, 89–92
  CRAFT formula in, 85–86
  design of, xvi, 81–83, 85–86
  examples of,
    Business education: Web Site Design
      Proposal, 95–96. *See also* Business
      education; Marketing education
    Biology: Science Fiction Assignment,
      189. *See also* Biology; Geology;
      Physics; Science
    English: *To Kill a Mockingbird* News
      Story Assignment, 185. *See also*
      English; Drama and Speech
    Geology: LaPalma Brochure options,
      89–92. *See also* Biology; Geology;
      Physics; Science
    Health: Ask Dr. Abby Assignment,
      184–185. *See also* Health education;
      Physical education
    History: Creating Propaganda, 92–93.
      See also History; Psychology; Social
      studies
    Home economics: Healthy Choice Meal
      Proposal, 94–95. *See also* Consumer
      and family studies
    Mathematics: Wallpaper Puzzle
      Assignment, 186–187. *See also*
      Mathematics
    Music: Bach to Kappelmeister
      Assignment, 186. *See also* Music
      education; Fine arts education
    Physical education: Ultimate Frisbee,
      93. *See also* Health education; Physical
      education
    Social Studies: Family History Research
      Assignment, 187–189. *See also*
      History; Psychology; Social studies
Audience analysis, 87, 100–102, 118, 153, 159
Audiotape response, to writing, 118–119

Austin, Carol, 48, 53
Autobiography, Literacy (Case Study), 14,
  171–173. *See also* Narrative knowledge

Backman, Royce, 186
Balance, in learning, 10, 128–129, 164
Basic (struggling) writers
  acetate sheets in teaching, 69–71
  blocks for, 66
  closure clues for, 75
  dictation with, 67
  errors made by, 75–76
  fluency development in, 63–67
  learning logs and, 66
  novice writing of, 65
  paired practice of, 71
  scenario depicting, 77–78
  sentence combining with, 73–77
  spelling for, 71–73
  strategic teaching of, vii, 71
  summarizing and paraphrasing skills
    for, 68–71
  think-aloud demonstration for, 69
  transcribing skills for, 65–67
  wall text and, 62–63
Bean, John, 57, 83
Bernstein, Ruby, 134–135
Best American Essays, The (Fadiman
  and Atwan), 137
Biocrostic poem, 55
Biopoem, 56
Biology, writing in, 19–22, 27, 33, 36, 39,
  48–49, 55, 87–88
Blair, Jacoy, 140–141
Blending Genre, Altering Style (Romano), 145
Blogs (weblogs), 9, 157, 159–162
*Blogs, Wikis, Podcasts, and Other Powerful
  Web Tools* (Richardson), 160
Bowe, Warren, 143
Boyer, Ernest, x
Bradbury, Ray, 45, 85
Brainstorming. *See* Clustering
*Bridging: A Teacher's Guide to Metaphorical
  Thinking* (Pugh et al), 50
Brothers Karamazov, The (Dostoyevski), 56
Bruner, Jerome, xiv
Burningham, Natalie, 92–93
Business education, writing in, 25, 39, 87–88

Carone, Katie, 187–189
Cases (dramatic scenarios), 37–38
Catton, Bruce, 47
"Chestnuts" (poem), 45–46, 47–48
Checklists for writing, 104–108
Chopra, Deepak, 46
Christiansen, Kathy, vii, 145, 152–153
Churchill, Winston, 15, 28
Cinquain (poem), 53–54
Cisneros, Sandra, 39
Clustering (mapping, brainstorming), 4–5

Co-Authoring in the Classroom (Dale), 114
Coaching
    as response to drafts, 122–124
    principles of, xix–xx, 119–120
    sandwich formula for, 120, 129
    scenarios depicting, 13–14, 77–78, 99–100,
        116–117
    tips for, 124
    to prompt editing and proofreading,
        116–117
    up-front activities for, 121–122
    using audiotape for, 124–125
    versus judging, 118–119
    with insight, 165–166
    See also Basic (struggling) writers;
        Prewriting; Revising; Editing/
        Proofreading
Collaboration
    flexible teaming and, 61
    for sentence combining (SC) exercises,
        73–77
    in writing, 113–114
    management of, 113–114
    power of, x, 81, 113
College Entrance Examination Board
    (CEEB), xi
Collins, James, 71
Combining sentences. *See* Sentence
    combining
Concept Trigger Words (Tierney), 174–176
Conferencing, 3, 13–14, 77–78, 99–100,
    116–117
Consumer and family studies, writing in, 10,
    87–88
Content area writing, *See* Biology; Business
    education; Consumer and family
    studies; Drama and Speech; English;
    Fine arts education; Geology; Health
    education; History; Industrial arts
    education; Marketing education;
    Mathematics; Music education;
    Physical education; Physics;
    Psychology; Science; Social studies
Cook, Jeramy, 189
CRAFT formula, 85–85, 89–92
Crosbie, Amy, 94–95
Cubing activity (Wolfe), vii, 63, 177–178
Cycle 1 Activities (Prewriting), 104–106
Cycle 2 Activities (Revising), 106–111
Csikszentmihalyi, Mihalyi, ix

D'Aoust, Catherine, 135
Daiker, Donald, 124
Dale, Helen, 114
Daniels, Harvey, x
Dialogue writing, 41–42
Diamante (poem), 54
Dictation activity, 67
Discovery, in writing, 13, 19, 42–43, 164. *See
    also* Insight (Meaning)
Doctorow, E.L., 99
Domains of writing (framework), xv
Dorroh, John, 22
Double-entry journal, 20–22
Douglass, Fredrick, 47
"Dover Beach" (Arnold), 36
Drama and speech, writing in, 12, 87–88
Dramatic scenarios (cases), 37–38
Drawing metaphorically, 49
Duplichan, Staycie, 161–162
Dunne, John Gregory, 30

Earth science. *See* Geology.
Editing/proofreading stage, 101, 104, 108,
    121–122, 124
Education
    aims of, viii
    balance in, 10, 128–129, 164
    busywork and fear in, ix–x, 19, 80
    discovery and, 13, 19, 42–43, 164
    fakery in, ix, 19, 114, 128, 145–146
    personal meaning (insight) and, 42–43, 164
    resistance to change in, 15–16, 28–29
    thinking processes in, 24–25
Emerson, Ralph Waldo, 57
English, writing in, 12, 25, 32, 39, 55–57, 85,
    104, 150
English as a Second Language learners. *See*
    Basic (struggling) writers.
Essay planning exercise, 68
Exit slip, 23
Expressive (writing-to-learn) texts,
    as foundation for academic writing,
        xiv–xv
    content area examples of, 30–31
    formats for, xv, 33
    management of, 19–20, 32
    See also Activities for writing-to-learn;
        Learning logs; Writing-to-learn
    See also Biology; Business education;
        Consumer and family studies; Drama/
        speech; English; Fine arts education;
        Geology; Health education; History;
        Industrial arts education; Marketing
        education; Mathematics; Music
        education; Physical education;
        Physics; Psychology; Science; Social
        Studies

Fackrell, Jennifer, 7
Fact sheet, 69–70, 140–141
Fakery, ix, 19, 114, 128, 145–146
Far West Educational Laboratory, 38
Farenheit 451 (Bradbury), 85
Fear in writing, 19, 80
Feedback (response)
    from peers, 106–109
    from teacher, 117
    questions preceding, 123
    sandwich formula for, 120, 129
Felt sense (Perl), 160–161
Ferriter, Bill, 161
Fine arts, writing in, 11, 34, 39, 41–42, 87–88,
    145, 150
Fishbowl training, 107–109
Fisher, Marshall Jon, 138
Flexible teaming, vii, 61
Flow (optimal experience), ix
Fluency, 63–66
Formats (expressive writing), 33
Formats (real world), for research
    writing, 97
Forster, E.M., vii
Freewriting, 48, 59, 60, 66
Freewriting and drafting stage, 101–103
Freud, Sigmund, 106
Funk, Clark, 93

Gabriel, Trip, 147
Gale, Sarah, 88–89
Gallwey, W. Timothy, 47
Gardner, Howard, 103
Gawande, Atul, 137

Generating and planning stage, 101–102
Geology, writing in, 39, 145
Gere, Anne, 55–56
Gibran, Kahil, viii
Given language exercise, 68
Glog applications, in writing, 134–135
Gooch, Chris, 6–7, 40–41
Goodlad, John, x
Gopnik, Adam, 138
Government, writing in. *See* Social studies
    (government)
Grading (judging)
    characteristics of, 118–119
    contrasted with sampling, 18
    as classroom discipline strategy, 18, 80
    hidden curriculum and, 17–19
    lay readers and, 118
    management of, xvi, 86
    portfolios and, 127–128
    rubrics for, 82
    six-trait analytical model and, 125–126
    traditional ideas about, 17–19
    use of points in, 19–20
    See also Assessment of writing: Rubrics
        (grading criteria)
Graham, Steve, vii, 77, 164, 167–169
Graphic organizers, 179–183
Guided imagery, 35–37
Guided (traditional) research, 133, 145–146

Hademenos, George, 113–114
Harrison, Corbett, 23
Hidden curriculum
    characteristics of, xvi, 17–19
    grading practices and, 18–19
    resisting, 22–26
Hillocks, George, 77
Health education, writing in, 10, 30–31,
    33–35, 36, 39, 87–88, 135
Heilbroner, Robert, 47
History, writing in, 26, 32, 36, 37, 42, 53–57,
    87–88, 105, 136–137, 140–142, 150,
    157–158
House on Mango Street, The (Cisneros), 39
How Writing Shapes Thinking (Langer and
    Applebee), 9
How to Write to Learn Science (Tierney &
    Dorroh), 22
Huckleberry Finn (Twain), 26

"I Am" poem, 55
iPod applications, in writing, 149–150
I-Search paper. *See* Personalized (I-Search)
    Research
Industrial arts education, writing in, 39,
    57–58, 88
Insight (personal meaning),
    characteristics of, viii, 13, 42–43
    intelligence and, 115, 132
    sharing of, ix, 4, 164–165
    squelching, 80–81
    teaching for and with, 9. 42–43, 85–86,
        165–166
    writing and, ix–x, 42–43, 164
Instructional scaffolds. *See* Scaffolding

Jensen, Amy, 29
Johnson, Michael, 10
Johnson, Sara, 95–96
Johnson, Tana, 184–185
Johnston, Patricia, 55

Journal writing. *See* Learning logs
Judging. *See* Grading (judging)

Keller, Aleisha, 84
Kernel sentences, 73
Kirby, Dan, xix–xx
Knowledge
    construction of, xiv, 13–14, 42–43, 59
    narration and, 2–3, 7, 13–14
    See also Insight (personal meaning);
        Narrative knowledge
Koehne, Alice, 185

Lasky, Kathryn, 62
Langer, Judith, x, xiii, 9
Lay readers, 118
Learning logs,
    in process writing activities, 9, 19, 24–25, 67
    management of, 19–20, 32, 62,
    resistance to, 65
Learning histories, 2–3. See also Literacy
    Autobiography
Learning together, ix, 61, 81, 113–114.
        See also Collaboration
Lee, F.D., 38
Letters activity, 34
Lewis, C.S., 66
Librarian Who Measured the Earth, The
    (Lasky), 62
Limericks, 53
Lincoln, Abraham, 46
"Lines for an Interment" (Macleish), 36
Listening
    activities to model, 4, 107–109
    to students, 164
Literacy autobiography
    assignment for, 14, 171–172
    examples of, 6–8
    in Four Domains of Writing framework, xv
    rationale for, xvi, 13
    resistance to, 15–17
"Literacy Club" (poem), 65
Luke, Jeff, 112

Macleish, Archibald, 36
Macrorie, Ken, 138
Mapping. *See* Clustering
Marketing education, writing in, 39
Martin, Jaqueline, 62
Mathematics, writing in, 10, 11–12, 24–26,
    38, 42, 57, 83, 87–88, 105, 135, 150
Maxwell, Rhoda, 118
McKinney, Julie, 113–114
McManus, Roberta, 53–54
McMullin, Joyce, 8
McPhee, John, 80
Memory (semantic and story), 132
Memories of learning, 1–3
Meaning. *See* Insight (personal meaning)
Metaphor, 45–60
    concept trigger words and, 48–49, 174–176
    examples for "teaching," 58–59
    examples for "writing," 48–50, 60
    extended in prose, 57–59
    pattern poems and, 53–57
    photosynthesis drawing to illustrate, 49
    power of, in teaching, 46–48
    semantic charts and, 52–53
    stimulating, 48–58
    teaching about, xvi, 46–48, 50–52
    wall text and, 48

Meeks, Lynn, 48, 53
Microtheme, 38, 116
Miller, Laura, vii, 154–155
Minilessons (writing skills), 75–76, 104, 106–109
Mitchell, Diana, 32–34, 37, 39, 42, 121
Modeling
    examples of, 4
    personal artifacts and, 4
    to teach audience analysis, 87, 100–102,
        118, 153, 159
    to teach basic skills, 69–71, 77–78
Models (exemplars), 120
Morgan, Ruth, 53
Morrison, Toni, 116
Moser, Launa, vii, 30, 32, 34–35, 39
Multigenre research project, 140–145
Murray, Donald, 124
Music education, writing in, 32, 34, 39, 42,
    57, 150
Myths of writing, 166–167

Narrative knowledge
    conferences and, 2–3
    as default writing strategy, 10
    intelligence and, xvi, 132
    prompting of, 2–6
    reflections on, 13–14
    sharing of, ix, 42–43, 112
National Assessment of Educational Progress
    (NAEP), xi–xiv
National Center for Case Study Teaching, 38
National Commission on Writing in
    America's Schools and Colleges, xi, xiii
National Writing Project, xvii
Nature of Science Essay, 62–63, 84
Nelson, Brandon, 25–26
Neuron note, 22, 124
Nielsen Dave, 68–69
Nin, Anais, 1
North Central Educational Laboratory, xvii
Northern Nevada Writing Project, 23, 149
Northwest Regional Educational Laboratory,
    125–127
Note-taking and note-making, 20–22
Novice writing, 65

Ohio Writing Project, 154
Olson, Carol Booth, 135–136, 138–140
Oral negotiation activity, 39
Outsiders, The (Hinton), 154–155
Oversoul, 81

Paired practice, 62, 72
Peer response
    and revision, 103–104
    problems in, 8
    training students for, 106–109
Perin, Dolores, vii, 77, 164, 167–169
Perl, Sondra, 160–161
Personal artifacts activity, 4
Personalized (I-Search) Research, 133,
    138–140
Personification, 57
Peterson, Melanie, 58
Photosynthesis drawing, 49
Physical education
    guided imagery in, 36
    writing in, 10, 32, 40, 42, 57, 87–88
Physics, writing in, 34, 38, 113–114
Plessinger, Annie, 36
Poems, pattern, 53–57

Pollan, Michael, 137
Portfolios, 9, 127–128
    artifacts in, 9, 128
    cover letter for, 128
    working, 128
    learning (presentation), 9, 128
Possible Lives (Rose), 10
PowerPoint applications, in writing, 152–154
Prensky, M., 148
Prewriting (Cycle 1), 104–106
    in English, 104
    in History, 105
    in Psychology 106,
    in Mathematics, 105
    in Science, 105
Process model of writing (visual), 100
Process (academic) writing,
    assessing and publishing stage in, 101, 104
    editing and proofreading stage in, 101, 104
    freewriting and drafting stage in, 101, 103
    generating and planning stage in, 101–103
    shaping and revising stage in, 101, 103–104
    resistance to, 111–112, 166–167
Proofreading. *See* Editing/proofreading stage
Psychology, writing in, 27–28, 57, 83,
    87–88, 106
Public writing. *See* Academic (public writing)
    texts; Process (academic) writing
Pugh, Sharon, 50

Quick-writes, 24, 32, 61–62
Quotation prompts, 34–35

RAFT assignments, 87–88
Read, Sylvia, 160
Reading strategies, in revision, 111
*Reading/Writing Connection,
    The* (Olson), 140
Recursiveness in writing, 101–104
Reflective practioner, ix
Research, in writing instruction, vii, xii–xiii, xvii
    77, 167–170
Research writing, 131–147
    cheating, fakery, and plagiarism in,
        146–147
    challenged advanced students in, 143–145
    multigenre research project, 133, 140–145
    personalized (I-search) research), 133,
        138–140
    rationale for, 133–134
    real world formats for, 134, 145
    saturation report, 133–137
    story illustrating, 131–132
    traditional guided research, 133, 145–146
Resistance
    in academic writing, 111–112, 166–167
    in learning logs, 65
    scenario depicting, 15–16
    to education reform, 28–29
    See also Fakery
Response to writing. *See* Coaching; Feedback;
    Peer response; Response groups
Response groups, 106–109
    guidelines for, 106–107
    role-playing to train, 107–109
Revising (Cycle 2)
    problems with, 111–112
    response groups in, 106–109
    self-assessment and, 109–111
    training groups for, 107–109
    See also Coaching; Editing/proofreading

Richardson, Glenn, 36
Richardson, Will, 157, 160
Rico, Gabrielle, 4
Role-playing activity, 39–41
Roll of Thunder, Hear My Cry (Taylor), 26
Romano, Tom, 143–144
Rose, Mike, 10
Rosenberg, Ethel and Julius, 136–137
Rubrics (grading criteria), 86, 97, 120
    examples of, 82, 92–93, 95–96, 98, 126,
    143–144, 153, 185–189 *See also*
    Assessment of writing; Grading
    (judging)

Sandwich formula, in response, 120,129
Saturation report, 133–137
Scaffolding, instructional, xiv–xv, 100
Science, writing in, 12, 19–22, 38, 39, 42, 54,
    61–63, 82–84, 87–88, 105, 135, 150.
    See also Biology; Geology; Physics,
Schank, Roger, 14, 131–132
Schon, Donald, ix
Self-assessment (reports), 109–113
Semantic charts, 52–53
Sentence combining (SC), 73–77
    for basic skills, 75–76
    closure clues for, 75
    demonstration exercise in, 73–75
    kernel sentences and, 73
    research on, 77
Sentence Combining (Strong), 76
"Shadow-teacher," in writing, ix
Shaver, James P., 17
Shaping and revising stage, 101, 103
"Shaping up, Shipping out" visual model, 101
Sharing writing, ix, 42–43, 112
Sis, Peter, 62
Six-trait analytical model, 126
Sizer, Ted, x
Skiing and writing, viii–ix
Sloan, Chris, vii, 24, 156–161
SmartBoard applications, 24, 158–159
Smith, Brendan, 53
Smith, Frank, 59
Snowflake Bentley (Martin), 62
Social studies (government), writing in,
    13, 26, 33–34, 39, 87–88, 136–137,
    152–153. *See also* History; Psychology
Socratic dialogues, 44
Software and services, 6, 146–147
Special education learners. *See* Basic
    (struggling) writers
Spelling, 71–73
Stafford, William, ix
Star Wars scenario, 80–81
Stone, Rob, 149
"Stones" (poem), 45, 47–48
Starry Messenger: Galileo Galilei (Sis), 62
Strategies for Struggling Writers (Collins),
Strong, Laura and Dana, 148
Strong, William, iii, 76
Summarizing and paraphrasing, 68–71

Take a stand activity, 34
Tanner, Megan, 186–187
Taylor, Mildred, 26
Teacher Leader Network, 161
Teachers, role of, 28–29

Teachers Teaching Teacher broadcast/blog, 158
Technology (electronic, digital), vii, xvii
    blogs (weblogs), 9, 159–162
    blogging vs. writing, 157
    digital "natives" vs. "immigrants," 148
    glog applications, 134–135
    iPod applications, 149–150
    PowerPoint applications, 152–154
    SmartBoard applications, 24, 158–159
    software and services, 6, 146–147
    Teachers Teaching Teachers broadcast/
    blog, 156
    WebQuest applications, 150–152
    Youth Voices website, 156
Tell Me a Story, (Schank), 131
Tempered Radical, The (Ferriter), 161
Thesis and support, 121–122
Think-pair-share activity, 4, 64,
Thinking, in writing, 9, 24–25, 81
Thurow, Lester, 47
Three words activity, 33
Tierney, Bob, xvii, 19–22, 48–49, 124–125
Tierney, Missy, 136–137
To Kill a Mockingbird (Lee), 185
Topping, Donna, 53–54
Transcribing activity, 66–67
Tribute (graduation gift) essay, 158–159
Truman, Harry, 26
Tsunami, writing about, 89–92
Twain, Mark, 26

Underground railroad, 46–47
Ungraded writing, 12–20

Vader, Darth, 80–81, 96–97
Valery, Paul, 15
Vocabulary teaching, 72, 77–78

Wall Text, vii, 48–49, 62–63, 82
Wasatch Range Writing Project, 24, 156
Weblogs (blogs). *See* Technology (electronic,
    digital); Blogs (weblogs)
WebQuest applications, 150–152
Welty, Eudora, 61
What if . . . ? activity, 32
Wilber, Dana, 149
Wilensky, Sarah, 147
Wolfe, Macie, vii, 61–63, 82–83, 177–178
Wooden, John, xx
Workshop teaching, 75–77
Wotring, A.M., 22
Writing
    academic. *See* Academic (public writing)
        texts
    across curriculum, 87–88
    activities. *See* Activities for writing
    agenda for nation, xiii
    assessment. *See* Assessment of writing;
        Grading (judging)
    assignments. *See* Assignments, for writing
    balance in, 10, 128–129, 164
    checklists for, 104–108
    coaching of. *See* Coaching
    collaboration in. *See* Collaboration
    conferences, 3, 13–14, 77–78, 99–100,
        116–117
    discovery in, 13, 19, 42–43, 164. *See also*
        Insight (personal meaning)

expressive. *See* Expressive (writing-to-learn)
        texts; Activities for writing-to-learn
    fakery in, ix, 15–19, 114, 128, 145–146
    fear in, 19, 80
    fluency and, 63–66
    four domains of, xv
    functions of, in learning,
    grading of. *See* Grading (judging);
        Assessment of writing
    hidden curriculum of, 17. *See also* Hidden
        curriculum of writing
    instructional scaffolds for. *See* Scaffolding.
    managing, xvi, 24–25, 99–114
    peer response in, 106–109
    portfolios. *See* Portfolios
    process. *See* Process (academic) writing
    punishment, and, 18, 80
    reading strategies and, 111
    recursive model of, 101
    research about, vii, xii–xiii, xvii, 22, 77,
        167–170
    resistance to, 15–16, 65, 111–112, 166–167
    sharing of, ix, 42–43, 112
    skiing and, viii–ix,
    thinking and, 9, 24–25, 81
    transcribing and, 66–67
    as learning tool. *See* Writing-to-learn;
        Activities for writing-to-learn;
        Expressive (writing-to-learn) texts;
        Learning logs
Writing-to-learn
    formats for, 33
    management of, 24–25
    points for, 19–22
    research on, 22, 168–170
    samples of, 26–28
    scaffolding for academic tasks, xiv–xv
    thinking processes and, xiii–xiv, 24–25
    wall text for, 48–49, 62–63, 82
    without grades, 19–20, 43
    See also Activities for writing-to learn;
        Expressive (writing-to-learn) texts;
        Learning logs; Biology; Business
        education; Consumer and family
        studies; Drama/speech; English;
        Fine arts education; Geology; Health
        education; History; Industrial arts
        education; Marketing education;
        Mathematics; Music education;
        Physical education; Physics;
        Psychology; Science; Social sciences
        (government)
WritingFix website, 23, 149–150
Writing to Learn (Zinsser), xiv
Writing Multigenre Research Papers
    (Allen), 145
Writing Next Report (Graham & Perin), 164,
    167–169
Writing to Learn Science (Tierney and
    Dorroh), 22

Yoshida, Jessie, 56
You are there scenes, 34
Young, Jeremy, vii, 24
Youth Voices website, 156

Zimmerman, Priscilla, 41–42
Zinsser, William, xiv